CUDA Programming with Python

From Basics to Expert Proficiency

Contents

Introduction

CUDA (Compute Unified Device Architecture) is a parallel computing platform and application programming interface (API) model created by NVIDIA. It allows developers to use NVIDIA graphics processing units (GPUs) for general purpose processing—an approach known as GPGPU (General-Purpose computing on Graphics Processing Units). Over the past decade, CUDA has revolutionized industries that require high-performance computing, enabling advancements in scientific research, data analytics, machine learning, and more.

The purpose of this book is to provide a comprehensive and clear guide to CUDA programming using Python, primarily through the Numba library. Numba is an open-source JIT compiler that translates a subset of Python and NumPy code into fast machine code, handling the complexity of GPU programming and allowing developers to leverage powerful GPU resources with minimal hassle.

Understanding CUDA alongside Python is essential for those looking to harness the full potential of their hardware without delving into more complex languages like C++. This book is designed to be accessible to programmers who have a basic understanding of Python and want to expand their knowledge into parallel computing and GPU-accelerated applications. No prior experience with CUDA or GPU programming is required.

We'll begin by setting up a development environment that ensures compatibility and efficiency, covering installation steps, required tools, and verification processes to avoid common pitfalls. Following this, we will dive into CUDA's architecture, explaining key concepts such as the execution model, memory hierarchy, and the differentiation between GPU and CPU processing.

Basic concepts of CUDA programming will be explored in detail, including writing simple CUDA programs, managing memory between host and device, understanding kernel functions, and handling errors. These foundational topics are crucial for any developer aiming to write efficient CUDA applications.

Moreover, the book examines parallel programming concepts, offering insights into the design and implementation of parallel algorithms. This includes an understanding of data parallelism and task parallelism, synchronization techniques, and performance metrics critical to optimizing parallel computations.

In the realm of combining CUDA with Python, we delve into Numba's capabilities for GPU acceleration. The sections will cover setting up Numba, writing CUDA kernels in Python, managing GPU memory, and optimizing code. Advanced techniques and best practices are also discussed for readers aiming to push the performance boundaries of their applications.

Debugging and profiling are essential aspects of CUDA programming, ensuring correctness and achieving peak performance. This book includes sections dedicated to using tools such as NVIDIA Nsight and CUDA-GDB for debugging, and NVIDIA Visual Profiler for performance analysis. Profiling insights guide the optimization processes, providing a methodical approach to enhance program efficiency.

Finally, we explore advanced CUDA programming techniques and optimization strategies. Concurrent execution with streams, efficient memory management, dynamic parallelism, and interoperability with other GPU APIs are topics covered to equip readers with advanced skills necessary for complex and high-performance CUDA applications.

This book aims to serve as a thorough reference for beginners and intermediate programmers, providing the necessary knowledge and tools to develop efficient, high-performance parallel applications with CUDA and Python. Whether you are a researcher, a data scientist, or a software engineer, the principles and practices detailed within will significantly enhance your computational capabilities and performance.

Chapter 1

Introduction to CUDA Programming

CUDA is a parallel computing platform developed by NVIDIA, enabling efficient utilization of graphics processing units (GPUs) for general-purpose computing. This chapter provides an overview of CUDA, tracing its evolution and highlighting the significance of GPU computing in various applications. Readers will be introduced to fundamental concepts such as parallel processing, the distinctions between GPUs and CPUs, essential terminologies, and the basic programming models used in CUDA. Additionally, the chapter explores the practical applications and future prospects of CUDA in advancing computational performance across multiple domains.

1.1 What is CUDA?

CUDA, an acronym for Compute Unified Device Architecture, is a parallel computing platform and application programming interface (API) model created by NVIDIA. It allows software developers to harness the tremendous processing power of NVIDIA GPUs for general-purpose computing, referred to as General-Purpose computing on Graphics Processing Units (GPGPU). Unlike traditional usage of GPUs, which were strictly confined to graphics processing tasks, CUDA transforms these graphics devices into a versatile parallel computing powerhouse.

At its core, CUDA provides a layer of abstraction that enables developers to leverage the massive parallel processing capabilities inherent in GPUs. It extends the C, C++, and Fortran programming languages by providing constructs that express parallelism, allowing developers to write programs where each thread operates independently but simultaneously. CUDA is composed of both the CUDA runtime and the CUDA driver API, facilitating direct interactions with the GPU hardware.

A typical CUDA program consists of host code—executed on the Central Processing Unit (CPU)—and device code, which runs on the GPU. The host is responsible for handling general computation control and data transfer between the host memory and device memory, while the device executes the computationally intensive portions of a program. This segregation of tasks ensures optimal utilization of both the CPU and GPU resources.

A fundamental feature of CUDA is its hierarchical model of parallelism. Threads are organized into blocks, and blocks are grouped into a grid. This arrangement allows for scalability and flexibility in computing resources management. Each thread within a block can share data through shared memory, and multiple blocks can operate independently, making full use of the GPU's computational units.

To illustrate the introduction of CUDA, consider a simple example of adding two arrays using CUDA. Below is a code snippet demonstrating this in Python with PyCUDA:

```
import pycuda.driver as cuda
import pycuda.autoinit
from pycuda.compiler import SourceModule
import numpy as np

# Kernel code in CUDA C
kernel_code = """
__global__ void add_arrays(float *a, float *b, float *c, int n) {
    int idx = threadIdx.x + blockDim.x * blockIdx.x;
    if (idx < n) {
        c[idx] = a[idx] + b[idx];
    }
}
"""

# Compile the kernel code
mod = SourceModule(kernel_code)
add_arrays = mod.get_function("add_arrays")

# Define array size
N = 1000

# Initialize host arrays
a = np.random.randn(N).astype(np.float32)
b = np.random.randn(N).astype(np.float32)
c = np.empty_like(a)
```

```
# Allocate device memory and copy host arrays to device
a_gpu = cuda.mem_alloc(a.nbytes)
b_gpu = cuda.mem_alloc(b.nbytes)
c_gpu = cuda.mem_alloc(c.nbytes)

cuda.memcpy_htod(a_gpu, a)
cuda.memcpy_htod(b_gpu, b)

# Launch kernel
block_size = 256
grid_size = int(np.ceil(N / block_size))
add_arrays(a_gpu, b_gpu, c_gpu, np.int32(N), block=(block_size, 1, 1), grid=(
    grid_size, 1))

# Copy result back to host
cuda.memcpy_dtoh(c, c_gpu)

print("Array addition result:", c)
```

This code demonstrates the basic workflow of a CUDA program:

1. Definition of a Kernel: The kernel function, written in CUDA C, is defined to perform element-wise addition of two arrays. 2. Memory Allocation: Host memory is allocated and initialized, followed by allocation on the device (GPU) for the input and output arrays. 3. Data Transfer: Data is transferred from host to device memory. 4. Kernel Launch: The kernel is launched with specified grid and block dimensions. 5. Result Retrieval: The result is copied back from the device to the host memory.

The kernel function add_arrays takes four parameters:

- Pointers to the input arrays a and b.
- A pointer to the output array c.
- An integer n representing the number of elements in the arrays.

The function uses the built-in variables threadIdx, blockDim, and blockIdx to compute the global index idx for each thread. This index is utilized to perform the addition operation on corresponding elements that fall within the array bounds. The resulting values are stored in the output array c.

CUDA's architecture provides developers with fine-grained control over memory hierarchy, including:

- Global Memory: Large memory accessible by all threads but with higher latency.

- Shared Memory: Fast, low-latency memory shared among threads within the same block.
- Registers: Ultra-fast memory available to each thread.

This control allows for performance optimization by minimizing latency and maximizing throughput.

CUDA supports numerous libraries and tools, such as cuBLAS for linear algebra, cuFFT for Fast Fourier Transforms, and Thrust for parallel algorithms, significantly enhancing productivity and efficiency in application development. Integrating these libraries simplifies complex operations, allowing developers to focus on higher-level design rather than low-level optimizations.

Understanding CUDA's fundamental concepts and programming model is crucial for effectively leveraging GPU capabilities. Advanced topics such as memory coalescing, warp divergences, and occupancy management provide additional layers of optimization, crucial for attaining peak performance.

The ensuing sections of this chapter delve into the historical context, GPU computing overview, and detailed exploration of parallel processing aspects, setting the stage for deeper insights into CUDA's capabilities and applications.

1.2 History and Evolution of CUDA

CUDA, or Compute Unified Device Architecture, has its roots in the early developments of parallel computing, which sought to harness the power of multiple processing units working concurrently to solve computational problems more efficiently. Historically, parallel computing relied heavily on intricate programming models and specialized hardware, limiting its broad adoption. The advent of CUDA marked a significant shift by providing a more accessible and versatile framework for parallel computing, specifically leveraging NVIDIA's Graphics Processing Units (GPUs).

The origins of CUDA can be traced back to NVIDIA's introduction of the GPU. The concept of a GPU was pioneered to accelerate the rendering of images for computer graphics. Initially, these GPUs were designed with fixed-function pipelines, tailored to specific tasks in rendering graphics. However, as the demand for more complex and realistic graphics grew, so did the need for more programmable and flexible architectures.

In 2000, NVIDIA introduced the GeForce 256, which was termed the world's first GPU. This marked the beginning of a new era in graphical computation, focusing on programmable shading, which allowed developers to write custom shaders using languages like Cg and HLSL. These advancements laid the groundwork for a more generalized and programmable use of GPUs.

The real breakthrough for general-purpose GPU computing (GPGPU) arrived with the release of CUDA in 2007. CUDA 1.0 was developed in response to the limitations of earlier GPGPU efforts that utilized graphics APIs like OpenGL and Direct3D for non-graphical computations. These efforts were cumbersome and required deep expertise in graphics programming, making them inaccessible to many developers. CUDA provided a more straightforward and cohesive environment by allowing programmers to write scalable and efficient parallel code using a language similar to C.

The initial versions of CUDA were designed to provide essential building blocks for parallel computing, such as thread hierarchies, shared memory, and synchronization primitives. These features made it easier for scientists, engineers, and developers to write parallel code without needing to master the intricacies of traditional graphical APIs.

Subsequent versions of CUDA brought significant improvements and extensions to the initial model. CUDA 2.0, released in 2008, introduced double-precision floating-point support, making it suitable for high-performance computing applications in scientific research. CUDA 3.0, released in 2010, included features like unified addressing, which simplified memory management by consolidating the device and host memory spaces into a single address space.

A notable advancement came with the introduction of CUDA 5.0 in 2012, which provided dynamic parallelism. This allowed a GPU kernel to launch other kernels, enabling more complex and flexible computations directly on the device. This feature significantly enhanced the capability of GPUs to handle more sophisticated algorithms and workflows.

CUDA's evolution continued with enhancements aimed at improving performance, ease of use, and support for diverse applications. CUDA 6.0 introduced the concept of Unified Memory in 2014, which further simplified memory management by providing a shared memory space accessible by both the CPU and GPU. This advance reduced the need for explicit memory transfers between the host and device, making it easier to develop applications that leverage the GPU's computational power.

The development trajectory of CUDA has also emphasized backward compatibility, ensuring that existing applications continue functioning with newer versions of the framework. This feature has been instrumental in building a robust ecosystem around CUDA, encouraging long-term investment from academia and industry.

Over the years, CUDA has expanded its ecosystem with an extensive set of libraries and tools designed to accelerate specific types of computations. These include cuBLAS for linear algebra, cuFFT for fast Fourier transforms, and cuDNN for deep neural networks. Such libraries have been optimized to leverage the parallel architecture of GPUs, providing substantial performance improvements over their CPU counterparts.

The timeline of CUDA's evolution highlights a relentless pursuit of making parallel computing more accessible, potent, and applicable to a wide range of domains, from scientific research to machine learning and real-time data processing. The synergy between continuous hardware advancements and the progressing CUDA platform has cemented NVIDIA GPUs as a pivotal component in the landscape of high-performance computing.

```
import pycuda.autoinit
import pycuda.driver as drv
import numpy
from pycuda.compiler import SourceModule

mod = SourceModule("""
  __global__ void multiply_them(float *dest, float *a, float *b)
  {
    const int i = threadIdx.x;
    dest[i] = a[i] * b[i];
  }
  """)

multiply_them = mod.get_function("multiply_them")
a = numpy.random.randn(400).astype(numpy.float32)
b = numpy.random.randn(400).astype(numpy.float32)

dest = numpy.zeros_like(a)
multiply_them(drv.Out(dest), drv.In(a), drv.In(b), block=(400,1,1), grid=(1,1))

print(dest)
```

```
[ 0.15315579 -0.4211322  1.6233644 -0.25260237 0.9508752 -1.9649584
 -1.7057542  0.13941771 -0.14287743 -1.0599248 0.17026755 0.67843133
```

...
0.77307427 0.6395133]

1.3 Overview of GPU Computing

Graphics Processing Units (GPUs) were originally designed for the primary purpose of accelerating image rendering tasks. However, due to their highly parallel structure, GPUs have evolved to serve broader computational purposes beyond graphics rendering. GPU computing leverages this parallelism, allowing a significant acceleration in a wide range of computational tasks by offloading portions of the code from the Central Processing Unit (CPU) to the GPU. This section delves into the architecture of GPUs, the fundamental principles of GPU computing, and their implications for modern computing.

GPU Architecture

GPUs differ from CPUs in several key areas related to their architecture. While CPUs are optimized for single-thread performance, focusing on minimizing the latency of individual tasks, GPUs are optimized for parallel throughput, focusing on maximizing the number of simultaneous tasks that can be executed. This is achieved through several specific architectural designs:

- **Streaming Multiprocessors (SMs)**: GPUs contain hundreds or thousands of small cores organized into streaming multiprocessors. Each SM can execute many threads concurrently. These threads can share resources like registers and memory within the SM, allowing efficient parallel processing.

- **Warp Execution**: The basic execution unit in a GPU is called a warp, typically consisting of 32 threads. Warps are executed in a Single Instruction, Multiple Threads (SIMT) model, where all threads of a warp execute the same instruction simultaneously but on different data.

- **Memory Hierarchy**: GPUs have a sophisticated memory hierarchy designed to maintain high data throughput. This includes global memory (large but relatively slow), shared memory (fast but limited in size and shared among threads in an SM), and various types of cache (e.g., L1, L2).

- **High Bandwidth**: GPUs are designed with high-bandwidth memory interfaces to handle the massive data requirements of parallel processing. Technologies like High-Bandwidth Memory (HBM) and GDDR6 significantly exceed the data transfer rates of typical CPU memory.

The combination of these architectural features enables GPUs to handle a massive number of operations concurrently, overshadowing CPUs in tasks suited to parallel execution.

Principles of GPU Computing

GPU computing, or GPGPU (General-Purpose computing on Graphics Processing Units), follows several principles to efficiently utilize the massively parallel nature of GPU architecture:

- **Parallelism**: Exploiting parallelism is crucial for making full use of GPU resources. In CUDA programming, this involves designing algorithms that can be decomposed into numerous small tasks that can be executed concurrently.
- **Data Locality**: Efficient use of GPU memory bandwidth and latency considerations necessitate careful management of data locality. Frequently accessed data should be placed in shared or local memory rather than global memory to reduce access times.
- **Memory Coalescing**: Memory access patterns should be optimized so that threads access contiguous blocks of memory, a process known as memory coalescing. This results in fewer, larger memory transactions rather than many small transactions, improving efficiency.
- **Minimizing Divergence**: Minimize thread divergence within warps; since all threads in a warp execute the same instruction sequence, divergence can lead to underutilization of GPU resources. This involves structuring code to reduce conditional statements and branches that adversely affect parallel execution.

Understanding these principles allows developers to write efficient CUDA programs that leverage the full power of GPUs.

Implications for Modern Computing

The adoption of GPU computing has heralded significant advancements across various fields:

- **Scientific Research**: GPUs have accelerated simulations and data processing in disciplines like physics, chemistry, and biology, enabling researchers to tackle larger and more complex problems. An example is the use of molecular dynamics simulations in drug discovery.
- **Machine Learning and AI**: The parallelism of GPUs is well-suited to the demands of training large neural networks. Frameworks like TensorFlow and PyTorch leverage GPUs to significantly reduce the time required for training and inference.
- **Real-Time Data Processing**: Applications that require real-time processing, such as video streaming, gaming, and autonomous driving, benefit from the low-latency and high-throughput characteristics of GPUs.
- **Financial Computing**: High-frequency trading and risk assessment in finance utilize GPUs for the rapid processing of large datasets, allowing for quicker decision-making.

GPU computing represents a paradigm shift in how complex computational tasks are approached. It underscores the importance of parallel processing in achieving superior computational performance and efficiency, laying the groundwork for advancements in numerous fields.

Example: CUDA Program for Vector Addition

To illustrate the practical application of GPU computing, consider the classic example of vector addition using CUDA. The following CUDA program adds two vectors on the GPU.

```
#include <cuda_runtime.h>
#include <stdio.h>

__global__ void vectorAdd(const float *A, const float *B, float *C, int
    numElements) {
    int i = blockDim.x * blockIdx.x + threadIdx.x;
    if (i < numElements) {
        C[i] = A[i] + B[i];
    }
}

int main(void) {
    int numElements = 50000;
    size_t size = numElements * sizeof(float);
    float *h_A = (float *)malloc(size);
    float *h_B = (float *)malloc(size);
    float *h_C = (float *)malloc(size);

    for (int i = 0; i < numElements; ++i) {
        h_A[i] = rand()/(float)RAND_MAX;
```

```
        h_B[i] = rand()/(float)RAND_MAX;
    }

    float *d_A = NULL;
    float *d_B = NULL;
    float *d_C = NULL;
    cudaMalloc((void **)&d_A, size);
    cudaMalloc((void **)&d_B, size);
    cudaMalloc((void **)&d_C, size);

    cudaMemcpy(d_A, h_A, size, cudaMemcpyHostToDevice);
    cudaMemcpy(d_B, h_B, size, cudaMemcpyHostToDevice);

    int threadsPerBlock = 256;
    int blocksPerGrid = (numElements + threadsPerBlock - 1) / threadsPerBlock;
    vectorAdd<<<blocksPerGrid, threadsPerBlock>>>(d_A, d_B, d_C,
        numElements);

    cudaMemcpy(h_C, d_C, size, cudaMemcpyDeviceToHost);

    for (int i = 0; i < numElements; ++i) {
        if (fabs(h_A[i] + h_B[i] - h_C[i]) > 1e-5) {
            fprintf(stderr, "Result verification failed at element %d!\n", i);
            exit(EXIT_FAILURE);
        }
    }

    printf("Test PASSED\n");

    cudaFree(d_A);
    cudaFree(d_B);
    cudaFree(d_C);
    free(h_A);
    free(h_B);
    free(h_C);

    printf("Done\n");
    return 0;
}
```

The program initializes two vectors, copies them to device memory on the GPU, and then launches a kernel to add corresponding elements in parallel. Memory from the GPU is copied back to the host, and the result is verified.

```
Test PASSED
Done
```

This example encapsulates the essence of GPU computing: significant parallel performance that accelerates computation-intensive tasks.

1.4 Importance of Parallel Processing

Parallel processing refers to the simultaneous execution of multiple computations, which can significantly accelerate data processing tasks.

The traditional approach, which employs serial processing, executes tasks sequentially on a single processing core. This linear approach has inherent limitations, particularly in processing large datasets or complex computational tasks. By contrast, parallel processing subdivides a problem into smaller, more manageable chunks, which are processed concurrently across multiple cores, leading to substantial performance improvements.

In the context of CUDA (Compute Unified Device Architecture), parallel processing is a cornerstone of leveraging the capabilities of modern GPUs (Graphics Processing Units). GPUs consist of hundreds or even thousands of cores that can perform numerous computations simultaneously, making them highly efficient for tasks amenable to parallelization. The importance of parallel processing can be elucidated through various fundamental aspects:

- **Performance Enhancement:** The primary advantage of parallel processing is the remarkable increase in computational speed. By dividing tasks across multiple cores, the processing time can be reduced proportionally. For example, a task that would take hours to complete using serial processing can be finished in minutes or seconds using parallel processing.
- **Scalability:** Parallel processing offers scalability, allowing applications to leverage the increasing number of cores available in modern GPUs. As the number of cores increases, the potential for parallel processing improves, enabling the handling of more complex and larger scale computations.
- **Energy Efficiency:** Parallel processing can result in better energy efficiency compared to serial processing, particularly for high-performance computing (HPC) tasks. By completing tasks faster, the overall energy consumption can be lower because the system can return to a lower power state sooner.
- **Solving Complex Problems:** Many scientific, engineering, and data analysis applications involve complex computations that are impractical to solve with traditional serial processing. Parallel processing enables the efficient handling of such problems by breaking them down into smaller subtasks that can be solved concurrently.

The CUDA programming model is designed to simplify parallel processing on GPUs. It provides scalability, enabling developers to harness the full potential of modern GPU architectures. At the core of CUDA's parallel processing capabilities is the concept of threads and blocks. A thread represents the smallest unit of execution, and threads are grouped into blocks, which are further grouped into a grid. This hierarchical organization ensures that CUDA applications can efficiently utilize the GPU hardware without explicit management of individual cores.

Consider the following CUDA kernel that illustrates simple parallel processing by adding two vectors:

```
__global__ void vector_add(float *A, float *B, float *C, int N) {
    int i = blockIdx.x * blockDim.x + threadIdx.x;
    if (i < N) {
        C[i] = A[i] + B[i];
    }
}
```

In this example, the vector_add kernel function performs element-wise addition of two vectors A and B, storing the result in vector C. By using CUDA's thread and block indexing, each thread computes a single element of the resulting vector in parallel. The execution configuration determines the number of threads per block (blockDim.x) and the number of blocks (gridDim.x). This allows the addition operation to be parallelized across all available cores on the GPU:

```
int N = 1024;
float *A, *B, *C;
cudaMallocManaged(&A, N * sizeof(float));
cudaMallocManaged(&B, N * sizeof(float));
cudaMallocManaged(&C, N * sizeof(float));

// Initialize vectors A and B
for (int i = 0; i < N; i++) {
    A[i] = static_cast<float>(i);
    B[i] = static_cast<float>(i * 2);
}

// Define number of threads per block and number of blocks per grid
int blockSize = 256;
int numBlocks = (N + blockSize - 1) / blockSize;

// Launch the kernel
vector_add<<<numBlocks, blockSize>>>(A, B, C, N);

// Synchronize to ensure all threads have completed
cudaDeviceSynchronize();

// Check the result
for (int i = 0; i < N; i++) {
    assert(C[i] == A[i] + B[i]);
}

cudaFree(A);
cudaFree(B);
cudaFree(C);
```

The parallel nature of the vector_add kernel significantly enhances performance compared to a serial implementation. For a large number of elements, the reduction in execution time is substantial due to the concurrent computations performed by the threads.

Understanding the architecture of GPUs is crucial to maximizing the benefits of parallel processing. GPUs have a large number of ALUs (Arithmetic Logic Units) capable of performing many arithmetic operations simultaneously. Each ALU can execute a single thread, and multiple threads execute concurrently within a streaming multiprocessor (SM). The SM schedules threads and manages their resources, including registers and shared memory, to optimize performance.

The importance of parallel processing extends beyond performance improvements. It also enables the resolution of previously intractable problems. For instance, applications in scientific research, such as simulations of physical phenomena, bioinformatics, and real-time data processing, benefit immensely from parallel processing. It allows researchers to model and analyze complex systems more accurately and in finer detail within practical timeframes.

Parallel processing also democratizes access to high-performance computing. With GPUs becoming more accessible and affordable, a broader range of industries and researchers can leverage the computational power that was once reserved for specialized supercomputers. This democratization accelerates innovation across diverse fields, from artificial intelligence and machine learning to real-time image and video processing.

The integration of CUDA with high-level programming languages like Python further simplifies the development of parallel applications. Python's rich ecosystem of numerical and scientific libraries, combined with CUDA's parallel processing capabilities, offers a powerful toolkit for developers and researchers. They can rapidly develop and iterate on complex parallel algorithms, taking advantage of Python's ease of use and CUDA's performance.

Overall, the significance of parallel processing in modern computing cannot be overstated. As data volumes grow and computational demands increase, the transition from serial to parallel processing is not just advantageous but essential for maintaining progress and enabling new technological advancements. The CUDA platform encapsulates this paradigm shift, providing the tools and frameworks necessary to harness the power of parallel processing effectively.

1.5 GPU vs CPU: Key Differences

Graphic Processing Units (GPUs) and Central Processing Units (CPUs) are integral components of modern computing systems, each designed to handle different types of tasks with varying efficiency. Understanding their key differences provides a foundational understanding necessary for leveraging CUDA effectively.

Architectural Design and Functionality
The fundamental difference between GPUs and CPUs lies in their architectural design. CPUs are designed for general-purpose computing tasks. They contain a few cores optimized for sequential serial processing. These cores are capable of high out-of-order execution and have complex control logic to handle various instructions efficiently. CPUs often have large unified caches to store data temporarily for quick access.

In contrast, GPUs consist of thousands of smaller, simpler cores designed to perform parallel operations across a vast amount of data concurrently. Unlike CPUs, the focus is not on reducing latency but maximizing throughput. GPUs have high arithmetic logic unit (ALU) to control unit (CU) ratios, which means more of the chip area is dedicated to data processing rather than data control. GPU architecture includes many threads executing simultaneously, which is highly beneficial for data-parallel tasks such as rendering images, performing matrix multiplications, and running simulations.

Parallelism and Computational Power
One of the most significant differences is how these components handle parallelism. CPUs implement instruction-level parallelism (ILP) and limited data-level parallelism (DLP) with a few cores. They excel at executing complex instructions one after another, which suits tasks requiring low latency and high single-thread performance.

GPUs, however, utilize massive data parallelism with thousands of threads running concurrently. This configuration makes GPUs exceptionally powerful for workloads that can be divided into many small, independent tasks executed simultaneously. This is commonly seen in applications like graphics rendering, neural network training, and scientific computations.

Use Cases and Efficiency
CPUs are best suited for tasks requiring high single-thread performance and low latency such as operating systems, managing input/out-

put (I/O) operations, running sequential instructions, and executing complex algorithms with non-parallelizable tasks.

GPUs are designed for tasks that can benefit from parallel execution, like rendering multiple pixels simultaneously in graphics applications, performing large-scale matrix operations in machine learning, and accelerating scientific simulations. They deliver superior performance and efficiency in these areas compared to CPUs because of their ability to process numerous simultaneous threads.

Memory Architecture
CPU memory architecture typically includes a well-organized cache hierarchy (L1, L2, and sometimes L3 caches), which helps in reducing the latency of fetching data for processors. The main memory (DRAM) is usually linked directly to the CPU, providing a relatively straightforward but latency-sensitive memory access model.

GPUs, on the other hand, utilize a more complex memory architecture optimized for throughput. This includes high-bandwidth memory such as GDDR5 or HBM, with a memory hierarchy that involves shared memory spaces, local memory, and constant caches. GPU memory systems are designed to optimize the massive amount of data transfer required for parallel tasks and to keep the many cores as busy as possible.

Energy Consumption and Thermal Design
Due to their specialization in sequential instructions and complex control logic, CPUs generally consume less power for each operation compared to GPUs. However, the focused design for high single-thread performance often results in higher consumption for prolonged complex tasks.

GPUs have higher power consumption overall due to their massive parallel architecture but are designed to optimize performance per watt for data-parallel tasks. The nature of parallel computation ensures GPUs are more energy-efficient when workload can be distributed over many threads, although their peak power usage tends to be higher.

Programming Models
Programming for CPUs is straightforward with traditional programming languages and development environments, allowing for direct, sequential, imperative programming paradigms.

Programming GPUs involves understanding parallel computing concepts and using specialized programming models such as CUDA or OpenCL. CUDA's programming model includes managing threads, memory sharing, and optimizing parallel executions, which can be a steep learning curve but is essential for maximizing GPU capabilities.

Inserting CUDA programming into a computing workflow involves recognizing these architectural and functional differences and leveraging the strengths of each. CPUs provide versatility and low-latency handling for a broad range of tasks, while GPUs offer unparalleled performance for parallelizable tasks. Properly utilizing both can lead to highly efficient and powerful computing solutions. Understanding the underpinnings of these processing units is fundamental as we delve deeper into CUDA programming and the utilization of GPU computing in advanced applications.

1.6 CUDA Software and SDK

CUDA, or Compute Unified Device Architecture, is NVIDIA's parallel computing architecture that enables dramatic increases in computing performance by harnessing the power of the GPU. The CUDA Software Development Kit (SDK) provides developers with a full suite of development tools, libraries, and resources that facilitate the creation and deployment of GPU-accelerated applications.

CUDA Toolkit

The CUDA Toolkit includes a compiler (nvcc), libraries for standard mathematical functions and parallel algorithms, and an extensive set of development tools. The nvcc compiler is specifically designed for compiling CUDA C/C++ code, converting it into the intermediate PTX (Parallel Thread Execution) code which is executed by the GPU.

1. **Compiler (nvcc)**: The CUDA Toolkit provides the nvcc compiler which is responsible for compiling the CUDA programs. Developers write code in CUDA C/C++ and nvcc compiles this code to PTX code that can be executed on the GPU.

2. **Libraries**: The Toolkit includes several libraries which provide optimized implementations of standard algorithms. Some of the principal libraries included in CUDA are:

    - **cuBLAS**: CUDA Basic Linear Algebra Subroutine library.
    - **cuDNN**: CUDA Deep Neural Network library.
    - **cuFFT**: CUDA Fast Fourier Transform library.

- **Thrust**: A parallel algorithms library which resembles the C++ Standard Template Library (STL).

3. **Development Tools**: The Toolkit comes with a range of tools to assist in debugging, profiling, and optimizing GPU code.

   - **Cuda-gdb**: A powerful debugger for GPU applications.
   - **NVIDIA Visual Profiler (nvprof)**: A graphical profiling tool that helps in analyzing performance.
   - **CUDA-MEMCHECK**: A tool for detecting memory errors in CUDA applications.

Developing with the CUDA Toolkit typically involves writing a host program that runs on the CPU and one or more kernel functions that run on the GPU. The host program is responsible for setting up the GPU environment, memory management, and launching kernel functions. The kernel functions are where the parallel computations are specified.

Below is an example of a simple CUDA program that adds two arrays:

```
// Kernel function to add the elements of two arrays
__global__
void add(int n, float *x, float *y)
{
  int index = threadIdx.x;
  int stride = blockDim.x;
  for (int i = index; i < n; i += stride)
      y[i] = x[i] + y[i];
}

int main(void)
{
  int N = 1<<20; // 1M elements
  float *x, *y;

  // Allocate Unified Memory -accessible from CPU or GPU
  cudaMallocManaged(&x, N*sizeof(float));
  cudaMallocManaged(&y, N*sizeof(float));

  // initialize x and y arrays on the host
  for (int i = 0; i < N; ++i) {
    x[i] = 1.0f;
    y[i] = 2.0f;
  }

  // Launch kernel on 1M elements on the GPU
  add<<<1, 256>>>(N, x, y);

  // Wait for GPU to finish before accessing on host
  cudaDeviceSynchronize();

  // Check for errors (all values should be 3.0f)
  for (int i = 0; i < N; ++i) {
    if (y[i] != 3.0) {
      printf("Error: value of y[%d] = %f\n", i, y[i]);
```

```
            return -1;
        }
    }

    printf("Success!\n");

    // Free memory
    cudaFree(x);
    cudaFree(y);

    return 0;
}
```

In this program, the cudaMallocManaged function allocates memory that is accessible by both the CPU and GPU, simplifying memory management. The kernel function add is executed by GPU threads where each thread computes an array element addition. The cudaDeviceSynchronize function ensures that the CPU waits for the GPU to complete before proceeding.

CUDA Drivers

CUDA software requires drivers that support the CUDA Toolkit and provide the interface between the operating system and the hardware. These drivers ensure the hardware capabilities of NVIDIA GPUs are fully utilized by the CUDA Toolkit.

CUDA Runtime and Driver API

The CUDA Runtime API and Driver API provide two programming interfaces to manage and work with CUDA. While the Runtime API is easier to use and is recommended for most applications, the Driver API offers more flexibility and control for advanced use cases.

Third-party Libraries and Ecosystem

Along with CUDA's standard libraries, there exists a vibrant ecosystem of third-party libraries and tools that complement and extend CUDA's capabilities. These include machine learning libraries (TensorFlow, PyTorch), scientific computing libraries (cuML, RAPIDS), and various domain-specific libraries.

The scope of CUDA Software and SDK is broad, encompassing tools, libraries, drivers, and APIs that collectively enable developers to harness the unparalleled computational capabilities of modern GPUs. As the field of GPU computing continues to evolve, staying updated with the latest updates and enhancements in the CUDA ecosystem remains crucial for achieving peak performance and efficiency in parallel computing tasks.

1.7 Basic Terminologies in CUDA

Understanding CUDA, or Compute Unified Device Architecture, requires familiarity with a set of fundamental terminologies. These terms form the foundation for more complex concepts and programming practices within CUDA. This section will enumerate and define these key terminologies, aiding readers in grasping how CUDA leverages GPUs for parallel computing.

1. Kernel: A kernel in CUDA refers to a function that runs on the GPU. It is written in a CUDA-enabled language such as CUDA C or CUDA Python. When a kernel is executed, it is launched across multiple threads, allowing parallel execution. Kernels are declared using the __global__ keyword in CUDA C.

```
// Example of a CUDA kernel in CUDA C
__global__ void myKernel() {
    // Code that will be executed by each thread
    int idx = threadIdx.x;
    printf("This is thread: %d\n", idx);
}
```

2. Thread: A thread is the smallest unit of execution in CUDA. Each thread executes the kernel function independently and in parallel. Threads are uniquely identified within their block by the threadIdx variable.

```
Output:
This is thread: 0
This is thread: 1
This is thread: 2
...
```

3. Block: Threads are grouped into thread blocks. Each block is a three-dimensional structure consisting of threads, identified by the blockIdx. A block can have up to 1024 threads in CUDA, spanning three dimensions: x, y, and z.

```
// Example of CUDA kernel utilizing block and thread indexes
__global__ void myKernel() {
    int idx = threadIdx.x + blockIdx.x * blockDim.x;
    printf("This is thread: %d\n", idx);
}
```

4. Grid: A grid is a collection of thread blocks. The grid dimensions can also span three dimensions. When a kernel is launched, its execution configuration specifies the number of blocks per grid and the number of threads per block.

```
// Launching a kernel on a grid
```

```
dim3 threadsPerBlock(16, 16);
dim3 numBlocks(2, 2);
myKernel<<<numBlocks, threadsPerBlock>>>();
```

5. Warp: A warp is a fixed-size group of 32 threads within a block that execute instructions in a lock-step manner. Warps are the fundamental unit of scheduling in CUDA. All threads in a warp start execution at the same program counter and follow the same instructions.

6. Memory Hierarchy: CUDA programming involves multiple types of memory, each with distinct usage and performance characteristics:

a. Global Memory: Accessible by all threads and blocks, with high latency. It provides large storage capacity but slow access speed.

b. Shared Memory: Located on the chip, accessible by threads within the same block, with much lower latency compared to global memory. Optimizing the use of shared memory can significantly improve performance.

c. Local Memory: Used privately by individual threads, stored in the global memory, but typically registers are used wherever possible to enhance speed.

d. Constant Memory: Read-only memory with low latency, utilized for storing constant values across all threads.

e. Register: Fastest memory available, each thread has a limited number of registers.

7. CUDA Runtime API: A set of high-level APIs provided by NVIDIA for managing and executing kernels, memory allocation, and data transfer between the host (CPU) and the device (GPU). The runtime API simplifies the development process compared to the lower-level driver API.

8. CUDA Driver API: Offers lower-level control over the device. It provides functionalities for device management, memory management, and kernel execution, requiring more detailed programming compared to the runtime API.

9. Streams: CUDA streams allow concurrent execution of multiple operations, such as kernel execution and memory transfers. By default, all operations are serialized in a single stream (stream 0). Creating multiple streams can enhance computational efficiency by overlapping execution and memory transfers.

```
// Example of CUDA stream creation and usage
cudaStream_t stream;
cudaStreamCreate(&stream);
```

```
myKernel<<<numBlocks, threadsPerBlock, 0, stream>>>();
```

10. Synchronization: Ensuring the correct order of operations across threads and blocks is essential. CUDA provides various synchronization mechanisms:

a. __syncthreads(): Function to synchronize threads within the same block.

b. cudaDeviceSynchronize(): Function to synchronize the host with the device, ensuring all preceding CUDA operations are completed.

```
// Example of synchronization functions
__global__ void myKernel() {
    __syncthreads();
    // Code that requires all threads to reach this point
}
cudaDeviceSynchronize();
```

These terminologies form the basis for understanding and writing efficient CUDA programs. Familiarity with these terms will enable comprehension of more advanced CUDA features and techniques. Each concept builds upon the previous ones, forming a structured approach to GPU programming.

1.8 CUDA Programming Models

CUDA programming models are designed to leverage the power of GPUs for parallel computation, allowing programmers to write scalable and efficient code. These models define how a task can be broken down into smaller subtasks, which can then be executed concurrently by multiple threads on the GPU. Here, we cover the key components of CUDA programming models, including threads, blocks, grids, and memory hierarchy. Understanding these components is crucial for creating effective CUDA programs.

Thread Hierarchy

In CUDA, the concept of thread hierarchy is fundamental. Threads are the smallest units of execution and are organized into blocks. Each block contains a group of threads that can cooperate by sharing data through shared memory and synchronizing their execution. The threads within a block can be indexed using a unique identifier, threadIdx, which helps in the parallel execution of a task.

A two-dimensional example of thread indexing in a CUDA kernel is as follows:

```
__global__ void matrixAdd(int *A, int *B, int *C, int N) {
    int row = threadIdx.y;
    int col = threadIdx.x;
    int idx = row * N + col;
    C[idx] = A[idx] + B[idx];
}
```

This example demonstrates how threads are indexed in a 2D grid to perform a matrix addition operation. Each thread computes the sum of corresponding elements from matrices A and B, storing the result in matrix C.

Block Hierarchy

Blocks are further organized into grids, where each grid comprises multiple blocks. The size and dimension of both blocks and grids can be specified at runtime, allowing for flexible and scalable parallel computations. Blocks are indexed uniquely within a grid using blockIdx.

Here is how a grid of blocks can be defined:

```
dim3 gridSize(2, 2);
dim3 blockSize(16, 16);
matrixAdd<<<gridSize, blockSize>>>(d_A, d_B, d_C, N);
```

In this setup, a grid with 2x2 blocks and each block consisting of 16x16 threads is used to execute the matrixAdd kernel.

Memory Hierarchy

CUDA's memory hierarchy is designed to optimize data access and minimize latency. The primary types of memory in CUDA are global memory, shared memory, constant memory, and local memory.

- **Global Memory**: This is the main memory space accessible by all threads. Although it has high capacity, it is relatively slow. Accessing global memory is efficient when performed coalesced, where neighboring threads access contiguous memory locations.
- **Shared Memory**: It is shared among threads within the same block, providing low-latency data access. Shared memory acts as a user-managed cache, significantly improving performance, especially in scenarios requiring frequent data reuse.
- **Constant Memory**: This read-only memory is optimized for storage of data constants that remain unchanged across kernel executions. It is cached, providing quick access to multiple threads.

- **Local Memory**: Though named 'local,' this memory resides in global memory space and is used for storing variables private to each thread.

The strategic placement of data across these memory types can enhance memory access patterns and performance.

Synchronization Mechanisms

CUDA provides synchronization mechanisms to coordinate the execution of threads. The __syncthreads() function is commonly used to synchronize threads within a block, ensuring that all threads have reached the same point of execution before proceeding.

An example using synchronization is as follows:

```
__global__ void reduceSum(int *input, int *output, int N) {
    extern __shared__ int sharedData[];
    int tid = threadIdx.x;
    int global_tid = blockIdx.x * blockDim.x + tid;

    // Load data into shared memory
    sharedData[tid] = (global_tid < N) ? input[global_tid] : 0;
    __syncthreads();

    // Perform parallel reduction
    for (int s = blockDim.x / 2; s > 0; s >>= 1) {
        if (tid < s) {
            sharedData[tid] += sharedData[tid + s];
        }
        __syncthreads();
    }

    // Write result for this block to global memory
    if (tid == 0) {
        output[blockIdx.x] = sharedData[0];
    }
}
```

This reduction example illustrates how shared memory and synchronization can be used to sum elements in an array in parallel.

CUDA Execution Model

In the CUDA execution model, the host (CPU) launches kernels on the device (GPU), where a kernel is a function executed by a grid of threads. The execution configuration specifies the grid and block dimensions and is provided in the triple-angle-bracket syntax («< ... »>).

For example:

```
int gridSize = ...;
int blockSize = ...;
kernel<<<gridSize, blockSize>>>(...);
cudaDeviceSynchronize();
```

This segment ensures that the kernel is launched with the given configuration and that the host waits for the kernel's completion using cudaDeviceSynchronize().

CUDA Streams and Asynchronous Execution

CUDA streams enable concurrent execution of multiple tasks, allowing overlapping of kernel execution, memory transfers, and computations. By default, all operations occur in a single, implicit stream, often referred to as the "default stream". Explicit streams can be created to define independent sets of operations.

For instance:

```
cudaStream_t stream1, stream2;
cudaStreamCreate(&stream1);
cudaStreamCreate(&stream2);

kernel1<<<gridSize, blockSize, 0, stream1>>>(...);
kernel2<<<gridSize, blockSize, 0, stream2>>>(...);

cudaStreamSynchronize(stream1);
cudaStreamSynchronize(stream2);

cudaStreamDestroy(stream1);
cudaStreamDestroy(stream2);
```

This example demonstrates how to create multiple streams, execute kernels within these streams, and synchronize their execution.

Understanding CUDA programming models involves mastering the concepts of threads, blocks, grids, and the memory hierarchy, along with efficient synchronization and concurrent execution strategies. This knowledge forms the foundation of writing high-performance CUDA programs capable of exploiting the full computational power of GPUs.

1.9 Applications of CUDA: Real-World Examples

CUDA (Compute Unified Device Architecture) has substantially impacted various fields by leveraging the immense computational power of GPUs. By facilitating massive parallelism, CUDA has enhanced performance and efficiency in numerous applications, enabling new methods and solutions for complex problems. This section presents detailed examples of real-world applications of CUDA across different domains: scientific research, medical imaging, artificial intelligence and machine learning, finance, and real-time data processing.

Scientific Research

One of the most prominent applications of CUDA lies in scientific computation and simulation. Researchers across various disciplines employ CUDA to accelerate computational tasks that were previously either infeasible or extremely time-consuming on traditional CPUs. For example, molecular dynamics simulations, which predict the physical movements of atoms and molecules, greatly benefit from CUDA's parallel processing capabilities. Consider the open-source software package GROMACS (GROningen MAchine for Chemical Simulations), widely used for protein simulations and other molecular dynamics studies. GROMACS utilizes CUDA to offload computation-intensive tasks to GPUs, significantly reducing simulation times.

```
__global__ void molecularDynamicsKernel(float *positions, float *forces, int n) {
    int idx = blockIdx.x * blockDim.x + threadIdx.x;
    if (idx < n) {
        // Kernel code to compute force on each particle
        forces[idx] = computeForce(positions, idx);
    }
}
```

This kernel exemplifies the parallel nature of molecular dynamics calculations, where each particle's force is computed concurrently across different threads.

Medical Imaging

Medical imaging is another domain where CUDA has made significant contributions. Techniques such as Magnetic Resonance Imaging (MRI) and Computed Tomography (CT) scans generate massive amounts of data requiring extensive processing. CUDA enables real-time image reconstruction and enhancement, improving both the speed and quality of medical diagnostics.

For example, in CT imaging, the process of image reconstruction involves solving a set of linear equations derived from the X-ray projections. CUDA accelerates this reconstruction process by parallelizing the projections and backprojection operations, crucial steps in the algorithm.

```
__global__ void backProjectionKernel(float *projections, float *image, int
    numProjections) {
    int idx = blockIdx.x * blockDim.x + threadIdx.x;
    if (idx < numProjections) {
        // Code to perform backprojection
        image[idx] = backProject(projections, idx);
    }
}
```

The above kernel back-projects the acquired projections to reconstruct the CT image slice by slice, leveraging the parallel capabilities of CUDA.

Artificial Intelligence and Machine Learning

CUDA plays a crucial role in the field of artificial intelligence (AI) and machine learning (ML). The training processes of deep learning models typically involve large datasets and complex computations, making them particularly suited for GPU acceleration. Frameworks such as TensorFlow and PyTorch utilize CUDA to perform tensor operations, matrix multiplications, and other heavy computational tasks more efficiently.

Consider a simple example of a matrix multiplication kernel, a fundamental operation in training neural networks:

```
__global__ void matrixMultiplyKernel(float *A, float *B, float *C, int width) {
    int tx = threadIdx.x;
    int ty = threadIdx.y;
    float value = 0;
    for (int k = 0; k < width; ++k) {
        value += A[ty * width + k] * B[k * width + tx];
    }
    C[ty * width + tx] = value;
}
```

This kernel demonstrates the parallel computation of elements in the result matrix C, crucial for speeding up the training of deep learning models.

Finance

In the finance industry, CUDA accelerates computational finance applications, such as option pricing, risk management, and trading strategies, by executing complex calculations in parallel. Monte Carlo simulations, which are widely used for pricing derivatives and assessing risk, benefit enormously from the parallelism offered by CUDA.

An example kernel for a simple Monte Carlo simulation for option pricing:

```
__global__ void monteCarloKernel(float *randomNumbers, float *results, int
    numSimulations) {
    int idx = blockIdx.x * blockDim.x + threadIdx.x;
    if (idx < numSimulations) {
        results[idx] = simulateOptionPrice(randomNumbers[idx]);
    }
}
```

This kernel leverages CUDA to simulate multiple scenarios concurrently, significantly speeding up the risk analysis process.

Real-Time Data Processing

Real-time data processing applications, such as video streaming, signal processing, and network traffic monitoring, also leverage CUDA's capabilities. For instance, CUDA enables the real-time encoding and decoding of high-definition video streams, crucial for applications requiring minimal latency, such as video conferencing and online gaming.

An example of a CUDA kernel for video frame processing might look like this:

```
__global__ void processFrameKernel(unsigned char *inputFrame, unsigned char *
    outputFrame, int width, int height) {
    int x = blockIdx.x * blockDim.x + threadIdx.x;
    int y = blockIdx.y * blockDim.y + threadIdx.y;
    if (x < width && y < height) {
        int idx = y * width + x;
        // Process pixel value
        outputFrame[idx] = processPixel(inputFrame[idx]);
    }
}
```

This kernel processes each pixel of the input frame in parallel, enabling real-time video processing capabilities.

CUDA's versatility and power have thus enabled advances across these diverse fields, transforming how complex computations and data processing tasks are approached and executed. Real-world examples illustrate CUDA's capacity to address challenging computational problems efficiently, thereby facilitating innovation and progress in various domains.

1.10 Future of CUDA and GPU Computing

The future of CUDA and GPU computing holds immense potential for advancing computational capabilities across diverse domains. As we delve into this dynamically evolving field, it is crucial to examine emerging trends, projected technological advancements, and the broad spectrum of applications poised to benefit from these developments.

As NVIDIA continues to innovate with each successive generation of GPUs, both hardware and software advancements are expected to drive significant improvements in performance, efficiency, and programmability. The introduction of newer architectures, such as the Ampere and Hopper architectures, exemplifies how GPU technology is pushing the envelope of computational power. These architectures integrate numerous technological enhancements, including increased core counts, improved memory hierarchies, and fine-tuned parallel processing capabilities.

```
/* Example of CUDA code using Ampere features */
__global__ void matrixMultiply(float *A, float *B, float *C, int N) {
    int row = blockIdx.y * blockDim.y + threadIdx.y;
    int col = blockIdx.x * blockDim.x + threadIdx.x;
    float value = 0;

    for (int k = 0; k < N; ++k) {
        value += A[row * N + k] * B[k * N + col];
    }

    C[row * N + col] = value;
}

int main() {
    // Host memory allocation and initialization
    float *h_A, *h_B, *h_C;
    int N = 1024; // Example size

    // Allocate memory and define grid/block dimensions
    dim3 threadsPerBlock(16, 16);
    dim3 numBlocks(N / threadsPerBlock.x, N / threadsPerBlock.y);

    // Kernel launch
    matrixMultiply<<<numBlocks, threadsPerBlock>>>(d_A, d_B, d_C, N);

    // Synchronize and deallocate memory
    cudaDeviceSynchronize();
    cudaFree(d_A);
    cudaFree(d_B);
    cudaFree(d_C);

    return 0;
}
```

Another key aspect of future developments is the integration of advanced memory technologies. High-bandwidth memory (HBM2) and GDDR6 are already enhancing data transfer rates, and future iterations promise even greater improvements. The NVLink interconnect is also a pivotal technology that allows for higher bandwidth and faster communication between GPUs, essential for large-scale parallel applications.

Emerging software advancements will continue to elevate the capabilities of CUDA. The introduction of CUDA Graphs facilitates the execution of complex workflows by capturing a series of CUDA operations and executing them as a graph. This offers reduced overhead and increased efficiency in managing asynchronous tasks. Furthermore, the expanding ecosystem of libraries, such as cuBLAS, cuFFT, and TensorRT, provides optimized solutions for specific computational tasks, significantly simplifying the development process for researchers and developers.

```
/* Utilizing CUDA Graphs for optimizing workflows */
cudaStream_t stream;
cudaStreamCreate(&stream);

cudaGraph_t graph;
cudaGraphExec_t instance;

cudaGraphCreate(&graph, 0);

// Insert graph nodes here, for example, kernel launches, memory copies, etc.
// cudaGraphAddKernelNode, cudaGraphAddMemcpyNode, etc.

cudaGraphInstantiate(&instance, graph, NULL, NULL, 0);
cudaGraphLaunch(instance, stream);

cudaStreamSynchronize(stream);
cudaGraphDestroy(graph);
cudaGraphExecDestroy(instance);
cudaStreamDestroy(stream);
```

The integration of artificial intelligence and machine learning applications has led to the development of specialized GPU hardware, such as Tensor Cores, which are designed to accelerate matrix operations critical to deep learning algorithms. As these technologies evolve, GPUs will play a fundamental role in advancing AI research, with CUDA providing the foundational programming model to harness this power.

Quantum computing is another frontier where GPUs may play a significant role. Hybrid quantum-classical algorithms, which leverage classical computations performed on GPUs to complement quantum processing, represent an exciting area of research. The combination of CUDA's parallel processing with quantum computing's unique capabilities could lead to breakthroughs in solving complex problems that are currently intractable.

The evolution of software paradigms, including the refinement of parallel programming models, will further enhance the accessibility and efficiency of GPU computing. For instance, the integration of heterogeneous computing frameworks, where CPUs, GPUs, and other accelerators work in tandem, is an area of active research. The SYCL and OpenCL frameworks are examples of efforts aimed at achieving seamless interoperability between different types of processing units.

```
/* Example of heterogeneous computing using CUDA with OpenCL */
#ifdef __cplusplus
extern "C" {
#endif
    #include <CL/cl.h>
#ifdef __cplusplus
}
#endif
```

```
#include <stdio.h>
#include <stdlib.h>
#include <cuda_runtime.h>

// Example function that invokes both CUDA and OpenCL functionalities
void hybridComputation() {
    // CUDA computation
    float *d_A, *d_B, *d_C;
    cudaMalloc((void**)&d_A, sizeof(float) * ARRAY_SIZE);
    cudaMalloc((void**)&d_B, sizeof(float) * ARRAY_SIZE);
    cudaMalloc((void**)&d_C, sizeof(float) * ARRAY_SIZE);

    // Kernel launch and CUDA synchronization
    cudaKernel<<<numBlocks, threadsPerBlock>>>(d_A, d_B, d_C);
    cudaMemcpy(h_C, d_C, sizeof(float) * ARRAY_SIZE, cudaMemcpyDeviceToHost)
        ;

    // OpenCL setup and computation (hypothetical example)
    cl_platform_id platform;
    cl_device_id device;
    cl_context context;
    cl_command_queue queue;
    // ... OpenCL initialization and kernel execution ...

    // Clean up resources
    cudaFree(d_A);
    cudaFree(d_B);
    cudaFree(d_C);
}

int main() {
    hybridComputation();
    return 0;
}
```

The impact of CUDA and GPU computing extends to various real-world applications, driving innovation in scientific research, medical imaging, autonomous vehicles, financial modeling, and more. In scientific simulations, GPUs accelerate calculations involved in complex systems such as climate models and molecular dynamics. In medical imaging, GPUs enhance diagnostic precision by facilitating faster and more accurate image processing.

Additionally, the widespread adoption of edge computing and the Internet of Things (IoT) is fueling demand for powerful, energy-efficient computing solutions. Next-generation GPUs, combined with CUDA, are well-positioned to meet these demands by offering robust performance in compact, low-power form factors.

As we anticipate future advancements, it is evident that CUDA and GPU computing will continue to redefine what is possible in the realm of high-performance computing. Continued innovation in hardware and software will empower researchers, developers, and engineers to tackle increasingly complex challenges, unlocking new possibilities across various industries and scientific disciplines.

Chapter 2

Setting Up the Development Environment

This chapter details the requirements and steps for setting up a development environment for CUDA programming with Python. It covers the installation of necessary tools including the CUDA Toolkit, Visual Studio Code, and Anaconda, alongside configuring Numba for GPU development. Verification of the installation and management of CUDA libraries are explained to ensure a smooth setup. Additionally, the chapter addresses setting up Jupyter Notebooks for CUDA, common installation issues, and their troubleshooting solutions.

2.1 System Requirements for CUDA Development

Before embarking on CUDA programming with Python, ensuring that your system meets the necessary hardware and software requirements is pivotal for a smooth and efficient development experience. This section examines the essential system components, including hardware and operating system prerequisites, that facilitate CUDA development.

Hardware Requirements

To develop CUDA applications, your system must be equipped with an NVIDIA GPU that supports CUDA. It's important to verify the compute capability of your GPU. The compute capability determines the features supported by the GPU. A list of NVIDIA GPUs and their corresponding compute capabilities can be found on NVIDIA's official website. Generally, a compute capability of 3.0 or higher is recommended for modern CUDA development.

The following hardware components are required:

- **NVIDIA GPU:** Ensure that the GPU is CUDA-capable. Compatibility can be verified by consulting the CUDA GPUs list available on the NVIDIA website.
- **Memory:** At least 4GB of system RAM is recommended; however, 8GB or more is preferable for handling high computational demands.
- **Disk Space:** Approximately 10GB of free disk space is needed for the CUDA Toolkit, auxiliary libraries, and development tools.
- **Processor:** A multi-core processor is recommended to handle the parallel processing tasks effectively.

Operating System Requirements

CUDA development is supported on various operating systems. The following outlines the software requirements for each major platform:

- **Windows:**
  - Versions: Windows 10 (version 1709 or later) is recommended. Earlier versions might still work but are not officially tested.
  - Compiler: Microsoft Visual Studio 2019 or later (Community, Professional, or Enterprise editions). Visual Studio is required for integration with the CUDA Toolkit.
- **Linux:**
  - Distributions: Ubuntu 18.04 or later, CentOS 7/8, or Fedora 29/30 are recommended. CUDA supports a variety of distributions, but newer versions ensure better compatibility.

    - Compiler: GCC 6.0 or later is required. GCC (GNU Compiler Collection) is widely used and compatible with CUDA.

- **macOS:**
    - Versions: macOS Mojave (version 10.14) or later. It should be noted that CUDA support on macOS has become limited.
    - Compiler: Xcode 10.1 or later is required. Earlier versions of Xcode may have compatibility issues.

Software Requirements

In addition to the operating system-specific requirements, there are several general software prerequisites that must be satisfied:

- **CUDA Toolkit:** The CUDA Toolkit provides a comprehensive development environment for CUDA applications. It includes libraries, debugging and optimization tools, and a runtime compiler.
- **Python:** Python 3.6 or later, preferably installed via Anaconda for ease of managing dependencies and environments.
- **Numba:** Numba is an essential library for CUDA development in Python. It translates Python functions to optimized machine code at runtime using industry-standard libraries like LLVM.
- **Anaconda:** Anaconda is a package manager, an environment manager, and Python distribution that is widely used in data science and scientific computing.

Driver Requirements

The NVIDIA display driver must be installed and correctly configured. The driver version must be compatible with the installed CUDA Toolkit version. Each version of the toolkit has specific driver version requirements, details of which can be found in the CUDA Toolkit release notes.

```
sudo apt-get install nvidia-driver-440
```

The above command installs version 440 of the NVIDIA driver on an Ubuntu system. The exact package name and version number might vary based on the distribution and the version of the CUDA Toolkit installed.

Additional Considerations

- **Permissions:** Ensure that your user account has the necessary administrative permissions to install software and configure drivers.
- **Internet Access:** Although not mandatory for CUDA development, having an active internet connection simplifies the installation of dependencies and allows access to online resources, documentation, and updates.

With these requirements met, your system will be well-equipped to develop and run CUDA applications effectively, enabling you to leverage the considerable computational power of NVIDIA GPUs for high-performance computing tasks.

2.2 Installing CUDA Toolkit

The CUDA Toolkit comprises development tools, the CUDA runtime, and libraries necessary for building, debugging, and optimizing applications using NVIDIA GPUs. This section provides a step-by-step guide for installing the CUDA Toolkit on various operating systems and verifying the installation.

Prerequisites: Before proceeding with the installation, verify that your system meets the following prerequisites:

- A compatible NVIDIA GPU that supports CUDA.
- An appropriate operating system (Windows, Linux, or macOS).
- Sufficient disk space and administrative privileges.

Step-by-Step Installation:

For Windows Users:

1. **Download the CUDA Toolkit:** Visit the official NVIDIA CUDA Toolkit webpage and download the installer for Windows. Select the version compatible with your GPU and operating system.
2. **Run the Installer:** Execute the downloaded installer. The installation wizard will guide you through the setup process.

3. **Choose Installation Options:** Select the components to install. For most users, it is recommended to install the default options, including the CUDA Toolkit, the CUDA Samples, and the driver.

4. **Verify the Installation:** Once the installation is complete, open the Command Prompt and run the following command to verify the toolkit and driver installation:

```
nvcc --version
```

```
C:\Program Files\NVIDIA GPU Computing Toolkit\CUDA\v11.0\bin\nvcc.exe
Copyright (c) 2005-2020 NVIDIA Corporation
Built on Mon_Jun_1_19:29:26_PDT_2020
Cuda compilation tools, release 11.0, V11.0.194
Build cuda_11.0_bu.relgpu_drvr445TC.10177936_0
```

For Linux Users:

1. **Download the CUDA Toolkit:** Navigate to the CUDA Toolkit download page and select the appropriate version and distribution for your Linux system.

2. **Add the CUDA Repository:** Follow the instructions on the website to add the CUDA repository to your system's package manager. For example, on Ubuntu:

```
sudo dpkg -i cuda-repo-<distro>_<version>_amd64.deb
sudo apt-key adv --fetch-keys http://developer.download.nvidia.com/
    compute/cuda/repos/<distro>/x86_64/7fa2af80.pub
sudo apt-get update
```

3. **Install the CUDA Toolkit:** Use the package manager to install the CUDA Toolkit and drivers:

```
sudo apt-get install cuda
```

4. **Set Environment Variables:** Add CUDA to your PATH by including the following lines in your ~/.bashrc or ~/.zshrc file:

```
export PATH=/usr/local/cuda-11.0/bin${PATH:+:${PATH}}
export LD_LIBRARY_PATH=/usr/local/cuda-11.0/lib64\
    ${LD_LIBRARY_PATH:+:${LD_LIBRARY_PATH}}
```

After modifying the file, refresh the environment variables:

```
source ~/.bashrc
```

5. **Verify the Installation:** Ensure the toolkit is correctly installed by running:

```
nvcc --version
```

```
nvcc: NVIDIA (R) Cuda compiler driver
Copyright (c) 2005-2020 NVIDIA Corporation
Built on Mon_Jun_1_19:29:26_PDT_2020
Cuda compilation tools, release 11.0, V11.0.194
Build cuda_11.0_bu.relgpu_drvr445TC.10177936_0
```

For macOS Users:

1. **Download the CUDA Toolkit:** Go to the CUDA Toolkit download page and choose the macOS version.
2. **Install Xcode:** Ensure that Xcode is installed on your system as it is necessary for compiling CUDA applications. Xcode can be downloaded from the Mac App Store.
3. **Run the Installer:** Open the downloaded .dmg file and install the CUDA Toolkit by following the on-screen instructions.
4. **Verify the Installation:** Open a terminal and verify the installation:

```
nvcc --version
```

```
nvcc: NVIDIA (R) Cuda compiler driver
Copyright (c) 2005-2020 NVIDIA Corporation
Built on Mon_Jun_1_19:29:26_PDT_2020
Cuda compilation tools, release 11.0, V11.0.194
Build cuda_11.0_bu.relgpu_drvr445TC.10177936_0
```

Post-Installation: After installation, it is crucial to test a few CUDA samples to ensure everything is functioning optimally. The CUDA Toolkit includes sample programs that can be compiled and executed.

1. **Compile Samples:** Change directory to the CUDA samples directory:

```
cd ~/NVIDIA_CUDA-11.0_Samples/1_Utilities/deviceQuery
make
```

2. **Run the Sample Program:** Execute the compiled sample program to validate the installation:

```
./deviceQuery
```

```
./deviceQuery Starting...

CUDA Device Query (Runtime API) version (CUDART static linking)

Detected 1 CUDA Capable device(s)

Device 0: "GeForce GTX 1080"
  CUDA Driver Version / Runtime Version          11.0 / 11.0
  CUDA Capability Major/Minor version number:    6.1
  Total amount of global memory:                 8119 MBytes (8507830272 bytes)
  (20) Multiprocessors, (128) CUDA Cores/MP:     2560 CUDA Cores
  GPU Max Clock rate:                            1733 MHz (1.73 GHz)
  Memory Clock rate:                             5005 Mhz
  Memory Bus Width:                              256-bit
  L2 Cache Size:                                 2097152 bytes
  ...
```

2.3 Setting Up Visual Studio Code for CUDA

Visual Studio Code (VS Code) is a highly extensible and versatile code editor that supports a multitude of programming languages, including Python and CUDA. It is crucial to configure Visual Studio Code correctly for CUDA programming to leverage GPU capabilities efficiently within your Python projects.

To begin, download Visual Studio Code from the official website: https://code.visualstudio.com/. Follow the installation instructions specific to your operating system. Once the installation is complete, launch Visual Studio Code to start configuring it for CUDA development.

First, install the necessary extensions. Open the Extensions view by clicking on the Extensions icon in the Activity Bar on the side of the window or by pressing *Ctrl+Shift+X*. Search for and install the following extensions:

- **Python** by Microsoft - Provides rich support for the Python language, including features like IntelliSense (Pylance), linting, debugging, and code navigation.
- **Cuda Snippets** - Offers snippets for CUDA C++ code, which can be useful when writing CUDA kernels.
- **C/C++** by Microsoft - Adds language support for C and C++ to VS Code, necessary for writing and debugging CUDA C++ code

contained within Python through Numba or custom extensions.

Next, configure the Python environment. If Anaconda or Miniconda is installed, VS Code should automatically detect the Python environment. To select the correct Python interpreter, open the Command Palette with *Ctrl+Shift+P* and type *Python: Select Interpreter*. Choose the appropriate Conda environment that you will be using for CUDA development.

Set up VS Code for CUDA debugging by configuring launch.json. This configuration file enables setting up custom debug configurations for your workspace. Create or modify the launch.json by opening the Command Palette and selecting *Debug: Open launch.json*. Add the following configuration:

```
{
    "version": "0.2.0",
    "configurations": [
        {
            "name": "Python: Current File",
            "type": "python",
            "request": "launch",
            "program": "${file}",
            "console": "integratedTerminal"
        },
        {
            "name": "CUDA Debugging",
            "type": "cppdbg",
            "request": "launch",
            "program": "${workspaceFolder}/path_to_executable",
            "args": [],
            "stopAtEntry": false,
            "cwd": "${workspaceFolder}",
            "environment": [],
            "externalConsole": false,
            "MIMode": "gdb",
            "setupCommands": [
                {
                    "description": "Enable pretty-printing for gdb",
                    "text": "-enable-pretty-printing",
                    "ignoreFailures": true
                }
            ],
            "preLaunchTask": "build",
            "miDebuggerPath": "/usr/bin/gdb",
            "miDebuggerArgs": "",
            "logging": {
                "trace": true,
                "traceResponse": true,
                "engineLogging": true
            }
        }
    ]
}
```

Ensure the C++ build tools are correctly configured in your system to facilitate the building and debugging of CUDA C++ extensions within Python. On Windows, these tools are part of the Microsoft Visual Studio build tools. On Linux, install g++ and related utilities through your package manager.

Create a .vscode/tasks.json to automate building CUDA code. Add the following configuration for tasks specific to compiling CUDA code:

```
{
    "version": "2.0.0",
    "tasks": [
        {
            "label": "build",
            "type": "shell",
            "command": "nvcc",
            "args": [
                "${file}",
                "-o",
                "${fileDirname}/${fileBasenameNoExtension}.out"
            ],
            "group": {
                "kind": "build",
                "isDefault": true
            },
            "problemMatcher": [
                "$gcc"
            ]
        }
    ]
}
```

This configuration allows you to compile CUDA files directly from within VS Code by using the *Terminal* or the *Tasks* interface.

To validate that the setup is correct, create a sample CUDA file, sample.cu, containing a basic kernel function:

```
#include <stdio.h>

__global__ void kernel() {
    printf("Hello, CUDA world!\n");
}

int main() {
    kernel<<<1,1>>>();
    cudaDeviceSynchronize();
    return 0;
}
```

Compile this file using the task automation or manually with the terminal command:

```
nvcc sample.cu -o sample.out
```

Run the resulting executable to verify the CUDA setup:

```
./sample.out
```

The output should display:

```
Hello, CUDA world!
```

If the execution and output are as expected, the VS Code environment is properly set up for CUDA development. Continue enhancing the configuration by customizing settings in .vscode/settings.json to tailor the environment to specific preferences or project requirements.

2.4 Installing Anaconda and Python

Anaconda is a popular open-source distribution of Python and R designed for scientific computing and data science. It simplifies package management and deployment, making it a preferred choice for developing CUDA-enabled Python applications. This section provides a detailed guide on installing Anaconda and setting up Python to ensure a seamless development environment for CUDA programming.

Downloading Anaconda

Begin by downloading the latest version of Anaconda from the official website: https://www.anaconda.com/products/individual. Choose the installer that matches your operating system (Windows, macOS, or Linux).

Installing Anaconda on Windows

1. Locate the downloaded installer and double-click to start the installation process. 2. In the Anaconda Installer window, click Next. 3. Read and accept the license agreement by checking the I Agree option, then click Next. 4. Choose if you wish to install Anaconda for **Just Me** or **All Users**, and click Next. 5. Select the installation location. It is recommended to keep the default installation path. Click Next. 6. On the **Advanced Installation Options** screen, it is crucial to check the option Add Anaconda to my PATH environment variable. This ensures the Anaconda will be accessible from the command line. Click Install to continue. 7. Once the installation completes, click Next, and then Finish to close the installer.

Installing Anaconda on macOS

1. Open the Terminal application. 2. Navigate to the directory where the Anaconda installer is downloaded. Use the command:

```
cd /path/to/your/download/directory
```

3. Run the installer script using:

```
bash Anaconda3-2022.05-MacOSX-x86_64.sh
```

4. Follow the on-screen instructions. Press Enter to review the license agreement, then type yes to agree. 5. Confirm the installation location, or press Enter to install in the default directory. 6. Optionally, allow the installer to initialize Anaconda by modifying the .bashrc or .zshrc file. 7. Once completed, close and re-open the Terminal.

Installing Anaconda on Linux

1. Open a terminal window. 2. Change to the directory containing the Anaconda installer:

```
cd /path/to/your/download/directory
```

3. Execute the installer script:

```
bash Anaconda3-2022.05-Linux-x86_64.sh
```

4. Follow the prompts to accept the license agreement by pressing Enter, then type yes. 5. Confirm the installation path, or press Enter to proceed with the default location. 6. Let the installer run, and afterwards, it will prompt to initialize Anaconda3:

```
Do you wish the installer to initialize Anaconda3 by running conda init? [yes|no]
```

Type yes and press Enter. 7. Once the installation is finished, close and reopen the terminal.

Verifying Anaconda Installation

To ensure that Anaconda is properly installed, open a terminal or command prompt and type:

```
conda --version
```

A successful installation displays the version of conda, indicating that Anaconda is accessible from the command line.

Creating a Virtual Environment with Python

A best practice for managing dependencies and keeping your development environment clean is to use virtual environments. To create a virtual environment with Python, follow these steps:

1. Open a terminal or command prompt. 2. Create a new virtual environment named cuda-env with Python version 3.9 (or the version com-

patible with CUDA toolkit):

```
conda create -n cuda-env python=3.9
```

3. Activate the virtual environment:

```
conda activate cuda-env
```

You should notice the prompt now prefixes (cuda-env) indicating the environment is active.

Installing Additional Python Packages

With the virtual environment activated, you can install additional Python packages necessary for CUDA development. For instance, to install Numba and numpy, run:

```
conda install numba numpy
```

To validate the installation of these packages, you can run a basic Python script that imports Numba and numpy to check for any issues:

```
python -c "import numba; import numpy; print('Numba and Numpy are installed
    successfully.')"
```

The expected output should confirm successful installation:

```
Numba and Numpy are installed successfully.
```

Following these steps ensures that you have a well-configured Python environment suitable for CUDA development.

2.5 Setting Up Numba for CUDA Programming

Numba is a powerful Python library that translates Python functions to optimized machine code at runtime using the industry-standard LLVM compiler library. This includes the ability to execute code on CUDA-capable GPUs. With Numba, you can significantly speed up execution of array-oriented and math-heavy Python functions by running them on the GPU. This section will walk through the detailed process of setting up Numba for CUDA programming.

First, ensure that you have already installed Anaconda on your system as detailed in the previous section. Anaconda simplifies package management and deployment, making it straightforward to handle dependencies for CUDA development.

1. Open Anaconda Prompt (Windows) or your terminal of choice (macOS and Linux).

2. Create a new Conda environment specifically for CUDA development. This helps in managing dependencies more effectively and prevents conflicts with other projects.

```
conda create -n cuda_env python=3.8
```

After creating the environment, activate it:

```
conda activate cuda_env
```

Update Conda to ensure that all package metadata is current:

```
conda update conda
```

Install the CUDA Toolkit within your Conda environment. This step ensures that Numba has access to CUDA libraries:

```
conda install -c anaconda cudatoolkit
```

Next, install Numba. The Conda package manager will handle the installation of Numba along with its dependencies, including LLVM and CUDA libraries.

```
conda install numba
```

To verify the installation, create a Python script and check if Numba recognizes the CUDA-enabled GPU. Open your favorite text editor or IDE, such as Visual Studio Code, and create a new Python file named verify_numba.py:

```
from numba import cuda

print("CUDA is available:", cuda.is_available())
```

Run the script in the terminal:

```
python verify_numba.py
```

The expected output within the terminal should be:

```
CUDA is available: True
```

If the output indicates that CUDA is not available, ensure that your system has a compatible NVIDIA GPU, the CUDA toolkit is correctly installed, and that all environment variables are correctly configured.

Numba's features for CUDA programming represent a substantial advancement for Python's computational capabilities. It supports JIT (Just-In-Time) compilation for running high-performance functions on the GPU. Let's examine a simple example to illustrate the use of Numba for CUDA programming.

Create a new Python file called cuda_example.py, and include the following code:

```
from numba import vectorize
import numpy as np
import time

@vectorize(['float32(float32, float32)'], target='cuda')
def vector_add(a, b):
    return a + b

def main():
    N = 1000000
    A = np.random.rand(N).astype(np.float32)
    B = np.random.rand(N).astype(np.float32)

    start_time = time.time()
    C = vector_add(A, B)
    print("Time taken:", time.time() - start_time)
    print("First 10 elements of C:", C[:10])

if __name__ == "__main__":
    main()
```

This script demonstrates a vector addition operation accelerated with Numba on a CUDA-capable GPU. The @vectorize decorator, with the target='cuda' parameter, tells Numba to compile the vector_add function for the GPU.

Execute the script:

```
python cuda_example.py
```

The output would provide the time taken for the operation and the first 10 elements of the resulting vector C:

```
Time taken: 0.031
First 10 elements of C: [0.79824364 0.8403859  1.3087263  1.0277536  1.0447648  0.9714701
 0.52774286 0.5797565  1.2673703  0.9938056 ]
```

This example shows how straightforward it is to use Numba for writing GPU-accelerated code. The integration with CUDA provides significant performance improvements while allowing the use of existing Python code and libraries.

Finally, for consistently managing dependencies and ensuring compatibility, it's good practice to create a requirements file for your Conda environment. This can be done with the following command:

```
conda list --explicit > requirements.txt
```

This command generates a requirements.txt file containing all the packages installed in your current environment, which can be shared and re-used on different machines or setups.

Setting up Numba for CUDA programming in Python provides a seamless and efficient way to leverage GPU computing capabilities, significantly enhancing the performance of mathematical and array-based computations.

2.6 Verifying the Installation

Verifying the successful installation of the CUDA Toolkit, Visual Studio Code, Anaconda, and Numba is critical to ensure that your development environment is correctly set up for CUDA programming with Python. This section outlines the steps and commands needed for verification.

First, ensure that your system's environment variables are correctly set. The CUDA Toolkit should automatically add the necessary paths to your system's environment variables during installation. To confirm this, open a terminal (Command Prompt on Windows, Terminal on macOS/Linux) and execute:

```
nvcc --version
```

The command should return the version of the CUDA compiler. A sample expected output is:

```
nvcc: NVIDIA (R) Cuda compiler driver
Copyright (c) 2005-2023 NVIDIA Corporation
Built on Fri_Jan_26_19:25:23_PST_2023
Cuda compilation tools, release 11.4, V11.4.48
```

If the command returns the CUDA version, the CUDA Toolkit is correctly installed.

Next, verify the installation of the NVIDIA driver by running:

```
nvidia-smi
```

This should provide details about the GPU on your system, including the GPU model, driver version, and CUDA version compatibility. Sample output looks like:

```
Wed Sep 29 11:33:44 2023
+-----------------------------------------------------------------------------+
| NVIDIA-SMI 470.57.02    Driver Version: 470.57.02    CUDA Version: 11.4     |
|-------------------------------+----------------------+----------------------+
| GPU  Name        Persistence-M| Bus-Id        Disp.A | Volatile Uncorr. ECC |
| Fan  Temp  Perf  Pwr:Usage/Cap|         Memory-Usage | GPU-Util  Compute M. |
|                               |                      |               MIG M. |
|===============================+======================+======================|
|   0  GeForce GTX 108...  On   | 00000000:01:00.0 Off |                  N/A |
| 40%   58C    P2    50W / 250W |      0MiB / 11178MiB |      0%      Default |
|                               |                      |                  N/A |
+-------------------------------+----------------------+----------------------+
```

For verifying Anaconda and the creation of a suitable environment for CUDA programming, execute:

```
conda --version
```

This confirms that Anaconda is installed. Next, create a new environment:

```
conda create -n cuda_env python=3.8
conda activate cuda_env
```

With the environment activated, install Numba:

```
conda install numba
```

To verify Numba installation and its CUDA compatibility, use the following Python commands:

```
python -c "import numba; print(numba.__version__)"
```

For GPU support, install the CUDA-enabled version of Numba:

```
conda install numba cudatoolkit=<appropriate-version>
```

Replace <appropriate-version> with the actual CUDA Toolkit version, for instance, 11.4. Testing a simple Numba CUDA program ensures that everything is correctly configured. Save and run the following code in a Python file (e.g., test_numba.py):

```
from numba import cuda
import numpy as np

@cuda.jit
def add_kernel(a, b, c):
    i = cuda.grid(1)
    if i < a.size:
        c[i] = a[i] + b[i]

n = 1000000
a = np.ones(n, dtype=np.float32)
b = np.ones_like(a)
c = np.zeros_like(a)
```

```
threadsperblock = 1024
blockspergrid = (a.size + (threadsperblock - 1)) // threadsperblock

add_kernel[blockspergrid, threadsperblock](a, b, c)
print("c[:5] =", c[:5])
```

Execute the Python script with:

```
python test_numba.py
```

The expected output should show the initial elements of array c, verifying the GPU computation:

```
c[:5] = [2. 2. 2. 2. 2.]
```

This confirms the CUDA toolkit is functional with Numba in the Python environment.

Finally, confirm the configuration of Jupyter notebooks for CUDA. Install Jupyter if not already installed:

```
conda install jupyter
```

Launch Jupyter with:

```
jupyter notebook
```

Create a new notebook and execute the same Numba code as within the Python script above. Ensure the output matches the previous run to confirm successful configuration.

By following these steps, one can ascertain that the CUDA development environment for Python is properly set, ensuring smooth, productive development processes.

2.7 Introduction to CUDA Samples

When embarking on CUDA programming with Python, examining and understanding CUDA samples provides a practical and comprehensive way to grasp core concepts and implementations. CUDA samples are well-crafted, illustrative programs and scripts that demonstrate various functionalities and applications of CUDA. These samples can serve as a substantial learning resource, enabling developers to see firsthand how theoretical CUDA concepts manifest in code.

The CUDA Toolkit includes numerous sample programs designed to support a diverse range of CUDA features, from basic operations to complex algorithms. These samples are essential for learning effective CUDA programming practices and optimizing code for performance. This section will delve into how to access, compile, and execute these sample programs, followed by an analysis of a couple of core examples.

To begin with, it's pivotal to understand how to locate and set up these samples on your system. Once the CUDA Toolkit is installed, the samples are also placed in a default directory. The following steps outline how to access and copy these samples to your working directory:

```
$ cd /usr/local/cuda/samples
$ cp -r . ~/<desired-location>
```

This operation copies the entire samples directory to your specified location, allowing you to modify and compile them without impacting the original files in the CUDA installation directory.

Post copying the samples, it is crucial to build them. The samples come with predefined makefiles which simplify the build process. Navigate to the desired sample directory and execute the following commands to build a sample:

```
$ cd ~/<desired-location>/<sample-directory>
$ make
```

Once executed, the make command compiles the sample, producing an executable file in the same directory. To run the compiled sample, issue the following command:

```
$ ./<sample-executable>
```

For instance, consider you navigate to and build the 'deviceQuery' sample, a basic yet significant program that queries and displays properties of the available CUDA-capable devices. The build and execution flow would be:

```
$ cd ~/cuda-samples/1_Utilities/deviceQuery
$ make
$ ./deviceQuery
```

The output from 'deviceQuery' provides comprehensive details about the GPU devices, including:

```
deviceQuery, CUDA Driver = CUDART, CUDA Driver Version = XX.YY, CUDA Runtime Version = XX.YY, NumDevs = 1, Device 0: "NVIDIA GPU Name"
Device 0: "NVIDIA GPU Name"
  CUDA Capability Major/Minor version number: X.X
  Total amount of global memory: 8192 MBytes
  ( X) Multiprocessors, ( Y) CUDA Cores/MP: Y CUDA Cores
  ...
```

Reading this output helps ascertain the capabilities and configuration of the CUDA-enabled device, which is vital for performance tuning and optimization.

Another prominent example is the 'vectorAdd' sample, which demonstrates a simple yet fundamental CUDA operation—adding two vectors. The process involves copying data to the GPU, executing the kernel, and retrieving the results. This is illustrated through the following source code:

```
// Vector addition kernel
__global__ void vectorAdd(const float *A, const float *B, float *C, int N) {
    int i = blockDim.x * blockIdx.x + threadIdx.x;
    if (i < N) {
        C[i] = A[i] + B[i];
    }
}
```

Building and running the 'vectorAdd' sample involves:

```
$ cd ~/cuda-samples/0_Simple/vectorAdd
$ make
$ ./vectorAdd
```

When executed, it performs the vector addition on GPU and prints out the time taken for both memory transfer and computation, which is critical for analyzing the efficiency of GPU operations over CPU counterparts.

In-depth examination of these CUDA samples illuminates the practical usage of GPU computing, pinpointing critical facets such as memory management, parallel execution model, and kernel launches. Furthermore, customizing these samples by altering parameters or integrating additional functionalities augments understanding and hones skills essential for proficient CUDA programming. As we progress further into more advanced examples, the foundational knowledge obtained through these standard samples will become increasingly valuable.

2.8 Managing CUDA Libraries and Dependencies

Efficient management of CUDA libraries and dependencies is pivotal to maintain smooth and robust CUDA application development. CUDA, being a parallel computing platform, leverages various libraries to optimize processing tasks. Key libraries such as cuBLAS, cuFFT, and cuDNN play significant roles in enhancing performance. This section elucidates the management of these libraries and the necessary configurations to ensure seamless integration in your Python-based CUDA projects.

Installing NVIDIA CUDA Libraries

Various CUDA libraries can be installed via the CUDA Toolkit installer or separately from the NVIDIA official website. The installation involves downloading the library packages and configuring the system paths to recognize these libraries.

Example for installing CUDA Toolkit:

```
wget https://developer.download.nvidia.com/compute/cuda/11.4.2/local_installers/
    cuda_11.4.2_470.57.02_linux.run
sudo sh cuda_11.4.2_470.57.02_linux.run
```

To ensure libraries such as cuBLAS and cuFFT are correctly installed:

```
sudo apt-get install libcublas-11-0 libcufft-11-0
```

Configuring Environment Variables

Post-installation, it is critical to configure your system paths to include the CUDA binaries and libraries. This is typically achieved by adding the following lines to your shell configuration file (e.g., '.bashrc', '.zshrc'):

```
export PATH=/usr/local/cuda-11.4/bin:$PATH
export LD_LIBRARY_PATH=/usr/local/cuda-11.4/lib64:$LD_LIBRARY_PATH
```

After modifying the shell configuration file, reload it to apply the changes:

```
source ~/.bashrc
```

Managing Dependencies with Anaconda

Anaconda is a powerful tool for managing Python environments, including CUDA libraries and dependencies. Using Anaconda, you can create isolated environments tailored to specific project requirements, thereby avoiding conflicts between library versions.

Create a new Anaconda environment with Python and essential CUDA packages:

```
conda create --name cudadev python=3.8 numpy
conda activate cudadev
```

Install necessary CUDA libraries such as Numba and CuPy within the environment:

```
conda install numba cupy
```

List all installed packages to verify the installation:

```
conda list
```

Linking CUDA Libraries in Python

In Python, linking to installed CUDA libraries often involves directly pointing to the library paths or using wrappers like Numba and CuPy, which manage low-level details. For instance, Numba automatically recognizes the CUDA Toolkit path configured in your environment variables.

Using CuPy to perform a simple vector addition:

```
import cupy as cp

# Define two vectors
a = cp.array([1, 2, 3, 4, 5], dtype=cp.float32)
b = cp.array([10, 20, 30, 40, 50], dtype=cp.float32)

# Perform vector addition
c = a + b

print(c)
```

Expected output:

```
[11. 22. 33. 44. 55.]
```

Verify that the computation is performed on the GPU by inspecting CuPy's device context:

```
print(cp.cuda.Device().count) # should output the number of CUDA-capable GPUs
```

Handling Version Conflicts

Library and dependency version conflicts can pose significant challenges. Consistently monitoring compatibility between the CUDA Toolkit, Python, and library versions is recommended. Anaconda facilitates this by allowing the specification of package versions during installation.

To install specific versions:

```
conda install numba=0.53.1 cupy=8.6.0
```

Conflicting dependencies can be managed using Conda or pip, ensuring that incompatible versions do not get installed.

Check dependency versions aligned:

```
conda list
```

Updating libraries to the latest compatible versions:

```
conda update numba cupy
```

Manually manage and resolve conflicts by reviewing the dependency graph using:

```
conda info --envs
```

Verifying Dependencies

Ensuring the correct placement and accessibility of CUDA libraries ensures stability. To verify if libraries such as cuBLAS and cuDNN are properly installed, simple tests can be conducted:

For cuDNN:

```
python -m cupy.cuda.cudnn.check
```

Successful output indicates proper installation.

For cuBLAS and other libraries, Numba's CUDA extensions can be verified:

```
from numba import cuda
cuda.detect()
```

The output should list the CUDA-capable GPUs and their properties if the libraries are correctly configured.

2.9 Setting Up Jupyter Notebooks for CUDA Development

To enable effective development and testing of CUDA code within an interactive environment, Jupyter Notebooks provide a highly versatile tool that supports a blend of code execution, visualization, and markdown documentation. This section guides through the process of setting up Jupyter Notebooks for CUDA development, ensuring seamless integration with the CUDA Toolkit and Python.

Firstly, install Jupyter using the Anaconda distribution, as it encapsulates essential data science libraries and provides a manageable environment. Open the Anaconda Prompt and execute the following command to install Jupyter:

```
conda install jupyter
```

Launching Jupyter Notebook is straightforward. Within the Anaconda Prompt, type:

```
jupyter notebook
```

This command starts the Jupyter Notebook server and opens a new tab in the default web browser at http://localhost:8888/tree, displaying the Jupyter dashboard.

To incorporate CUDA within Jupyter Notebooks, install the necessary Python packages like Numba. Numba transforms Python functions into optimized machine code at runtime using the industry-standard LLVM compiler library. Ensure Numba is installed by running:

```
conda install numba
```

Additionally, verify that cudatoolkit is installed within your Anaconda environment:

```
conda install cudatoolkit
```

Create a new Jupyter Notebook and initialize your development environment. Import the required libraries by executing the following Python code within a cell:

```
import numba
from numba import cuda
import numpy as np
```

This code ensures that Numba and CUDA are accessible for subsequent operations. To validate the environment, a simple kernel test can ascertain proper configurations. Define a basic CUDA kernel that performs element-wise addition of two arrays:

```
@cuda.jit
def vector_add(a, b, c):
    idx = cuda.grid(1)
    if idx < a.size:
        c[idx] = a[idx] + b[idx]
```

This CUDA function uses cuda.grid(1) to determine the unique thread index within the grid, ensuring that each thread operates on a unique element in the input arrays.

Next, create sample arrays and allocate memory on the GPU. The following code demonstrates the data setup and kernel launch procedure:

```
n = 1 << 20 # Number of elements
a = np.ones(n, dtype=np.float32)
b = np.ones(n, dtype=np.float32)
c = np.empty(n, dtype=np.float32)

# Allocate device memory and copy input data to the device
d_a = cuda.to_device(a)
d_b = cuda.to_device(b)
d_c = cuda.device_array(n, dtype=np.float32)

# Define thread block and grid sizes
threads_per_block = 256
blocks_per_grid = (n + (threads_per_block - 1)) // threads_per_block

# Launch the kernel
vector_add[blocks_per_grid, threads_per_block](d_a, d_b, d_c)

# Copy the result back to the host
d_c.copy_to_host(c)
```

The above code assigns 1 million elements to arrays a and b, copies these arrays to the device memory, and sets up the device result array d_c. The kernel is launched with the specified grid and block sizes, and the resultant data is copied back from the GPU to the host for verification.

To confirm that the kernel executed correctly, verify the output array c. Execute the following command to check the first ten elements of the output:

```
print(c[:10])
```

The expected output should display ten elements, each with the value 2.0. This indicates correct addition of elements from arrays a and b.

```
[2. 2. 2. 2. 2. 2. 2. 2. 2. 2.]
```

Successful execution and correct results validate the setup, enabling further exploration and implementation of complex CUDA algorithms within Jupyter Notebooks.

Jupyter Notebooks also offer rich visualization capabilities to analyze and debug CUDA-based applications. Leverage libraries such as Matplotlib for graphical representations. Install Matplotlib if not already present:

```
conda install matplotlib
```

To visualize performance metrics or other data, import Matplotlib and plot the required graphs. For instance, generate a simple plot of the resultant array c:

```
import matplotlib.pyplot as plt

plt.plot(c[:100]) # Plot the first 100 elements
plt.title('Resultant Array Elements')
plt.xlabel('Index')
plt.ylabel('Value')
plt.show()
```

The plot should depict a flat line at 2.0 across all plotted indices, providing a visual confirmation of the CPU-GPU collaboration.

By integrating Jupyter Notebooks with CUDA, educators and practitioners can effortlessly combine teaching materials, executable code, and interactive visuals, fostering an enriching learning and development environment. This setup ensures that Python serves as a bridge between high-level coding ease and the computational prowess of CUDA-enabled GPUs.

2.10 Troubleshooting Common Installation Issues

When setting up a CUDA development environment, various issues can arise that may hinder the installation process or affect the functionality of the installed tools. This section addresses common problems encountered and their potential solutions, ensuring a smooth configuration and operation.

1. CUDA Toolkit Installation Issues

- **Driver Incompatibility:** Ensure that the NVIDIA driver version is compatible with the CUDA Toolkit version. Check the version compatibility matrix provided by NVIDIA on their official website. If the driver is incompatible, download and install the correct version.

- **Toolkit Path Configuration:** Verify that the CUDA Toolkit's installation path is correctly added to the system's environment variables. On Windows, ensure that the CUDA_PATH variable is set and that the bin directory under the CUDA installation path is included in the PATH variable. On Linux, add the following lines to your .bashrc or .zshrc file:

```
export PATH=/usr/local/cuda-<version>/bin:$PATH
export LD_LIBRARY_PATH=/usr/local/cuda-<version>/lib64:
    $LD_LIBRARY_PATH
```

  Replace <version> with the appropriate CUDA version number.

- **Unsupported GPU:** Ensure that the GPU is supported by the CUDA Toolkit. Verify the hardware compatibility list provided by NVIDIA. If the GPU is not supported, consider upgrading to a compatible GPU.

2. **Visual Studio Code Configuration Issues**

- **Extension Issues:** Ensure that the necessary extensions for CUDA and Python development are installed in Visual Studio Code. Extensions like **Python**, **C/C++**, and **Numba** are essential. Verify their installation from the Extensions view (Ctrl+Shift+X).

- **IntelliSense Problems:** If IntelliSense features are not working properly, check whether the configuration files (c_cpp_properties.json) are correctly set up. Adjust the includePath and browse.path variables to include the CUDA headers, for example:

```
{
    "configurations": [
        {
            "name": "Win32",
            "includePath": [
                "${workspaceFolder}/**",
                "C:/Program Files/NVIDIA GPU Computing Toolkit/CUDA/v<
                    version>/include"
            ],
            "compilerPath": "C:/Program Files (x86)/Microsoft Visual Studio/<
                version>/BuildTools/VC/bin/cl.exe",
            "intelliSenseMode": "msvc-x64"
        }
```

```
    ],
    "version": 4
}
```

Replace <version> with the appropriate CUDA and Visual Studio version numbers.

3. Anaconda and Python Installation Issues

- **Conda Environment Errors:** Ensure that the Conda environment is activated before installing any packages or running scripts. Use the following command to activate the desired environment:

```
conda activate <environment_name>
```

  Replace <environment_name> with the name of your Conda environment.

- **Package Conflicts:** Resolve any package version conflicts by specifying compatible versions during installation. For example, when installing Numba, ensure that the CUDA version is specified:

```
conda install numba cudatoolkit=<version>
```

  Replace <version> with the desired CUDA Toolkit version.

4. Numba Configuration Issues

- **CUDA Driver Errors:** Ensure that the CUDA driver is correctly installed and the GPU device is recognized. Test the installation by running a simple Numba CUDA program:

```
from numba import cuda
cuda.detect()
```

  If the GPU is not detected, recheck the driver installation or consult the system's GPU configuration.

- **Compatibility Issues:** Ensure that the versions of Numba, CUDA Toolkit, and NVIDIA drivers are compatible. Refer to the compatibility documentation on the Numba and NVIDIA websites for details on supported versions.

5. Jupyter Notebook Configuration Issues

- **Kernel Installation:** Ensure that the correct kernel is installed for Jupyter Notebooks to use the Conda environment. If the kernel is not appearing, install the **ipykernel** package and set up the kernel:

```
conda install ipykernel
python -m ipykernel install --user --name=<environment_name> --display-name
    "<Custom Name>"
```

  Replace <environment_name> with the name of the Conda environment and <Custom Name> with a name for the Jupyter Notebook kernel.

- **CUDA Import Errors:** Verify that the Jupyter Notebook environment is using the correct Conda environment. If there are import errors for CUDA or related libraries, ensure the kernel is set to the appropriate environment in the Jupyter interface.

6. General Debugging Tips

- **Log Files:** Review the log files for detailed error messages. These logs can provide insights into the root cause of installation or runtime issues.

- **Documentation and Forums:** Consult the official documentation for CUDA, Numba, and other tools. Community forums, GitHub issues, and StackOverflow are valuable resources for troubleshooting and obtaining solutions from developers who may have encountered similar issues.

- **Environment Isolation:** To prevent conflicts, isolate the development environment using virtual environments like Conda. This practice ensures that dependencies are correctly managed without interference from other installed packages.

```
!conda info --envs
```

The command above lists all Conda environments, providing a quick check for correct environment setup.

```
# conda environments:
#
base                  * /usr/local/anaconda3
cuda_env                /usr/local/anaconda3/envs/cuda_env
```

Confirming the active environment aids in verifying that the appropriate dependencies and configurations are applied to the development setup.

Chapter 3

Python and Numba Introduction

This chapter introduces Python's role in scientific computing and the importance of just-in-time (JIT) compilation. It covers the basics of installing and setting up Python and Numba, a JIT compiler that accelerates Python functions. Key topics include familiarizing with NumPy, understanding Numba's functionality, writing and optimizing Numba-accelerated code, and comparing Numba with other Python accelerators. Practical applications and integration with other Python libraries are also discussed.

3.1 Introduction to Python for Scientific Computing

Python has established itself as a formidable tool in the realm of scientific computing due to its simplicity, readability, and extensive ecosystem of libraries. Many scientists and engineers prefer Python for its straightforward syntax, which enables rapid development and prototyping. Additionally, Python's flexibility and ability to integrate seamlessly with other languages and tools further augment its utility in scientific research and engineering applications.

At the core of Python's appeal in scientific computing is its rich collection of libraries, such as NumPy, SciPy, and Pandas, which provide powerful tools for numerical computations, data manipulation, and statistical analysis. These libraries are foundational, offering highly optimized functions that can handle large datasets efficiently, making Python not just a convenient choice but a powerful one.

NumPy is perhaps the most fundamental library and forms the foundation for scientific computing in Python. It introduces the ndarray, a powerful N-dimensional array object, along with a suite of functions for performing efficient operations on these arrays. NumPy arrays are significantly faster and more memory-efficient than Python lists, especially as the size of the data increases. For example, consider the creation and manipulation of a large array:

```
import numpy as np

# Creating a large 1D array of 10 million elements
large_array = np.arange(1e7)

# Performing an element-wise multiplication
result_array = large_array * 2
```

```
# Output (first 5 elements of result_array)
array([0., 2., 4., 6., 8.])
```

The operations on large_array are vectorized, meaning they are performed in a highly efficient manner without the need for explicit loops in Python. This is one of the key reasons why NumPy is preferred for large-scale data processing tasks.

SciPy extends NumPy's functionality by adding a collection of algorithms and high-level commands for scientific and engineering tasks. It includes modules for optimization, integration, interpolation, eigenvalue problems, algebraic equations, and more. This allows researchers to solve complex mathematical problems with relatively simple and concise code. For instance, solving a system of linear equations can be achieved using:

```
from scipy.linalg import solve

A = np.array([[3, 2], [1, 4]])
b = np.array([1, 2])

# Solving the system of linear equations Ax = b
x = solve(A, b)
```

```
# Output
array([-0.14285714, 0.57142857])
```

Here, solve from the scipy.linalg module efficiently computes the solution to the system of linear equations $Ax = b$.

Pandas is a library designed for data manipulation and analysis. It introduces data structures such as DataFrame, which is akin to relational tables or dataframes in R. DataFrame objects make it easy to manipulate and analyze structured data, perform operations like filtering, grouping, statistical analysis, and merging datasets. Consider an example of handling a dataset:

```
import pandas as pd

# Creating a DataFrame
data = {'Name': ['Alice', 'Bob', 'Charlie'], 'Age': [25, 30, 35]}
df = pd.DataFrame(data)

# Selection and filtering
adults = df[df['Age'] > 28]
```

```
# Output
     Name  Age
1     Bob   30
2  Charlie  35
```

The power and flexibility of DataFrames in Pandas simplify working with large datasets, making the data analysis process more intuitive and efficient.

Alongside these core libraries, Python's ecosystem for scientific computing is enriched by visualization tools like **Matplotlib**, **Seaborn**, and **Plotly**. These libraries enable the creation of a wide range of visualizations from simple plots to complex interactive graphics. Visualization is crucial in scientific computing as it allows for the interpretation and communication of data insights. For example, generating a simple line plot with Matplotlib can be done as follows:

```
import matplotlib.pyplot as plt

# Generating data
x = np.linspace(0, 10, 100)
y = np.sin(x)

# Creating a line plot
plt.plot(x, y)
plt.xlabel('x')
plt.ylabel('sin(x)')
plt.title('Sine Wave')
plt.show()
```

```
# The output will be a graphical window displaying the sine wave.
```

Python's versatility is further demonstrated by its interoperability with other programming languages and technologies. Libraries such as **Cython** and **pybind11** allow embedding C/C++ code within Python, enabling performance-critical sections of code to be executed more efficiently without sacrificing the ease of Python's usage. Additionally, Python's integration with web technologies through frameworks like **Flask** and **Django** facilitates the deployment of scientific applications as web services.

Finally, the active Python community and extensive documentation provide a supportive environment for both novice and experienced developers. Numerous tutorials, forums, and collaborative platforms ensure that help is readily available, promoting continuous learning and improvement.

The combination of an extensive library ecosystem, ease of use, and strong community support makes Python an indispensable tool in the arsenal of scientists and engineers, enabling them to conduct research and solve complex problems efficiently.

3.2 Installing and Setting Up Python

To effectively utilize Python for scientific computing, it is essential to have a well-configured environment. This section delineates the sequential steps to install Python, configure your development environment, and ensure that all essential libraries are available.

The primary method for installing Python is through the official Python website (python.org) or by using a package manager like Anaconda. Below, we detail each approach.

Installation via the Official Python Website: 1. Navigate to https://www.python.org/downloads/. 2. Select the version compatible with your operating system and download the installer. For this book, we recommend Python 3.8 or later. 3. Run the installer: - On Windows: Execute the downloaded .exe file, ensure that "Add Python to PATH" is checked, and follow the installation prompts. - On macOS: Open the downloaded .pkg file and follow the prompts. - On Linux: Use your package manager. For example, on Ubuntu:

```
sudo apt update
sudo apt install python3
```

Installation via Anaconda: Anaconda is a popular distribution that includes Python and a suite of scientific computing libraries.

1. Navigate to https://www.anaconda.com/products/distribution. 2. Download the installer for your operating system. 3. Run the installer:

- On Windows: Follow the on-screen instructions. - On macOS: Open the downloaded .pkg file and follow the prompts. - On Linux:

```
bash ~/Downloads/Anaconda3-2020.02-Linux-x86_64.sh
```

4. Verify the installation:

```
conda list
```

Configuring the Development Environment: Post-installation, setting up a robust development environment is critical. We recommend using Jupyter Notebook or an Integrated Development Environment (IDE) like PyCharm or Visual Studio Code.

To install Jupyter Notebook via pip:

```
pip install notebook
```

To launch Jupyter Notebook:

```
jupyter notebook
```

This will open a browser window where you can create and manage Jupyter Notebooks, enabling an interactive computing environment ideal for data science workflows.

For those preferring an IDE:

1. **PyCharm**: Download from https://www.jetbrains.com/pycharm/download/. - Follow installation instructions specific to your operating system. - Configure a new project to use the Python interpreter from your Anaconda installation or the standard Python installation path.

2. **Visual Studio Code**: - Download from https://code.visualstudio.com/. - Install the Python extension via the Extensions Marketplace. - Configure the settings to use your preferred Python interpreter.

Ensuring Essential Libraries are Available: Scientific computing with Python relies heavily on various libraries. We will focus on installing NumPy, SciPy, pandas, and matplotlib, which form the cornerstone of many scientific computing tasks.

To install these libraries using pip:

```
pip install numpy scipy pandas matplotlib
```

For Anaconda users:

```
conda install numpy scipy pandas matplotlib
```

Verify installations by importing these libraries in a Python session:

```
python
>>> import numpy
>>> import scipy
>>> import pandas
>>> import matplotlib
>>> exit()
```

A successful import without errors confirms the libraries are properly installed.

Incorporating these tools and libraries into your development workflow ensures a smooth start to Python programming for scientific computing, allowing for efficient data analysis, visualization, and computational tasks.

3.3 NumPy: The Foundation for Data Science in Python

NumPy, which stands for Numerical Python, is a pivotal library for scientific and numerical computing in Python. It provides a high-performance multidimensional array object along with tools for working with these arrays. The key features of NumPy include a powerful N-dimensional array object, comprehensive mathematical functions, tools for generating random numbers, and essential routines for linear algebra, Fourier transforms, and more.

At the core of NumPy is the ndarray object, a multidimensional array, which forms the backbone of most data manipulation tasks in scientific computing.

1. NumPy Arrays

The primary object of NumPy is its powerful ndarray, aka n-dimensional array. These arrays are homogeneous in nature, meaning that they are composed of elements of the same data type. Creating arrays with NumPy is straightforward:

```
import numpy as np

# Creating a 1D NumPy array
array_1d = np.array([1, 2, 3, 4, 5])
```

```
# Creating a 2D NumPy array
array_2d = np.array([[1, 2, 3], [4, 5, 6]])

print(array_1d)
print(array_2d)
```

```
[1 2 3 4 5]
[[1 2 3]
 [4 5 6]]
```

2. Array Attributes

NumPy arrays come with several essential attributes:

```
# Shape of the array
print(array_2d.shape)

# Number of dimensions
print(array_2d.ndim)

# Number of elements in the array
print(array_2d.size)

# Data type of the array elements
print(array_2d.dtype)
```

```
(2, 3)
2
6
int64
```

3. Array Initialization

NumPy provides several functions to initialize arrays efficiently:

```
# Array of zeros
zeros_array = np.zeros((3, 3))

# Array of ones
ones_array = np.ones((2, 4))

# Identity matrix
identity_matrix = np.eye(3)

# Array with a range of elements
range_array = np.arange(1, 10, 2)

# Array with random numbers
random_array = np.random.random((3, 3))

print(zeros_array)
print(ones_array)
print(identity_matrix)
print(range_array)
```

```
print(random_array)
```

```
[[0. 0. 0.]
 [0. 0. 0.]
 [0. 0. 0.]]
[[1. 1. 1. 1.]
 [1. 1. 1. 1.]]
[[1. 0. 0.]
 [0. 1. 0.]
 [0. 0. 1.]]
[1 3 5 7 9]
[[0.61024477 0.53163524 0.16133902]
 [0.20218977 0.58275829 0.38668351]
 [0.56257722 0.14698735 0.78709386]]
```

4. Array Indexing

Indexing in NumPy arrays works similarly to Python lists but is more powerful with support for multidimensional access:

```
# 1D array indexing
print(array_1d[2])

# 2D array indexing
print(array_2d[1, 2])

# Slicing
print(array_2d[:, 1])
```

```
3
6
[2 5]
```

5. Array Operations

Element-wise operations, such as addition, subtraction, multiplication, and division, can be performed directly on NumPy arrays:

```
# Creating two NumPy arrays
array_a = np.array([[1, 2], [3, 4]])
array_b = np.array([[5, 6], [7, 8]])

# Element-wise addition
result_add = array_a + array_b

# Element-wise multiplication
result_mul = array_a * array_b

# Matrix multiplication
result_dot = np.dot(array_a, array_b)

print(result_add)
print(result_mul)
print(result_dot)
```

```
[[ 6  8]
 [10 12]]
[[ 5 12]
 [21 32]]
[[19 22]
 [43 50]]
```

6. Broadcasting

NumPy supports broadcasting, which allows arithmetic operations on arrays of different shapes. Broadcasting automatically expands the smaller array to match the shape of the larger array:

```
# Array and scalar broadcasting
array_c = np.array([1, 2, 3])
scalar = 2

result_broadcast = array_c * scalar

# Array and array broadcasting
array_d = np.array([[1], [2], [3]])

result_broadcast_2 = array_d + array_c

print(result_broadcast)
print(result_broadcast_2)
```

```
[2 4 6]
[[2 3 4]
 [3 4 5]
 [4 5 6]]
```

7. Universal Functions

NumPy provides a wide range of vectorized functions, known as universal functions (ufuncs), that perform element-wise operations on arrays:

```
# Applying universal functions
array_e = np.array([0, np.pi/2, np.pi])
sin_array = np.sin(array_e)

# Element-wise exponentiation
exp_array = np.exp(array_e)

print(sin_array)
print(exp_array)
```

```
[0.000000e+00 1.000000e+00 1.224647e-16]
[1.000000e+00 1.648721e+00 2.718282e+00]
```

8. Aggregations

Aggregations summarize data by reducing multiple elements to one through operations such as summing, finding the mean, or identifying the maximum value:

```
array_f = np.array([[1, 2, 3], [4, 5, 6]])

# Sum of all elements
total_sum = np.sum(array_f)

# Mean of all elements
mean_value = np.mean(array_f)

# Maximum value
max_value = np.max(array_f)

print(total_sum)
print(mean_value)
print(max_value)
```

```
21
3.5
6
```

9. Linear Algebra

NumPy includes various functions for performing linear algebra computations, including matrix multiplication and decompositions:

```
# Linear algebra functions
matrix_g = np.array([[1, 2], [3, 4]])

# Matrix inverse
inverse_matrix = np.linalg.inv(matrix_g)

# Eigenvalues and eigenvectors
eigenvalues, eigenvectors = np.linalg.eig(matrix_g)

print(inverse_matrix)
print(eigenvalues)
print(eigenvectors)
```

```
[[-2.   1. ]
 [ 1.5 -0.5]]
[5.37228132 -0.37228132]
[[ 0.82456484 -0.41597356]
 [ 0.56576746  0.90937671]]
```

10. Random Functions

NumPy also offers a set of random number generation functions for creating arrays of random values, which are critical in simulations and algorithms that require stochastic processes:

```
# Random samples from a standard normal distribution
random_array_1 = np.random.randn(3, 3)

# Random integers
random_integers = np.random.randint(1, 10, size=(3, 3))

print(random_array_1)
print(random_integers)
```

```
[[ 0.34234389  1.06917058 -0.47288384]
 [ 1.39984163 -0.44274954  0.39361719]
 [-0.92124535 -1.04610346  1.09119169]]
[[6 5 6]
 [6 9 6]
 [7 9 9]]
```

NumPy serves as the foundation for many other libraries in the Python ecosystem. Libraries such as Pandas, SciPy, Matplotlib, and scikit-learn are built on top of NumPy, leveraging its rich functionality, efficient computations, and robust performance. Understanding the core functionalities of NumPy is essential for anyone working in data science, as it forms the basis for data manipulation and computational tasks.

3.4 Understanding JIT Compilation

Just-In-Time (JIT) compilation is a technique that provides significant performance improvements for dynamic languages like Python by compiling code at runtime rather than prior to execution. This section delves into the principles of JIT compilation, how it contrasts with other compilation methods, and its relevance and application in Python, particularly with the Numba library.

JIT compilation aims to bridge the gap between the flexibility of interpreted languages and the performance of compiled languages. When a program is run, the JIT compiler translates parts of the intermediate representation or source code into machine code on-the-fly, enabling execution on the CPU. The machine code is then cached to avoid re-compilation of the same code regions, optimizing runtime performance.

The primary advantage of JIT compilation is its ability to optimize hot paths, which are frequently executed parts of the program. Since the compilation occurs during execution, the JIT compiler can gather runtime information to make more informed optimization decisions that static compilers cannot. These optimizations include inlining functions, eliminating redundant bounds checks, and utilizing work-specific pointers.

The JIT compilation process typically follows these steps:

- **Initial Execution:** The interpreter starts executing the bytecode without any optimizations.
- **Profiling:** As the code runs, performance-critical sections ("hot spots") are identified through profiling.
- **Optimization:** The identified hot spots are compiled into optimized machine code.
- **Execution of Compiled Code:** Subsequent executions of the hot spots use the optimized machine code, improving performance.

The contrast between JIT compilation and other compilation approaches can be summarized as follows:

- **Interpreted Languages:** In purely interpreted languages, the source code is translated into intermediate bytecode, which is directly executed by an interpreter. This approach is flexible but often slower due to the overhead of interpretation.
- **Ahead-Of-Time (AOT) Compilation:** AOT compilers translate the entire source code into machine code before execution. This results in faster execution as the code is pre-optimized, but it lacks the adaptive optimizations that JIT can provide.
- **JIT Compilation:** JIT compilers combine the benefits of interpreted and AOT compilation. They start by interpreting the code, then switch to compiling and optimizing frequently executed paths, thus adapting the optimizations based on runtime behavior.

In Python, several JIT compilers are available, such as PyPy, Numba, and Pyston. Each comes with unique features but shares the common goal of improving Python's runtime performance. Numba stands out due to its seamless integration with NumPy, enabling efficient scientific computing.

Numba, leveraging the LLVM (Low-Level Virtual Machine) framework for JIT compilation, allows for the on-the-fly conversion of Python functions into optimized machine code. This minimizes the overhead typical of interpreted languages and accelerates numerical computations significantly. Here is an example that shines light on how Numba's JIT compilation transforms a routine:

```
from numba import jit
import numpy as np

@jit(nopython=True)
def matrix_multiply(A, B):
    return np.dot(A, B)

A = np.random.random((1000, 1000))
B = np.random.random((1000, 1000))

# Executing the JIT-compiled function
C = matrix_multiply(A, B)
```

The `@jit` decorator enables the just-in-time compilation for the `matrix_multiply` function. The `nopython=True` argument ensures that the function is fully compiled rather than interpreted, leading to significant performance gains.

Execution Output:

```
Process finished with exit code 0
```

The compilation step happens upon the first invocation of the function, resulting in a slight delay initially because of the compilation overhead. Subsequent calls to `matrix_multiply` do not incur this cost, as the compiled machine code is reused, thus achieving speedups typically observed in compiled languages.

Understanding the interplay between interpreted, AOT, and JIT compilation provides critical insight into optimizing Python programs for high-performance computing. Numba leverages JIT compilation to give Python the performance characteristics necessary for intensive scientific applications without sacrificing the language's flexibility or ease of use.

3.5 Introduction to Numba

Numba is an open-source JIT compiler that translates a subset of Python and NumPy code into fast machine code using the LLVM compiler infrastructure. Developed by Anaconda, Inc., Numba allows Python functions to run at native machine code speed, vastly improving the performance of numerical computations.

Numba achieves its performance improvements by focusing on the optimization of numerical functions and supporting array-oriented computations. It integrates seamlessly with the Python scientific computing ecosystem, particularly NumPy, providing an efficient means to accelerate computations with minimal code changes.

To begin utilizing Numba, one imports the numba module and decorates Python functions with @jit or @njit decorators, specifying function signatures if needed. Numba then compiles these functions at runtime.

Consider a basic example where Numba is used to accelerate a simple numerical computation:

```
import numba
import numpy as np

@numba.jit
def sum_array(arr):
    sum = 0
    for i in range(arr.size):
        sum += arr[i]
    return sum

array = np.arange(1e7)
print(sum_array(array))
```

In this example, the sum_array function, which sums the elements of an array, is decorated with @jit. By doing so, Numba compiles this function to machine code, significantly improving execution speed.

It is crucial to understand the various decorators and options available in Numba:

1. @jit: The just-in-time decorator that tells Numba to compile the function. It can accept an optional signature argument. 2. @njit: A shorthand for @jit(nopython=True), enforcing Numba to operate in "nopython" mode where Python object handling is avoided entirely for maximum speed.

The following example highlights the effect of @njit:

```
@numba.njit
```

```
def fast_sum_array(arr):
    sum = 0
    for i in range(arr.size):
        sum += arr[i]
    return sum
```

By using @njit, we ensure that Numba compiles the function entirely to machine code, avoiding the overhead of Python's object model.

Numba supports advanced features like parallel computing and GPU acceleration. Using the @vectorize and @guvectorize decorators, one can compile functions that operate element-wise on arrays, similar to NumPy's ufuncs (universal functions).

```
from numba import vectorize

@vectorize([float64(float64, float64)], target='parallel')
def add_arrays(a, b):
    return a + b

a = np.arange(10**7, dtype=np.float64)
b = np.arange(10**7, dtype=np.float64)
c = add_arrays(a, b)
```

In this example, the add_arrays function is vectorized to operate element-wise and is parallelized across multiple CPU cores. The target='parallel' argument specifies the parallel computing target.

Moreover, Numba supports GPU programming using the CUDA platform. By using @cuda.jit, one can write functions that execute on NVIDIA GPUs.

```
from numba import cuda

@cuda.jit
def gpu_sum_array(arr, sum):
    i = cuda.grid(1)
    if i < arr.size:
        cuda.atomic.add(sum, 0, arr[i])

arr = np.arange(1e7, dtype=np.float32)
sum = np.array([0], dtype=np.float32)
gpu_sum_array[256, 256](arr, sum)
print(sum[0])
```

Here, gpu_sum_array demonstrates a sum reduction on the GPU using CUDA. The function is decorated with @cuda.jit and utilizes CUDA-specific constructs like cuda.grid and cuda.atomic.add.

Understanding when and how to apply Numba's decorators is essential for optimizing Python code effectively. Awareness of the computational patterns suited for JIT compilation and the limitations of Numba's current capabilities will guide developers in leveraging its power.

3.6 Installing and Setting Up Numba

Numba is an open-source JIT compiler that translates a subset of Python and NumPy code into fast machine code. This section covers the installation process and initial setup of Numba to ensure that your development environment is prepared for the subsequent sections.

Numba works best with a variety of configurations, including different operating systems and Python distributions. It is compatible with CPython, the standard Python interpreter, as well as Anaconda, a popular Python distribution for scientific computing.

Pre-requisites:

- **Python 3.6 or later:** Numba supports Python versions 3.6 and beyond. Ensure that you have an appropriate version installed.
- **pip:** A package installer for Python that simplifies the installation process for libraries.
- **NumPy:** Ensure that NumPy is already installed as Numba is designed to work with it.

Installation Steps:

Numba can be installed via pip or through the Anaconda distribution. Both methods will be described below.

Using pip:

If you are using the standard Python distribution with pip, the installation command is straightforward. Open your terminal or command prompt and execute:

```
pip install numba
```

Upon executing this command, pip will handle the download and installation of Numba and its dependencies. To verify the installation, you can initiate a Python interpreter session and import Numba:

```
import numba
print(numba.__version__)
```

If installed correctly, this series of commands will display the Numba version number.

Using Anaconda:

Anaconda users can take advantage of the conda package manager to install Numba efficiently. In your terminal or Anaconda prompt, execute the following:

```
conda install numba
```

This command will instruct conda to handle the installation process. Again, verifying the installation can be done by importing Numba in a Python interpreter session as shown above.

Testing the Installation:

To ensure the installation's success, it's useful to run a quick test compiling a simple function. Here is a basic example:

```
from numba import jit

@jit(nopython=True)
def add(a, b):
    return a + b

print(add(2, 3))
```

The expected output should be:

```
5
```

If the output matches the expected result without errors, Numba is properly installed and configured.

Optional Dependencies:

For advanced features, consider installing optional dependencies:

- **LLVM:** The Low-Level Virtual Machine (LLVM) project is required for some advanced compilation features.
- **CUDA Toolkit:** For leveraging GPU acceleration (detailing covered in future sections), ensure the CUDA Toolkit is installed.

These tools can be installed via pip or conda, depending on your primary package manager.

Configuration and Environment Setup:

After installation, configuring your development environment to efficiently work with Numba involves setting environment variables and verifying compilation tools. For instance, setting the environment variable $\mathrm{NUMBA\_DISABLE\_JIT}$ to 1 disables JIT compilation, useful for debugging purposes.

Modify your environment settings as follows:

```
export NUMBA_DISABLE_JIT=1
```

In Windows Command Prompt, you can use:

```
set NUMBA_DISABLE_JIT=1
```

Alternatively, use a Python script to set environment variables programmatically:

```
import os

os.environ['NUMBA_DISABLE_JIT'] = '1'
```

Ensuring your environment variables and paths are correctly set will streamline your development process with Numba.

Hardware Considerations:

Utilizing Numba's GPU capabilities requires CUDA-compatible hardware. Verify your GPU's compatibility with the CUDA Toolkit as mismatches can lead to compilation issues or runtime errors.

To summarize, having a correctly set up and configured installation of Numba is pivotal for your evolution through the subsequent sections focused on code acceleration and optimization. The steps above detail an exhaustive methodology ensuring your environment is well-prepared for advanced Numba applications.

3.7 Numba Basics: Accelerating Python Functions

Numba is a powerful library that brings the speed of compiled languages to Python code by allowing Just-In-Time (JIT) compilation. This section delves into the fundamental aspects of accelerating Python functions using Numba. By understanding how to utilize Numba effectively, significant performance improvements can be achieved in scientific computing tasks.

To begin using Numba, it is necessary to understand its primary decorator, `jit`, and its role in function compilation. The `jit` decorator enables the automatic conversion of Python code into optimized machine code at runtime. Consider the following example:

```
from numba import jit
```

```
@jit
def sum_array(arr):
    total = 0
    for val in arr:
        total += val
    return total

import numpy as np
arr = np.random.rand(1000000)
print(sum_array(arr))
```

In this code, the function sum_array is decorated with jit. When executed, numba translates the Python code into machine code just before execution, leading to a significant speedup for the loop operation.

One of Numba's strengths is its capacity to compile functions in different modes: nopython and object modes. By default, jit operates in object mode, which allows Python objects within the code. For optimal performance, the nopython mode can be explicitly enforced as follows:

```
@jit(nopython=True)
def sum_array_nopython(arr):
    total = 0
    for val in arr:
        total += val
    return total

print(sum_array_nopython(arr))
```

In nopython mode, Numba ensures that the code contains only native types, thereby eliminating overhead from Python object handling and achieving better performance.

Another useful Numba feature is the parallel option, which enables parallel execution for loops using multiple cores:

```
@jit(nopython=True, parallel=True)
def sum_array_parallel(arr):
    total = 0
    for i in numba.prange(len(arr)):
        total += arr[i]
    return total

print(sum_array_parallel(arr))
```

The numba.prange function is a parallel equivalent to Python's range, distributing loop iterations across available cores. This parallel execution leverages data-level parallelism inherent in many numerical computations.

A comprehensive exploration of Numba also includes understanding how to optimize more complex functions. Numba supports a variety of data structures as inputs and performs extensive type inference. Consider a function that operates on 2D arrays:

```
@jit(nopython=True)
def matmul(A, B):
    n, m = A.shape
    m2, p = B.shape
    assert m == m2
    C = np.zeros((n, p))
    for i in range(n):
        for j in range(p):
            for k in range(m):
                C[i, j] += A[i, k] * B[j, k]
    return C

A = np.random.rand(500, 500)
B = np.random.rand(500, 500)
print(matmul(A, B))
```

This matrix multiplication function, matmul, multiplies two 2D arrays and returns their product. The function uses loops to iterate over the matrix dimensions and perform element-wise operations, significantly improved through Numba's JIT capabilities.

Occasionally, users may encounter situations where Numba's type inference needs additional hints. In such cases, numba.typeof can identify variable types, while numba.extending provides tools to create new types and functions.

To extend functionalities further, Numba offers specialized decorators:

- vectorize – Compiles the function into a Universal Function (ufunc), enabling element-wise operations for arrays.
- guvectorize – Similar to vectorize but supports generalized ufuncs with more flexible broadcasting rules.

Example of vectorize usage:

```
from numba import vectorize

@vectorize(['float64(float64, float64)'], target='parallel')
def add_vectors(a, b):
    return a + b

print(add_vectors(arr, arr))
```

Here, add_vectors is compiled into a fast, element-wise ufunc.

Through these examples, it becomes apparent that Numba offers tools to greatly enhance the performance of Python functions, particularly for computationally intensive tasks. Its adaptability to various data types and array operations, combined with parallel processing capabilities, positions it as an essential library for scientific computing in Python.

3.8 GPU Acceleration with Numba

Leveraging the computational power of GPUs for accelerating Python code has become increasingly important in scientific computing, data science, and machine learning. Numba provides an efficient way to achieve GPU acceleration by enabling direct compilation of Python functions to CUDA code which can run on NVIDIA GPUs. This section delves into the concepts and practical implementations of GPU acceleration with Numba, illustrating how to write Python code that utilizes the GPU capabilities.

To use GPU features with Numba, it is imperative to have a fundamental understanding of CUDA, NVIDIA's parallel computing platform and programming model. CUDA allows the execution of concurrent threads on a GPU, making it feasible to handle large-scale computations which would be infeasible on a CPU.

Prerequisites: Before proceeding with GPU programming using Numba, ensure that your system meets the following requirements:

- A compatible NVIDIA GPU with CUDA Compute Capability 3.0 or higher.
- CUDA Toolkit installed on your system.
- Numba installed. Ensure it is correctly configured to recognize the CUDA toolkit.

The use of Numba for GPU acceleration is accomplished through CUDA.jit, which is a decorator to compile Python functions that can be executed on the GPU. Here is a step-by-step explanation to get started:

1. Importing Necessary Modules: First, import the necessary Numba and NVIDIA CUDA libraries:

```
from numba import cuda
import numpy as np
```

2. Writing CUDA Kernels with Numba: A CUDA kernel is a function that runs on the GPU. The @cuda.jit decorator is used to define such a kernel:

```
@cuda.jit
def vector_add(a, b, c):
    tid = cuda.grid(1)
    if tid < a.size:
        c[tid] = a[tid] + b[tid]
```

In this example, vector_add is a kernel that computes the element-wise addition of two arrays a and b, storing the result in array c. The cuda.grid(1) function calculates a 1D grid of thread indices, assigning each thread a unique index tid in the grid. The condition if tid < a.size ensures that the kernel only processes valid indices within the arrays.

3. Allocating and Transferring Data to the GPU: Data must be transferred from the host (CPU) to the device (GPU) before executing the kernel. This can be accomplished using special functions to allocate and copy memory:

```
n = 1024
a = np.random.random(n).astype(np.float32)
b = np.random.random(n).astype(np.float32)
c = np.empty(n).astype(np.float32)

a_device = cuda.to_device(a)
b_device = cuda.to_device(b)
c_device = cuda.device_array_like(a)
```

Here, numpy arrays a and b are created and filled with random values. cuda.to_device transfers these arrays to the GPU, and cuda.device_array_like(a) allocates memory on the GPU for the resulting array c.

4. Launching the Kernel: The next step is to execute or "launch" the kernel on the GPU:

```
threads_per_block = 256
blocks_per_grid = (a.size + (threads_per_block - 1)) // threads_per_block

vector_add[blocks_per_grid, threads_per_block](a_device, b_device, c_device)
```

The kernel launch configuration specifies the number of threads per block and the number of blocks per grid to be used by the GPU. This configuration is crucial for optimizing performance by ensuring adequate utilization of GPU resources. In this example, the grid size ensures that there are enough threads to process all elements of the vectors.

5. Copying the Result Back to the Host: Once the kernel finishes execution, the result must be copied back to the host:

```
c = c_device.copy_to_host()
print(c)
```

This will copy the data from the GPU back to the CPU and print the result.

Understanding Thread Hierarchies: The performance of CUDA kernels can be significantly improved by understanding how threads are organized. CUDA employs a hierarchical model where threads are grouped into blocks and blocks are grouped into a grid. Each block has a unique index, and within each block, threads have unique indices. This hierarchy allows for fine control over parallelization:

```
@cuda.jit
def matrix_mult(A, B, C):
    row, col = cuda.grid(2)
    if row < C.shape[0] and col < C.shape[1]:
        temp = 0.0
        for k in range(A.shape[1]):
            temp += A[row, k] * B[k, col]
        C[row, col] = temp
```

Here, a 2D CUDA kernel matrix_mult is defined for performing matrix multiplication. The cuda.grid(2) function returns a tuple representing the row and column indices. The thread hierarchy allows every element of the output matrix C to be computed in parallel, significantly reducing computation time for large matrices.

Synchronization and Atomic Operations: In certain applications, threads need to synchronize at a specific point to ensure correct execution. Numba provides synchronization primitives to handle such scenarios:

```
@cuda.jit
def synchronize_example(arr):
    tid = cuda.threadIdx.x

    arr[tid] += 1

    cuda.syncthreads()

    if tid == 0:
        arr[0] = cuda.blockIdx.x
```

cuda.syncthreads() ensures that all threads within a block reach this point before proceeding, preventing race conditions.

For scenarios requiring atomic operations (operations performed without interruption):

```
from numba import int32

@cuda.jit
def atomic_example(arr):
    for i in range(len(arr)):
        cuda.atomic.add(arr, i, 1)
```

Atomic operations like cuda.atomic.add guarantee that changes to the shared data by threads are correctly serialized.

Understanding and utilizing these advanced features can optimize your code further for performance improvements on GPUs.

3.9 Comparing Numba with Other Python Accelerators

Python's popularity in scientific computing and data science can, in part, be attributed to its rich ecosystem of libraries that can accelerate the execution of computationally intensive code. Among these, Numba, Cython, and PyPy stand out. Each of these tools offers unique advantages and has specific use cases. This section explores the distinctions, strengths, and limitations of Numba compared to these other Python accelerators.

Numba vs. Cython

Numba and Cython are two powerful tools for enhancing the performance of Python code, but they employ fundamentally different approaches. Numba uses just-in-time (JIT) compilation to convert a subset of Python and NumPy code into fast machine code at runtime. It is designed to be easy to use with minimal changes to the existing Python codebase. Numba excels in scenarios where runtime flexibility is required and where functions undergo repeated execution with varying input sizes or data types.

In contrast, Cython is a statically compiled ahead-of-time (AOT) compiler. It allows Python code to be written with C-like performance by integrating C data types and allows direct calls to C libraries. This method produces efficient C extensions for Python, which can markedly speed up the execution of statistical models, numerical simulations, and more. However, Cython requires learning its distinct syntax and often involves more extensive code refactoring.

The following example demonstrates the JIT compilation process with Numba. Consider a basic function to compute the sum of squares of an array:

```
import numpy as np
from numba import njit

@njit
```

```
def sum_of_squares(arr):
    result = 0.0
    for x in arr:
        result += x ** 2
    return result

arr = np.array([1.0, 2.0, 3.0, 4.0])
print(sum_of_squares(arr))
```

Using the @njit decorator, Numba seamlessly optimizes this function.

Now, achieving similar performance with Cython would require this transformation:

```
import numpy as np
cimport numpy as np

def sum_of_squares(np.ndarray[np.float64_t, ndim=1] arr):
    cdef double result = 0.0
    cdef int i
    for i in range(arr.shape[0]):
        result += arr[i] ** 2
    return result
```

This Cython version necessitates the explicit declaration of variable types and more intricate handling of arrays and loops.

Numba vs. PyPy

PyPy is an alternative Python interpreter that emphasizes JIT compilation to accelerate Python code execution. It works by translating Python bytecode to machine code at runtime, similar to Numba. However, PyPy aims to be a drop-in replacement for the standard CPython interpreter, meaning entire applications can benefit from performance improvements without any code modification. PyPy is particularly effective for speeding up long-running applications with complex control flow.

While PyPy improves the general execution speed of Python programs, Numba allows for more granular optimization of specific functions or code segments, especially those involving numerical computations and array manipulations. Numba's optimizations can often outperform PyPy for numerical tasks due to its specialized handling of NumPy arrays and mathematical functions.

In evaluating PyPy versus Numba, it is critical to consider the nature of the application. For full-program acceleration, opting for PyPy might be advantageous. For targeted performance boosts in scientific computing tasks, integrating Numba could yield better results.

Use Cases Alignment

- **Numba**: Ideal for numerical and scientific computing where functions contain loops and array operations. It works well with NumPy and GPU computing.
- **Cython**: Suitable for developing performance-critical sections of code where deep integration with C/C++ is beneficial. Commonly used for creating Python extensions.
- **PyPy**: Best for general-purpose Python acceleration without code modification, especially advantageous for interpretive workloads and pure Python codebases.

Performance Considerations

Empirical performance testing provides valuable insight into the applicability of these tools. Benchmarks often illustrate that Numba and Cython significantly exceed the performance of CPython in numerical tasks, while PyPy excels in pure Python scenarios with fewer dependencies.

The following performance test evaluates a numerical integration task using Numba and Cython. The benchmark demonstrates Numba's ability to expedite numerical computation with minimal code adjustment.

```
import numpy as np
from numba import jit

@jit(nopython=True)
def integrate(f, a, b, N):
    x = np.linspace(a, b, N)
    dx = (b - a) / N
    total = 0.0
    for xi in x:
        total += f(xi) * dx
    return total

def f(x):
    return np.sin(x)

print(integrate(f, 0, np.pi, 1000000))
```

The performance improvement realized by Numba manifests prominently in the reduced execution time, which is critical for large-scale computations.

Each accelerator has its niche, and the choice between them depends on the specific requirements of the projects undertaken. Robust knowledge of these tools facilitates informed decisions, optimizing performance and resource utilization in Python-based scientific computing.

Future Developments

The landscape of Python acceleration is continually evolving. Numba, Cython, and PyPy regularly receive updates that expand their capabilities and improve their performance. Emerging technologies and advancements in compiler optimization will further enhance their respective potentials.

Informed choice and application-specific optimization are crucial for leveraging Python's full capabilities in scientific computing, reflecting the diversity and specialized strengths of tools like Numba, Cython, and PyPy. This dynamic environment necessitates ongoing learning and adaptation to foster efficient and effective computational solutions.

3.10 Real-World Applications of Numba

Numba, as a Just-In-Time (JIT) compiler, accelerates numerical computations in Python, making it a powerful tool in scientific and applied computational fields. The practical benefits of leveraging Numba become evident when examining real-world applications where computational performance is a critical factor. Here, we explore several domains where Numba excels, directly impacting the efficiency and capability of Python-based projects.

Data Science and Machine Learning

Data scientists frequently deal with large datasets requiring efficient processing capabilities. Numba simplifies the task by speeding up feature extraction, transformation, and statistical computations. Below is an example illustrating the acceleration of a basic statistical function using Numba.

```
import numpy as np
from numba import jit

@jit(nopython=True)
def compute_mean(array):
    sum = 0.0
    for i in range(array.size):
        sum += array[i]
    return sum / array.size

data = np.random.rand(1000000)
mean_value = compute_mean(data)
```

```
print(mean_value)
```

Implementing the function compute_mean with Numba drastically reduces computation time compared to its pure Python counterpart, providing an edge in processing high-dimensional data commonly encountered in data science tasks.

Financial Modeling

The finance industry benefits immensely from Numba's accelerated computations, particularly in the realms of quantitative analysis, risk management, and derivative pricing. For instance, Monte Carlo simulations, used to predict future asset prices and perform risk assessments, see significant performance boosts.

```
from numba import jit
import numpy as np

@jit(nopython=True)
def monte_carlo_simulation(S0, r, sigma, T, N):
    dt = T / N
    paths = np.zeros(N)
    paths[0] = S0
    for t in range(1, N):
        z = np.random.standard_normal()
        paths[t] = paths[t - 1] * np.exp((r - 0.5 * sigma**2) * dt + sigma * np.sqrt(dt)
            * z)
    return paths

S0 = 100 # Initial stock price
r = 0.05 # Risk-free rate
sigma = 0.2 # Volatility
T = 1.0 # Time to maturity in years
N = 1000 # Number of time steps

simulated_paths = monte_carlo_simulation(S0, r, sigma, T, N)
print(simulated_paths)
```

The accelerated function monte_carlo_simulation allows for efficient pricing of derivatives and other financial instruments, which is critical for making timely and informed investment decisions.

Physics Simulations

Simulating physical systems involves solving differential equations that describe phenomena such as fluid dynamics, electromagnetism, and particle physics. Numba can speed up these computations, enabling more complex and higher-resolution simulations.

```
from numba import jit, prange
import numpy as np

@jit(nopython=True, parallel=True)
def compute_wave_propagation(u, dx, dt, c, steps):
```

```
    nx = u.shape[0]
    for n in range(steps):
        for i in prange(1, nx - 1):
            u[i] = u[i] - c * dt / dx * (u[i] - u[i - 1])
    return u

nx = 1000
dx = 0.01
dt = 0.001
c = 1.0
steps = 100

u = np.sin(np.linspace(0, 4 * \np.pi, nx)) # Initial condition
wave_u = compute_wave_propagation(u, dx, dt, c, steps)
print(wave_u)
```

Here, compute_wave_propagation leverages parallel execution facilitated by Numba, handling large grid sizes more effectively than standard Python implementations. This capability is valuable in research and industry applications involving computational physics.

Bioinformatics

Bioinformatics incorporates substantial computational tasks in analyzing biological data, such as DNA sequence alignment, protein structure prediction, and evolutionary studies. Numba's acceleration abilities can enhance these bioinformatics computations.

```
from numba import jit
import numpy as np

@jit(nopython=True)
def sequence_alignment(seq1, seq2):
    len1, len2 = len(seq1), len(seq2)
    dp = np.zeros((len1+1, len2+1))
    for i in range(1, len1+1):
        for j in range(1, len2+1):
            match = dp[i-1, j-1] + (1 if seq1[i-1] == seq2[j-1] else 0)
            delete = dp[i-1, j] - 1
            insert = dp[i, j-1] - 1
            dp[i, j] = max(match, delete, insert)
    return dp[-1, -1]

seq1 = "AGCTGAC"
seq2 = "AGCTGGA"
alignment_score = sequence_alignment(seq1, seq2)
print(alignment_score)
```

Bioinformaticians can observe significant gains in performance for sequence alignment algorithms, facilitating large-scale genomic data analysis.

Image Processing

Image processing requires intensive computation for tasks such as convolution, transformation, and feature extraction. Numba can expedite these processes, making real-time image analysis and computer vision applications feasible in Python.

```
from numba import jit
import numpy as np

@jit(nopython=True)
def apply_filter(image, kernel):
    kernel_size = kernel.shape[0]
    offset = kernel_size // 2
    filtered_image = np.zeros_like(image)
    for x in range(offset, image.shape[0] - offset):
        for y in range(offset, image.shape[1] - offset):
            filtered_image[x, y] = np.sum(kernel * image[x - offset:x + offset + 1, y -
                offset:y + offset + 1])
    return filtered_image

image = np.random.rand(512, 512).astype(np.float32) # Simulated image
kernel = np.ones((3, 3), np.float32) # Simple averaging kernel
filtered_image = apply_filter(image, kernel)
print(filtered_image)
```

Through the accelerated convolution function, application performance in image filtering tasks is enhanced considerably, supporting real-time processing needs in fields such as medical imaging and autonomous driving.

These examples demonstrate the broad applicability and impact of Numba in accelerating Python code across diverse scientific and engineering domains. The ability to integrate seamlessly with existing Python workflows while providing high-performance computational capabilities positions Numba as an invaluable tool for practical applications requiring efficient numerical processing.

Chapter 4

CUDA Architecture and Memory Model

This chapter provides an in-depth exploration of CUDA architecture and its memory model. It introduces the components of CUDA, including streaming multiprocessors (SMs) and CUDA cores, and examines the memory hierarchy such as global, shared, constant, and texture memory. The concepts of memory coalescing, access patterns, latency, and bandwidth are discussed, along with strategies for efficient memory management. Furthermore, the chapter explains the CUDA execution model and its impact on optimization.

4.1 Overview of CUDA Architecture

CUDA, or Compute Unified Device Architecture, is a parallel computing platform and application programming interface (API) model created by NVIDIA. It allows developers to use NVIDIA GPUs for general-purpose processing, an approach commonly referred to as GPGPU (General-Purpose computing on Graphics Processing Units). The architecture of CUDA is designed to leverage the high throughput and parallelism inherent in GPUs to accelerate complex computations. Understanding the architecture is crucial as it influences how programs are structured and optimized for peak performance.

At the heart of CUDA architecture are streaming multiprocessors (SMs) which contain CUDA cores. These cores execute the actual computations. The architecture is organized to maximize throughput by handling numerous threads concurrently. CUDA's execution model is built on a hierarchy of threads, blocks, and grids, where threads are the basic unit of execution. Threads are organized into blocks, which in turn are organized into grids. This hierarchical structure allows developers to define fine-grained parallelism in their programs.

CUDA includes a diverse memory hierarchy designed to balance speed and size to meet the varying requirements of different types of memory accesses. The primary memory types include global memory, shared memory, constant memory, and texture memory. Global memory is the largest and can be accessed by all threads but has the highest latency. Shared memory is much faster but only accessible by threads within the same block. Constant and texture memories are read-only, offering specialized access patterns that can be exploited for specific types of computations.

The flexibility of CUDA's memory model is complemented by a thorough execution model. This model dictates how threads are dispatched, executed, and synchronized. The threads within a block can cooperate through shared memory and can be synchronized using barrier synchronization, allowing more sophisticated parallel algorithms to be implemented efficiently. However, global memory accesses need careful optimization to avoid performance bottlenecks due to their high latency.

To illustrate, consider a simple CUDA program that adds two vectors. The following code snippet demonstrates the structure and usage of threads and blocks:

```
__global__ void vector_add(float *a, float *b, float *c, int N) {
    int idx = blockIdx.x * blockDim.x + threadIdx.x;
    if (idx < N) {
        c[idx] = a[idx] + b[idx];
    }
}
```

Here, the __global__ keyword defines a kernel function that runs on the device (GPU). The function vector_add computes the sum of vectors a and b, storing the result in vector c. The blockIdx.x, blockDim.x, and threadIdx.x built-in variables help identify the index of the thread currently executing the code. By efficiently organizing data and computations, developers can leverage the massive parallelism CUDA offers.

The following example shows how to launch this kernel from the host side in Python using the PyCUDA library:

```
import pycuda.driver as cuda
import pycuda.autoinit
from pycuda.compiler import SourceModule
import numpy as np

N = 1024
a = np.random.rand(N).astype(np.float32)
b = np.random.rand(N).astype(np.float32)
c = np.empty_like(a)

a_gpu = cuda.mem_alloc(a.nbytes)
b_gpu = cuda.mem_alloc(b.nbytes)
c_gpu = cuda.mem_alloc(c.nbytes)

cuda.memcpy_htod(a_gpu, a)
cuda.memcpy_htod(b_gpu, b)

mod = SourceModule("""
__global__ void vector_add(float *a, float *b, float *c, int N) {
    int idx = blockIdx.x * blockDim.x + threadIdx.x;
    if (idx < N) {
        c[idx] = a[idx] + b[idx];
    }
}
""")

vector_add = mod.get_function("vector_add")
vector_add(a_gpu, b_gpu, c_gpu, np.int32(N), block=(256,1,1), grid=(N//256,1))

cuda.memcpy_dtoh(c, c_gpu)

print(c[:10]) # Display the first 10 elements of c
```

The execution of the above code would result in an output similar to:

```
[1.276078   0.8760913  0.94769627 1.2266245  0.7391665  1.5014677
 1.1882235  1.4558091  1.0952548  1.5506284 ]
```

This example emphasizes several key points about CUDA architecture. First, understanding how threads and blocks are organized is essential for writing efficient CUDA code. Second, memory management plays a critical role; moving data between host (CPU) and device (GPU) memory must be performed carefully to avoid unnecessary delays.

The performance of CUDA programs heavily relies on effective usage of all hierarchical memory types. Directly accessing global memory is slower due to its size and latency, so an optimal approach often involves using shared memory for intermediate computations within a block, reducing the frequency and latency of global memory accesses. Efficient CUDA programming requires an iterative process of profiling and refining code to maximize resource utilization, minimize memory latency, and balance the workload across threads and blocks.

By understanding the fundamental components and structure of the CUDA architecture, developers can better design their applications to exploit the parallel computing capabilities of modern GPUs fully. This knowledge serves as the foundation for diving deeper into CUDA specifics and optimizing performance, setting the stage for more advanced implementations and optimizations in subsequent sections.

4.2 Streaming Multiprocessors (SMs)

Streaming Multiprocessors (SMs) are the fundamental building blocks of NVIDIA's CUDA architecture. They play a critical role in defining the capabilities and performance characteristics of the GPU. Each SM houses multiple CUDA cores and various types of memory, orchestrating the parallel execution of threads.

An SM consists of several key components:

- **CUDA Cores**: These are the primary execution units within an SM. They can execute integer and floating-point arithmetic operations in parallel.
- **Warp Scheduler**: The warp scheduler manages the execution of warps, which are groups of 32 threads. It can switch between different warps to maximize device utilization and hide latency.
- **Instruction Cache**: Stores instructions for the warp scheduler, reducing the need to fetch instructions from the global memory.
- **Shared Memory/ L1 Cache**: Provides a fast, low-latency memory space for threads within a block, facilitating data sharing and synchronization.
- **Registers**: Fast, small memory locations local to each thread, used for storing temporary data.
- **Special Function Units (SFUs)**: Designed for executing complex mathematical operations like trigonometric functions, logarithms, and exponentiation.
- **Memory Load/Store Units**: Handle reading and writing data between the various levels of the memory hierarchy and the CUDA cores.

The architecture of the SM allows for highly concurrent execution of numerous threads. The warp scheduler is responsible for managing and scheduling the execution of these threads in warps. When a warp is stalled, perhaps due to a memory access delay, the scheduler can switch to another warp that is ready to execute, thereby utilizing the processing units effectively.

```
__global__ void simpleKernel(float *d_a) {
    int idx = blockIdx.x * blockDim.x + threadIdx.x;
    d_a[idx] = d_a[idx] * d_a[idx];
}
```

In the code above, each thread performs a simple operation on a global memory array. The warp scheduler in each SM will handle the execution of these threads. If the memory access to d_a is delayed, the warp scheduler will switch to another warp, keeping the CUDA cores busy.

The interaction between different SM components can have significant implications for performance. For example, high dependency on memory operations might lead to a scenario where warp schedulers spend substantial time waiting for data. Proper use of shared memory and register can mitigate such bottlenecks.

Shared memory within an SM acts as a programmable cache. It allows threads within a block to share data quickly. This is utilized in various applications, such as matrix multiplication, where threads need to access and manipulate shared data.

Consider a practical example of matrix multiplication using shared memory:

```
__global__ void matMulKernel(float *A, float *B, float *C, int N) {
    __shared__ float sA[TILE_WIDTH][TILE_WIDTH];
    __shared__ float sB[TILE_WIDTH][TILE_WIDTH];

    int col = blockIdx.x * TILE_WIDTH + threadIdx.x;
    int row = blockIdx.y * TILE_WIDTH + threadIdx.y;
    float value = 0;

    for (int t = 0; t < (N / TILE_WIDTH); ++t) {
        sA[threadIdx.y][threadIdx.x] = A[row * N + (t * TILE_WIDTH + threadIdx.x)
            ];
        sB[threadIdx.y][threadIdx.x] = B[(t * TILE_WIDTH + threadIdx.y) * N + col];

        __syncthreads();

        for (int i = 0; i < TILE_WIDTH; ++i) {
            value += sA[threadIdx.y][i] * sB[i][threadIdx.x];
        }

        __syncthreads();
    }
    C[row * N + col] = value;
}
```

Here, sA and sB are shared memory arrays used to store sub-matrices of A and B. By utilizing shared memory, the kernel minimizes global memory accesses, thus improving the overall performance.

The memory controllers and load/store units coordinate with the shared memory and the rest of the memory hierarchy to ensure efficient data movement. Optimizing the usage of these components is crucial for achieving high performance in CUDA applications.

The balance between computational throughput and memory bandwidth within an SM is another critical factor. Efficient instruction scheduling and memory access patterns can significantly enhance performance. Techniques such as memory coalescing, where memory accesses are aligned and grouped to minimize latency, are essential for leveraging the full potential of an SM's architecture.

To illustrate the impact of coalescing, consider the following two scenarios for memory access:

```
// Non-coalesced memory access
for (int i = 0; i < N; i++) {
    arr[idx + i * stride] = arr[idx + i * stride] * 2.0f;
}

// Coalesced memory access
for (int i = 0; i < N; i++) {
    arr[idx + i] = arr[idx + i] * 2.0f;
}
```

In the first case, memory accesses are scattered, leading to inefficient utilization of memory bandwidth. In the second case, memory accesses are sequential, allowing for coalesced memory transactions that are more efficient.

Overall, the architecture of Streaming Multiprocessors is designed to handle diverse workloads efficiently. Understanding the interplay between various SM components, optimizing memory usage, and employing effective scheduling techniques are crucial for writing high-performance CUDA applications.

4.3 CUDA Cores and Their Functionality

CUDA cores are the fundamental processing units within the NVIDIA GPU architecture, analogous to CPU cores but optimized for parallel computation at a massive scale. A single GPU can house thousands of CUDA cores, enabling substantial computational throughput when executing parallelizable tasks.

Each CUDA core is a lightweight, scalar processor capable of executing simple arithmetic and logical operations. These cores are grouped within Streaming Multiprocessors (SMs), where they share resources such as registers and shared memory. Understanding the operational nuances of CUDA cores is crucial for optimizing performance in GPU-accelerated applications.

Execution of Instructions

CUDA cores execute instructions based on the Single Instruction, Multiple Threads (SIMT) architecture. In this model, a set of threads, known as a warp (typically 32 threads), is synchronized to execute the same instruction concurrently. This efficient instruction dispatch mechanism enables high throughput for vectorizable workloads.

When a program is executed on a GPU, the CUDA runtime system schedules warps on available SMs. Each SM dynamically manages its warps, switching contexts as needed to hide instruction latencies and maximize utilization of arithmetic units.

Warp Scheduling and Instructions

Instruction execution within a warp is highly efficient due to the SIMT paradigm. If all threads in a warp follow the same control path, they execute in a lock-step manner, with all threads processing the same instruction simultaneously. However, divergence in the control path, such as through conditionals, can lead to inefficient execution as the warp must serialize the divergent paths before converging back to a synchronous state.

```
# CUDA kernel with potential warp divergence
__global__ void warp_divergence_example(int *data) {
    int tid = threadIdx.x;
    if (tid % 2 == 0) {
        data[tid] *= 2; // Path A
    } else {
        data[tid] += 1; // Path B
    }
}
```

In the example above, warp divergence occurs because not all threads within a warp take the same branch of the conditional statement. To minimize divergence, developers should design their algorithms to maintain uniform control flow within warps whenever possible.

Arithmetic Units and Throughput

CUDA cores are equipped with arithmetic logic units (ALUs) to perform integer and floating-point operations. The performance of these operations can vary depending on the type of arithmetic used. For instance, floating-point operations might have different latencies and throughput compared to integer operations due to the underlying hardware design.

The throughput of arithmetic operations is an essential factor for performance optimization. High computational throughput can be achieved by ensuring that the CUDA cores are kept busy with arithmetic operations, thereby maximizing the usage of ALUs. This can be done by reducing idle times through efficient memory access patterns and minimizing warp divergence as discussed previously.

Memory Access and Coalescing

Efficient memory access patterns are critical for maintaining high throughput in CUDA applications. CUDA cores access various types of memory such as global memory, shared memory, and local memory. The memory access speed can significantly impact the overall performance.

Memory coalescing is a mechanism that combines multiple memory accesses into a single transaction, thereby reducing the number of memory requests and improving bandwidth utilization. For effective memory coalescing, threads within a warp should ideally access consecutive memory addresses.

```
# Efficient memory coalescing
__global__ void coalesced_memory_access(int *input, int *output) {
  int tid = threadIdx.x + blockIdx.x * blockDim.x;
  output[tid] = input[tid] * 2;
}
```

In the example above, all threads within a warp access consecutive elements of the input array, enabling coalesced memory accesses and thus improved performance.

Latency Hiding and Occupancy

Latency hiding is an essential feature of CUDA cores. When a warp is waiting for memory operations to complete, the SM can switch to another warp that is ready to execute, thereby hiding the latency of the memory operation. This warp scheduling strategy helps to keep the CUDA cores busy and improves overall throughput.

Occupancy, defined as the ratio of active warps to the maximum number of warps supported by an SM, is a critical factor affecting latency hiding. Higher occupancy typically enables better latency hiding, though it can also lead to resource contention. Therefore, achieving optimal performance often requires balancing occupancy with effective resource utilization.

```
# Kernel with different resource requirements
__global__ void compute_kernel(float *a, float *b, float *c) {
    int idx = threadIdx.x + blockIdx.x * blockDim.x;
    float x = a[idx];
    float y = b[idx];
    c[idx] = x * y + sinf(x);
}
```

In this kernel, the use of floating-point arithmetic, combined with intrinsic functions like $\sin f()$, affects both the resource usage and execution latency. Careful consideration of these factors is essential for optimizing occupancy and latency hiding.

Efficient usage of CUDA cores involves minimizing warp divergence, adopting coalesced memory access patterns, and leveraging the latency hiding capabilities of the architecture. By focusing on these aspects, developers can harness the full computational power of CUDA-enabled GPUs.

4.4 The Memory Hierarchy in CUDA

In CUDA, understanding the memory hierarchy is critical for writing efficient programs. Each type of memory available on the GPU serves specific purposes and has distinct characteristics in terms of size, latency, and bandwidth. An efficient utilization of the memory hierarchy can significantly impact the performance of CUDA applications.

The CUDA memory hierarchy can be broadly categorized into: **global memory**, **shared memory**, **constant memory**, **texture memory**, and **registers and local memory**. Each type offers different performance characteristics, making it essential for developers to choose the appropriate memory for the given task.

Global Memory is the largest and most flexible memory space on the GPU, but it has the highest latency and lowest bandwidth. This memory is accessible by all threads and functions within a kernel and across multiple kernel launches. Its primary advantage is its capacity, which can be in the order of gigabytes. However, accessing global memory can introduce significant delays if not handled optimally. Therefore, minimizing access latency through techniques such as memory coalescing – where contiguous threads access contiguous memory locations – is crucial.

Shared Memory resides within each Streaming Multiprocessor (SM) and is significantly faster than global memory. Shared among threads in the same thread block, shared memory enables efficient data sharing and synchronization, making it ideal for tasks requiring frequent exchange of data between threads, such as tiled matrix multiplication. However, its size is limited, typically to 48 KB or 96 KB per SM, depending on the GPU architecture. Programs must be written to effectively partition work and data to fit within this space.

Consider an example kernel using shared memory for matrix multiplication:

```
__global__ void matrixMulShared(float *A, float *B, float *C, int N) {
    __shared__ float subTileA[TILE_SIZE][TILE_SIZE];
    __shared__ float subTileB[TILE_SIZE][TILE_SIZE];

    int tx = threadIdx.x;
    int ty = threadIdx.y;
    int row = blockIdx.y * TILE_SIZE + ty;
    int col = blockIdx.x * TILE_SIZE + tx;

    float value = 0;

    for (int m = 0; m < N / TILE_SIZE; ++m) {
        subTileA[ty][tx] = A[row * N + (m * TILE_SIZE + tx)];
        subTileB[ty][tx] = B[(m * TILE_SIZE + ty) * N + col];
        __syncthreads();

        for (int k = 0; k < TILE_SIZE; ++k)
            value += subTileA[ty][k] * subTileB[k][tx];
        __syncthreads();
    }
    C[row * N + col] = value;
}
```

In the code snippet, shared memory is used to load submatrices (or tiles) from the global memory, allowing threads within a block to collaboratively compute portions of the output matrix without frequently accessing global memory.

Constant Memory is read-only memory cached on-chip for optimized access by the SMs. It is accessible by all threads, but only for reading, and is cached to make access efficient. This memory space is best suited for storing variables such as constants that are frequently read but infrequently written. For example, look-up tables for mathematical functions can be stored in constant memory. It can hold up to 64 KB of data.

Texture Memory is another read-only memory, specifically optimized for spatial data access. It is cached and provides hardware support for spatial locality, which can be beneficial for 2D and 3D spatial access patterns, such as those found in image processing tasks. Similar to constant memory, texture memory helps reduce the number of global memory accesses by leveraging its caching mechanisms.

Registers are the fastest memory available on the GPU, allocated per thread. Registers hold variables that are most frequently accessed. However, their number is limited, typically just a few dozen per thread. Efficient use of registers is pivotal for achieving high performance, but excessive register usage can lead to what is known as *register spilling* – where extra register values are temporarily stored in local memory (part of global memory), introducing latency penalties.

Local Memory is a misnomer in CUDA terminology. It does not imply on-chip memory; rather it refers to memory local to each thread but located in the global memory space. It is utilized for thread-private data that does not fit into registers. Although accessed similarly to global memory, its usage should be minimized because it shares the same high latency characteristics.

Efficient CUDA programming necessitates a thorough understanding of these memory types and appropriate strategies for their usage. For instance, using shared memory for intermediate computations, constant memory for frequently accessed constants, texture memory for spatial-dependent data, and minimizing global and local memory accesses.

In the next sections, we delve deeper into each type of memory, exploring their benefits, use cases, and optimal strategies to harness their potential within your CUDA programs.

4.5 Global Memory and Its Characteristics

Global memory in CUDA represents the largest and most flexible memory space accessible to both the host (CPU) and the device (GPU). This versatility comes at the cost of higher latency compared to other memory types. Understanding global memory and its characteristics is essential for writing efficient CUDA programs.

Global memory is allocated and freed by the host using CUDA API functions. The allocated memory can be transferred between the host and the device via explicit memory copy functions such as cudaMemcpy. The following example demonstrates how to allocate global memory and transfer data:

```
int N = 1000;
float *hostArray, *deviceArray;

// Allocate host memory
hostArray = (float*)malloc(N * sizeof(float));

// Fill the host array
for (int i = 0; i < N; i++) {
    hostArray[i] = i * 2.0;
}

// Allocate device memory
cudaMalloc((void**)&deviceArray, N * sizeof(float));

// Copy data from host to device
cudaMemcpy(deviceArray, hostArray, N * sizeof(float), cudaMemcpyHostToDevice);
```

After data processing on the device, the results can be copied back to the host using the same cudaMemcpy function with the direction specified as cudaMemcpyDeviceToHost. Proper synchronization should be ensured when accessing shared global memory data across different kernels or between the host and device.

Global memory offers ample space, but its high latency requires carefully optimized access patterns to minimize memory transaction overhead. Memory accesses must be coalesced, meaning consecutive threads should access consecutive memory addresses. For example, if thread index tid reads or writes element tid in an array, the access pattern is perfectly coalesced. Accesses that are not coalesced will result in multiple memory transactions, negatively impacting performance. Here is an example of a coalesced memory access:

```
__global__ void simpleKernel(float *array) {
    int tid = threadIdx.x + blockIdx.x * blockDim.x;
    array[tid] = array[tid] + 1.0;
}
```

Conversely, scattering memory access patterns lead to inefficient memory operations. An example of non-coalesced access would be if each thread accessed non-contiguous memory elements:

```
__global__ void scatterKernel(float *array, int stride) {
    int tid = threadIdx.x + blockIdx.x * blockDim.x;
    array[tid * stride] = array[tid * stride] + 1.0; // Non-coalesced access
}
```

Global memory reads and writes can significantly benefit from caching mechanisms. CUDA devices employ a read-only data cache known as the L1 cache, introduced since compute capability 3.x, which can cache global memory for read-only data. This cache can substantially reduce latency for repetitive reads of the same data. The __restrict__ keyword can be used in kernel function arguments to indicate that pointers won't alias, allowing for better optimization.

Latency and bandwidth are critical factors when dealing with global memory. The theoretical bandwidth is determined by the GPU's hardware specifications. However, achieving peak bandwidth requires careful management of memory access patterns to avoid bottlenecks. Strided and irregular memory accesses, as shown in the earlier scatter example, prevent the coalescing of transactions, thereby decreasing effective bandwidth.

The hierarchical nature of memory emphasizes the importance of minimizing global memory usage when possible, leveraging faster memory types such as shared memory and registers (discussed in subsequent sections). Nonetheless, in scenarios where large data sets exceed the capacity of faster memory types, optimizing global memory use becomes pivotal.

Efficient memory management in global memory can be achieved through the following strategies:

- Ensuring coalesced access patterns for both reads and writes.
- Utilizing caching mechanisms effectively, primarily through read-only data caching.
- Minimizing frequent memory transfers between host and device.
- Using appropriate memory allocation and deallocation functions to avoid memory leaks.
- Profiling memory access patterns and optimizing based on insights from tools like NVIDIA's Visual Profiler or Nsight.

Here is an example of optimized memory access using the read-only cache:

```
__global__ void optimizedKernel(const float *__restrict__ input, float *
    __restrict__ output) {
    int tid = threadIdx.x + blockIdx.x * blockDim.x;
    float value = input[tid]; // Cached in L1
    output[tid] = value * 2.0;
}
```

Understanding global memory and its effective utilization is essential for achieving high performance in CUDA programming. By applying the described strategies, programmers can significantly mitigate latency and maximize bandwidth, leading to more efficient and faster CUDA applications.

4.6 Shared Memory: Benefits and Usage

In CUDA, shared memory is an important feature designed to provide significant performance gains when utilized effectively. Shared memory, available within a Streaming Multiprocessor (SM), plays a crucial role in accelerating data access and computation. It is a form of programmer-managed cache memory that supports low-latency, high-bandwidth data exchanges among threads within a block. Understanding the benefits and appropriate usage of shared memory requires an in-depth examination of its characteristics and operational nuances.

Shared memory is on-chip, enabling faster data access compared to the global memory that resides off-chip. This on-chip memory is accessible by all threads within a block, facilitating data sharing and synchronization. Each SM has a fixed amount of shared memory, usually on the order of tens of kilobytes (e.g., 48KB or 96KB depending on the CUDA compute capability). This shared resource is limited and must be allocated carefully to accommodate the needs of threads within a block.

The benefits of shared memory primarily stem from its low-latency access. In contrast to global memory access, which can take hundreds of clock cycles, accessing shared memory typically incurs a delay of only a few clock cycles. This advantage makes shared memory an ideal candidate for designing efficient parallel algorithms, especially those involving collaborative computations among threads.

One of the common use cases for shared memory is to act as a tile cache for matrix multiplication. In a simple matrix multiplication kernel, each thread typically accesses global memory elements repeatedly, leading to redundant global memory accesses and increased latency. To optimize such a kernel, we can load tiles of matrices into shared memory, allowing threads to reuse the data efficiently and thereby minimizing global memory accesses.

Consider the following CUDA kernel for matrix multiplication utilizing shared memory:

```
__global__ void matrixMulShared(float *A, float *B, float *C, int N) {
    __shared__ float tile_A[TILE_SIZE][TILE_SIZE];
    __shared__ float tile_B[TILE_SIZE][TILE_SIZE];
```

```
    int row = blockIdx.y * TILE_SIZE + threadIdx.y;
    int col = blockIdx.x * TILE_SIZE + threadIdx.x;
    float value = 0;

    for (int tileIdx = 0; tileIdx < (N + TILE_SIZE - 1) / TILE_SIZE; ++tileIdx) {
        if (row < N && tileIdx * TILE_SIZE + threadIdx.x < N)
            tile_A[threadIdx.y][threadIdx.x] = A[row * N + tileIdx * TILE_SIZE +
                 threadIdx.x];
        else
            tile_A[threadIdx.y][threadIdx.x] = 0.0;

        if (col < N && tileIdx * TILE_SIZE + threadIdx.y < N)
            tile_B[threadIdx.y][threadIdx.x] = B[(tileIdx * TILE_SIZE + threadIdx.y) *
                 N + col];
        else
            tile_B[threadIdx.y][threadIdx.x] = 0.0;

        __syncthreads();

        for (int k = 0; k < TILE_SIZE; ++k)
            value += tile_A[threadIdx.y][k] * tile_B[k][threadIdx.x];

        __syncthreads();
    }

    if (row < N && col < N)
        C[row * N + col] = value;
}
```

In this kernel, matrices A and B are divided into smaller sub-matrices or tiles. These tiles are loaded into shared memory, allowing threads to perform matrix multiplication on these sub-matrices. The __shared__ keyword denotes shared memory arrays tile_A and tile_B, which are accessed collaboratively by threads within the same block. This reduces the number of global memory accesses and exploits data locality efficiently.

Synchronization among threads within a block is achieved using __syncthreads(). This barrier synchronization ensures that all threads have completed the loading of tiles into shared memory before proceeding with the computation. Efficient use of shared memory in this manner results in notable performance improvement over a naïve approach that involves frequent global memory accesses.

Shared memory is also beneficial in scenarios involving stencil computations, reduction operations, and algorithms necessitating frequent data reuse among threads. For example, in a reduction operation where an array of elements needs to be summed, shared memory can be used to store intermediate results, reducing the overhead of writing to and reading from global memory.

Optimization of shared memory usage requires careful consideration of the following factors:

- **Bank Conflicts:** Shared memory is divided into banks, which can be accessed simultaneously. However, if multiple threads access the same bank, bank conflicts occur, leading to serialization of accesses and performance degradation. To avoid bank conflicts, ensure that accesses are spread across different banks effectively. CUDA compute capabilities provide mechanisms to handle bank conflicts more efficiently.

- **Memory Allocation:** The amount of shared memory required per block impacts the maximum number of active blocks per SM. Therefore, optimal allocation is necessary to balance between the advantages of shared memory usage and resource utilization.

- **Thread Cooperation:** Threads within a block should be programmed to cooperate, utilizing shared memory to exchange data and perform computations collectively. This cooperative approach minimizes redundant work and leverages the high-bandwidth access to shared memory.

Effective use of shared memory involves profiling and tuning the memory access patterns to minimize latency and maximize throughput. The nvprof profiler and NSight tools are invaluable in analyzing the performance impact of shared memory and identifying potential bottlenecks.

Shared memory enhances the capabilities of CUDA by allowing threads within a block to communicate and share data at high speeds. Properly leveraging this memory model is essential for developing high-performance CUDA applications that fully utilize the computational power of modern GPUs.

4.7 Constant and Texture Memory

Constant and texture memory are types of read-only memory spaces in the CUDA architecture that serve specific purposes to optimize performance for certain kinds of data access patterns. Both of these memory types offer caching benefits and support specific use cases that can lead to significant performance improvements when used correctly. Understanding how to effectively utilize constant and texture memory is essential for optimizing CUDA applications.

Constant Memory

Constant memory is a read-only memory space designed for variables that remain unchanged throughout the kernel's execution. It is cached, which allows for faster access compared to global memory, especially when multiple threads access the same data. The size of constant memory is limited to 64 KB, so it must be used judiciously.

Data stored in constant memory can be accessed by kernels using the __constant__ qualifier. The cache is optimized for scenarios where all threads in a warp read the same address simultaneously, as this allows the memory access to be serviced by a single read operation from the cache, reducing the need for multiple accesses to global memory.

Example usage of constant memory:

```
__constant__ float constData[256];

__global__ void kernelFunction(float *outputData) {
    int idx = threadIdx.x;
    outputData[idx] = constData[idx] * 2.0f;
}

void setupConstantMemory(float *hostData) {
    cudaMemcpyToSymbol(constData, hostData, 256 * sizeof(float));
}
```

In this example, the kernel function reads from the constData array, which is stored in constant memory. By using the cudaMemcpyToSymbol function, the data is transferred from the host to the constant memory on the device before kernel execution.

Texture Memory

Texture memory, unlike constant memory, is designed for two primary benefits: caching and access pattern flexibility. It is especially beneficial for applications that involve frequent and irregular read access patterns, such as those found in image and signal processing applications. Texture memory supports a variety of data types and provides address modes and filtering options, making it suitable for more complex access patterns.

Texture memory is cached similarly to constant memory but offers additional flexibility by providing spatial locality and filtering features. Spatial locality means that threads accessing addresses that are close to each other in memory benefit from the same cache line, and filtering options provide linear interpolation and other texture sampling features.

To use texture memory, data is bound to a texture using the cudaBindTexture function. Access to texture memory is performed through texture references or objects, which are defined at a higher level than plain pointers.

Example of texture memory usage:

```
texture<float, 1, cudaReadModeElementType> texRef;

__global__ void kernelFunction(float *outputData) {
    int idx = threadIdx.x;
    outputData[idx] = tex1Dfetch(texRef, idx) * 2.0f;
}

void setupTextureMemory(float *devData, size_t size) {
    cudaChannelFormatDesc channelDesc = cudaCreateChannelDesc<float>();
    cudaBindTexture(NULL, texRef, devData, channelDesc, size);
}
```

In this example, the tex1Dfetch function is used to fetch data from the texture memory, and the texture reference texRef is used to bind the data. By utilizing texture memory, the access patterns that benefit from caching and the inherent filtering capabilities can yield performance improvements.

Performance Considerations

The use of constant and texture memory can lead to significant performance improvements, but they must be used appropriately within their constraints. Constant memory thrives when all or most threads in a warp access the same memory location, effectively reducing the memory bandwidth requirements. Texture memory excels with complex access patterns where caching and filtering add significant value.

However, both types of memory are read-only, meaning they cannot be written to by kernels during execution. This property makes them suitable for static data required across multiple kernel launches but not for dynamically changing data.

In situations where constant memory is used, careful planning of the memory layout and accesses is paramount to maximizing the use of the constant cache. Similarly, when using texture memory, consideration must be given to the spatial locality of the data and how threads access it, to make full use of the caching mechanisms.

Ultimately, integrating constant and texture memory into a CUDA application requires thoughtful analysis of the data access patterns and memory usage to fully leverage the benefits of these specialized memory spaces.

4.8 Registers and Local Memory

Registers and local memory play crucial roles in optimizing the performance of CUDA applications. Understanding their characteristics and correct usage is essential for achieving high efficiency.

Registers in CUDA are the fastest form of memory available to each thread. They reside within the Streaming Multiprocessors (SMs) and provide immediate access to frequently used variables. The primary characteristic of registers is their low latency and high bandwidth, making them ideal for storing variables that require rapid access.

Each thread has its dedicated set of registers, typically referred to as register files. The number of registers available per SM is finite, and this limited number can impact the execution of CUDA kernels. The CUDA compiler allocates registers based on usage within kernels, and exceeding the maximum number leads to the spilling of registers into local memory, which is significantly slower.

To define variables in registers, one simply declares them normally within the CUDA kernel. For instance:

```
__global__ void kernelFunction() {
    int a, b, c; // These variables are stored in registers by default
    a = 2;
    b = 3;
    c = a + b;
}
```

In this example, variables a, b, and c are placed in registers. The efficiency of register usage can be monitored using tools like nvcc compiler flags, which provide insights into register allocation and usage.

Local memory in CUDA, despite its name, is not to be confused with shared memory. Local memory is a type of global memory and has higher access latency compared to registers or shared memory. It is used when the register allocation exceeds the available register resources, or when arrays or structures too large to fit into registers need to be stored.

Local memory is allocated per-thread but resides in the GPU's global memory. Consequently, accessing local memory involves higher latency and lower bandwidth compared to registers. Local memory usage should be minimized to reduce performance degradation.

The usage of local memory typically occurs implicitly when the compiler spills registers. For example:

```
__global__ void kernelFunction() {
    int largeArray[1000]; // This large array cannot fit into registers
    largeArray[0] = 1;
}
```

In this scenario, largeArray is too large to fit in the registers, so it gets allocated in local memory. Despite being accessible on a per-thread basis, it should be avoided for operations that need frequent and rapid access.

Optimizing register and local memory usage involves several strategies. First, developers should minimize the number of variables within CUDA kernels to reduce register pressure. Second, developers can utilize the maxrregcount flag with nvcc to limit the number of registers used per thread:

```
nvcc -maxrregcount=32 kernel.cu -o kernel
```

By setting a maximum register count, developers can control register usage and, consequently, manage local memory spills.

Analyzing performance data using the NVIDIA Visual Profiler or nvprof is critical for identifying register pressure and local memory utilization. These tools allow pinpointing bottlenecks and adjusting code to optimize memory usage.

A practical example of register and local memory usage can be observed in complex computational kernels. For instance:

```
__global__ void complexKernel(float *input, float *output, int N) {
    int idx = threadIdx.x + blockIdx.x * blockDim.x;
    if (idx < N) {
        float temp1 = input[idx] * 2.0f;
        float temp2 = temp1 + sinf(input[idx]);
        float result = temp2 / (temp1 + 1.0f);
        output[idx] = result;
    }
}
```

In this kernel, the variables temp1, temp2, and result are candidates for registers. If N is large and the register usage surpasses the limit, some of these variables may be spilled to local memory, impacting performance.

Fine-tuning register and local memory usage involves iterative profiling and code adjustments. Reducing unnecessary variable declarations, optimizing algorithms for minimal memory footprint, and carefully balancing the number of threads are imperative for maximizing CUDA performance.

4.9 Memory Coalescing and Access Patterns

Memory coalescing is a crucial optimization technique in CUDA programming that aims to increase memory access efficiency by minimizing warp divergence and ensuring that memory transactions are performed in a manner that maximizes throughput. In CUDA, global memory accesses are costly in terms of latency and bandwidth, making it crucial to optimize the way threads within a warp access memory.

A warp consists of 32 threads and GPUs perform memory transactions typically in sizes of 32, 64, or 128 bytes. Memory coalescing occurs when these threads access consecutive memory addresses, allowing the hardware to combine these accesses into a single memory transaction. This reduces the total number of transactions, thereby enhancing performance.

When threads in a warp access global memory in a scattered or non-sequential manner, memory transactions become inefficient due to the need for multiple transactions, leading to increased memory latency. Let's consider examples of both coalesced and non-coalesced memory accesses to illustrate this concept further.

```
# Coalesced memory access pattern
@cuda.jit
def coalesced_kernel(arr):
    idx = cuda.grid(1)
    if idx < arr.size:
        arr[idx] += 1.0
```

In the above kernel, each thread accesses a consecutive element in the array 'arr'. Threads within a warp access contiguous memory locations, allowing the hardware to coalesce these accesses into fewer memory transactions.

```
# Non-coalesced memory access pattern
@cuda.jit
def non_coalesced_kernel(arr):
    idx = cuda.grid(1)
    stride = 32
    if idx < arr.size // stride:
        arr[idx * stride] += 1.0
```

In this example, threads access elements with a stride of 32. Although each thread accesses only one element, these accesses are not contiguous, leading to multiple memory transactions per warp and resulting in poor performance.

To achieve optimal memory coalescing, several strategies can be employed:

Alignment: Ensure that data structures are appropriately aligned to the memory transaction size. CUDA devices favor memory accesses that align with 32, 64, or 128-byte boundaries. Unaligned accesses can result in additional memory transactions and inefficiencies.

Stride-1 Access: Opt for stride-1 access patterns where consecutive threads access consecutive memory addresses. This minimizes the number of memory transactions required per warp and maximizes coalescing efficiency.

Data Layout Transformation: In situations where stride-1 access is not naturally present, data layout transformations such as array transposition can help achieve coalesced accesses. By reorganizing data in memory to align with the access patterns of threads, the GPU can achieve efficient memory transactions.

Memory Padding: Introducing padding can sometimes resolve alignment issues. Although it introduces some memory overhead, proper padding can ensure that access patterns remain coalesced, particularly in multidimensional arrays.

Consider the following example of array transposition for better coalescing:

```
@cuda.jit
def transpose(arr, result):
    i, j = cuda.grid(2)
    if i < arr.shape[0] and j < arr.shape[1]:
        result[j, i] = arr[i, j]
```

In the 'transpose' kernel, threads access the input array 'arr' in a coalesced manner, leading to efficient memory transactions. The output array 'result' is organized such that threads write to contiguous memory locations, promoting coalescing upon write operations.

To diagnose and improve memory coalescing, developers can make use of profiling tools such as NVIDIA's NSight or the Visual Profiler. These tools provide insights into memory access patterns, memory transaction counts, and the effectiveness of coalescing. Metrics such as "global load efficiency" and "global store efficiency" help identify areas for improvement.

By understanding and implementing memory coalescing techniques, developers can significantly enhance the performance of CUDA applications. The patterns discussed in this section form a foundational aspect of efficient memory management, playing a crucial role in the overall optimization of CUDA kernels.

4.10 Latency and Bandwidth Considerations

Understanding latency and bandwidth is crucial for optimizing CUDA applications, ensuring that data transfers and kernel executions occur as efficiently as possible. Latency refers to the time delay before a transfer or computation begins, while bandwidth measures the rate of data transfer. These two metrics are pivotal in identifying bottlenecks and minimizing performance degradation.

Latency in the context of CUDA programming can be observed at multiple levels, including memory access latency and the latency associated with initiating kernels. Memory access latency refers to the delay experienced when data is being read from or written to various levels of memory. For instance, fetching data from global memory typically has higher latency compared to shared memory, due to the physical distance and complexity of accessing global memory. Understanding these differences allows developers to design their algorithms in a way that minimizes high-latency operations.

Bandwidth, on the other hand, is critical in determining how quickly data can be moved between different memory hierarchies or between the CPU and GPU. In CUDA, the global memory offers the highest capacity but also has the lowest bandwidth compared to shared memory, which provides faster access with relatively higher bandwidth due to its proximity to the SMs. Effectively utilizing memory with higher bandwidth can significantly enhance application performance.

Considering these two concepts, we can thus discuss several strategies for their optimization:

First, **coalescing global memory accesses** is essential for optimizing bandwidth usage. When threads within a warp access memory locations that are contiguous and aligned correctly, the memory controller can merge these accesses into fewer transactions, thus improving bandwidth utilization. The following example illustrates a coalesced versus non-coalesced access pattern:

```
# Example of non-coalesced memory access
__global__ void nonCoalescedAccess(float *data) {
    int idx = blockIdx.x * blockDim.x + threadIdx.x;
    for (int i = 0; i < N; i++) {
        data[idx + i * blockDim.x] = ...; # Strided access
```

```
    }
}

# Example of coalesced memory access
__global__ void coalescedAccess(float *data) {
    int idx = blockIdx.x * blockDim.x + threadIdx.x;
    for (int i = 0; i < N; i++) {
        data[idx + i] = ...; # Contiguous access
    }
}
```

Coalescing is more challenging when dealing with multi-dimensional arrays or complex data structures. For such cases, data layout transformation or padding might be necessary to ensure contiguous memory access patterns.

Second, **minimizing memory access latency** involves exploiting the various levels of memory hierarchy. Shared memory, due to its proximity to the CUDA cores, has significantly lower access latency compared to global memory. Therefore, frequently accessed data should be loaded into shared memory where possible. Consider the following example:

```
__global__ void useSharedMemory(float *data, float *result) {
    __shared__ float sharedData[BLOCK_SIZE];
    int idx = blockIdx.x * blockDim.x + threadIdx.x;

    sharedData[threadIdx.x] = data[idx];
    __syncthreads();

    // Perform computations with sharedData
    result[idx] = ...;
}
```

However, shared memory is limited in size, and its effective use often requires a balance between the amount of data stored and the resultant occupancy of the threads.

Third, **overlapping computation and data transfers** is an effective technique in reducing the overall impact of latency. CUDA streams and asynchronous memory copies allow for concurrent execution of computations and data transfers. Employing multiple CUDA streams to handle different parts of a computation can hide latency as illustrated below:

```
cudaMemcpyAsync(destination, source, size, cudaMemcpyDeviceToHost, stream1);
kernel<<<blocks, threads, 0, stream2>>>(...);

cudaStreamSynchronize(stream1);
cudaStreamSynchronize(stream2);
```

In this manner, computations in stream2 can be initiated while data transfer in `stream1` is still ongoing, thus hiding the latency of data transfers behind useful computation.

Lastly, **profiling tools** such as NVIDIA nvprof and Nsight Systems are invaluable for identifying latency and bandwidth issues. These tools provide detailed insights into the timeline of memory transactions, kernel execution, and data transfer bottlenecks. Using these tools effectively involves running the application with different configurations and carefully analyzing the profiling results to identify inefficient patterns.

The interplay of latency and bandwidth in CUDA programming necessitates careful attention to memory access patterns, the utilization of shared memory, concurrent execution capabilities, and profiling techniques. By optimizing these aspects, one can significantly enhance the performance and efficiency of CUDA applications.

4.11 Memory Management and Optimization Strategies

Efficient memory management is crucial for maximizing the performance of applications using CUDA. This section focuses on various strategies to manage memory effectively and optimize for the best possible performance on CUDA-enabled devices.

Optimizing memory access patterns and leveraging different types of memory correctly can lead to significant performance gains. It is important to understand the characteristics of each memory type and the associated access patterns to use them efficiently.

To begin with, one must understand the differences between the types of memory available in CUDA, specifically global, shared, constant, register, and local memory, as discussed in earlier sections.

- **Global Memory:** This is the largest and slowest type of memory, accessible by all threads. It should be used for data that needs to be accessed by multiple threads across different blocks.
- **Shared Memory:** This memory is shared among threads of a single block and is much faster than global memory. It is useful for data that requires frequent read/write access by threads within the same block.
- **Constant Memory:** This read-only memory is cached and should

be used for data that does not change during kernel execution.

- **Registers:** These are the fastest memory type and are private to each thread. They should be used for frequently accessed data that fits within the limited register space.

- **Local Memory:** This refers to thread-private memory stored in the global memory space. Its use should be minimized due to its latency.

Various strategies can be employed to manage these memory types efficiently.

1. Minimizing Global Memory Access: Global memory accesses have high latency, and minimizing these accesses can greatly improve performance. One common approach is to use shared memory to cache data that is frequently accessed by threads within a block. By loading data from global memory to shared memory, threads can then access this data with significantly lower latency.

2. Maximizing Memory Coalescing: Memory coalescing refers to the process of combining multiple memory accesses into a single transaction, thus reducing the number of accesses and improving performance. For efficient memory coalescing, threads in a warp should access consecutive memory addresses. This ensures that memory transactions are coalesced into fewer accesses.

```
__global__ void example_kernel(float *input, float *output) {
    int idx = threadIdx.x + blockIdx.x * blockDim.x;
    output[idx] = input[idx] + 1.0f;
}
```

In the example above, if input and output arrays are stored in consecutive global memory locations, the memory accesses will be coalesced, resulting in efficient memory transactions.

3. Efficient Use of Shared Memory: Shared memory allows for very fast data access when used correctly. However, it is essential to ensure that there are no bank conflicts. Shared memory is divided into banks, and accessing different memory addresses in the same bank simultaneously results in conflicts, leading to serialization of access.

```
__global__ void shared_mem_example(float *data) {
    __shared__ float shared_data[256];
    int idx = threadIdx.x;
    shared_data[idx] = data[idx];
    __syncthreads();

    // Process shared_data[idx]...
```

```
}
```

In this example, each thread copies data into its corresponding position in the shared_data array, ensuring that there are no bank conflicts, assuming a sufficient number of banks.

4. Leveraging Constant Memory: Constant memory is highly advantageous when the data does not change throughout the kernel execution. Because it is cached, accessing constant memory is significantly faster compared to global memory.

```
__constant__ float const_data[256];

__global__ void const_mem_example(float *output) {
    int idx = threadIdx.x;
    output[idx] = const_data[idx] * 2.0f;
}
```

The above code demonstrates how constant memory can be used. The const_data array is stored in constant memory, and each thread reads from it. Because this memory is cached, the reads are very fast.

5. Reducing Register Pressure: High register usage can limit the number of concurrent threads on a Streaming Multiprocessor (SM), reducing overall occupancy and potentially harming performance. It is important to balance the use of registers to maintain high occupancy.

```
__global__ void register_example(float *data) {
    int idx = threadIdx.x;
    float temp = data[idx]; // Minimum use of registers
    data[idx] = temp * 2.0f;
}
```

6. Avoiding Local Memory Bottlenecks: Local memory is actually global memory and should be avoided whenever possible due to its high latency.

7. Employing Asynchronous Memory Copy: CUDA provides asynchronous memory copy operations to overlap data transfer and computation. This can hide memory transfer latency and improve overall throughput.

```
cudaMemcpyAsync(dst, src, size, cudaMemcpyHostToDevice, stream);
cudaKernelExample<<<blocks, threads, 0, stream>>>(device_ptr);
```

Efficiently managing memory at different hierarchy levels and following optimization strategies can significantly enhance the performance of CUDA applications. Achieving optimal memory utilization ensures that data accesses are fast and concurrent executions are maximized, leveraging the full potential of the CUDA architecture.

4.12 Understanding the CUDA Execution Model

The CUDA execution model defines how parallel computations are structured and executed on NVIDIA GPUs. It is essential to understand this model to design efficient parallel algorithms. The key components of the CUDA execution model include threads, blocks, grids, and the hierarchy in which these elements are organized for execution on the GPU.

CUDA programs, or kernels, are executed by a large number of threads organized in a hierarchical structure. Each kernel is executed by a grid of thread blocks. A thread block is a group of threads that can cooperate among themselves through shared memory and synchronize their execution. Once a kernel is launched, the grid and blocks cannot be changed; their configuration must be defined at the time of the kernel's launch.

Threads and Thread Blocks:

Each thread within a block has a unique identifier accessible through built-in variables such as threadIdx. Similarly, each block within a grid has a unique identifier given by blockIdx. These identifiers are used to distinguish threads and coordinate their activities. Threads within a block can share data amongst themselves via shared memory, which is a small, on-chip memory accessible to all threads in the block. This characteristic makes shared memory suitable for data that needs quick access by multiple threads, allowing for efficient inter-thread communication.

The number of threads per block, often called the block size, and the number of blocks in the grid, or grid size, are crucial parameters that affect the performance and efficiency of kernel execution. The maximum number of threads per block is a hardware limit, which is contingent on the specific GPU architecture.

Grids:

A grid is a collection of thread blocks that execute the same kernel simultaneously. Grids are defined in one, two, or three dimensions, similarly to tread blocks. For example, one can declare a grid of 16x16x1 blocks, where each block comprises 32x32x1 threads. The indices of threads and blocks are accessible within the kernel using built-in variables such as blockIdx, threadIdx, blockDim, and gridDim. These variables provide a systematic way to organize and navigate through threads and blocks within the grid.

```
__global__ void matrixAdd(float* A, float* B, float* C, int N) {
    int row = blockIdx.y * blockDim.y + threadIdx.y;
    int col = blockIdx.x * blockDim.x + threadIdx.x;

    if (row < N && col < N) {
        C[row * N + col] = A[row * N + col] + B[row * N + col];
    }
}

int main() {
    ...
    dim3 threadsPerBlock(16, 16);
    dim3 numberOfBlocks((N + threadsPerBlock.x - 1) / threadsPerBlock.x,
                        (N + threadsPerBlock.y - 1) / threadsPerBlock.y);
    matrixAdd<<<numberOfBlocks, threadsPerBlock>>>(d_A, d_B, d_C, N);
    ...
}
```

In this example, the matrix addition kernel matrixAdd is configured such that each thread computes one element of the resulting matrix. The runtime API function launch configuration, <<<numberOfBlocks, threadsPerBlock >>>, defines the grid and block dimensions.

Warp and SIMD Execution:

A unique aspect of CUDA execution is the decomposition of thread blocks into warps. A warp is a group of 32 threads that get executed in a Single Instruction, Multiple Data (SIMD) fashion. When a kernel launches, the entire grid of thread blocks is scheduled for execution, but within each block, threads are executed in groups of 32, known as warps.

All threads in a warp execute the same instruction at any given time. This model implies that divergent paths within a warp, caused by conditional branching, can result in performance degradations due to serialized execution of different paths. Therefore, minimizing divergent branches within warps is crucial for optimizing performance.

Synchronization and Communication:

CUDA provides mechanisms to synchronize the operations of threads within a block using the __syncthreads function. This function acts as a barrier at which threads in a block must wait until all have arrived before any can proceed. This synchronization is critical when threads within a block share data via shared memory. However, synchronization across thread blocks is not inherently supported within a single kernel launch. Global synchronization can only be achieved by terminating the current kernel and launching a subsequent one.

Execution Configuration and Launch:

The execution configuration of a CUDA kernel, as shown earlier, is specified using the <<<gridSize, blockSize>>> syntax. This execution configuration defines the dimensions of the grid and blocks but also includes optional kernel parameters such as dynamically allocated shared memory size and stream identifiers.

```
void kernelLaunch() {
    int sharedMemSize = 1024;
    dim3 threadsPerBlock(32, 1);
    dim3 numberOfBlocks(128, 1);

    matrixAdd<<<numberOfBlocks, threadsPerBlock, sharedMemSize, 0>>>(d_A,
         d_B, d_C, N);
}
```

In this example, the kernel launch configuration allocates 1024 bytes of shared memory per block.

Understanding the CUDA execution model is crucial for harnessing the full potential of GPU computing. By judiciously organizing threads, blocks, and grids, and by optimizing synchronization and communication, one can achieve significant performance improvements in CUDA applications. The effective utilization of warp-based execution and memory hierarchies, along with precise configurations of grids and blocks, forms the foundation for developing high-performance CUDA programs.

Chapter 5

Basic CUDA Programming Concepts

This chapter introduces foundational concepts in CUDA programming, covering the structure of CUDA programs and the compilation process. Key topics include understanding kernels, thread hierarchy, grid, and block dimensions. It addresses memory allocation, data transfer between host and device, kernel launching, and thread synchronization. The chapter also highlights error handling, an overview of CUDA libraries, and best practices to avoid common pitfalls in CUDA programming.

5.1 Introduction to CUDA Programming Basics

CUDA (Compute Unified Device Architecture) is NVIDIA's parallel computing platform and application programming interface (API) that allows developers to use NVIDIA GPUs for general purpose processing. Understanding the basics of CUDA programming is essential for efficiently leveraging the computational power of GPUs to accelerate programs. This section delves into the foundational elements of CUDA, focusing on its essential components and basic constructs.

CUDA programs are written using the C/C++ language with some extensions provided by CUDA. These extensions include keywords for defining parallel functions (kernels), managing memory, and synchronizing threads. CUDA organizes computations in a hierarchical grid of thread blocks, where each block contains multiple threads. This section introduces key concepts such as kernels, thread hierarchy, grid and block dimensions, and the compilation process to provide a solid foundation for writing CUDA programs.

In CUDA, the smallest unit of execution is a **thread**. Multiple threads form a **block**, and multiple blocks form a **grid**. This hierarchical structure allows for significant flexibility and scalability in parallel execution.

Kernel Functions: The core of CUDA programming is the *kernel function*, which is a function that runs on the device (GPU). A kernel is defined using the __global__ keyword, indicating its execution on the GPU. Here is a simple example of a kernel function that adds two arrays:

```
__global__ void add(int *a, int *b, int *c) {
    int index = threadIdx.x;
    c[index] = a[index] + b[index];
}
```

In this example, the add kernel takes three integer pointers as parameters, representing the arrays to be added. The threadIdx.x intrinsic provides the thread index within the block, allowing each thread to access different elements of the input arrays.

Thread Hierarchy: To manage the complexity of parallel execution, CUDA introduces several built-in variables:

- threadIdx: Contains the index of the thread within its block.
- blockIdx: Contains the index of the block within the grid.
- blockDim: Contains the dimensions (number of threads) in the block.
- gridDim: Contains the dimensions (number of blocks) in the grid.

These variables enable threads to determine their unique index within the entire grid of threads. As an example, consider a kernel that computes the sum of two arrays using grid and block indices:

```
__global__ void addArrays(int *a, int *b, int *c, int N) {
    int index = blockIdx.x * blockDim.x + threadIdx.x;
    if (index < N) {
        c[index] = a[index] + b[index];
    }
}
```

In this example, the total index of the current thread is computed using both blockIdx.x and threadIdx.x. The check if (index < N) ensures that threads do not access out-of-bound memory, providing a safeguard in case the total number of threads exceeds the array size N.

Grid and Block Dimensions: When launching a kernel, the developer must specify the organization of the grid and blocks. This is done using the «<»> notation, which takes two parameters specifying the number of blocks and the number of threads per block, respectively. For instance, launching the above addArrays kernel could look like this:

```
int N = 1024;
int blockSize = 256;
int numBlocks = (N + blockSize - 1) / blockSize; // Compute number of blocks needed

int *d_a, *d_b, *d_c;
// Allocate memory on the device...
cudaMalloc(&d_a, N * sizeof(int));
cudaMalloc(&d_b, N * sizeof(int));
cudaMalloc(&d_c, N * sizeof(int));

// Kernel launch
addArrays<<<numBlocks, blockSize>>>(d_a, d_b, d_c, N);
```

In this snippet, numBlocks is calculated to ensure that each element in the arrays is processed, even if the size of the arrays is not a multiple of the block size. Memory allocation is done using cudaMalloc, allocating memory on the GPU for the arrays.

The GPU has its own memory space, separate from the host (CPU) memory. To utilize the GPU's computational power, data must be transferred between the host and device. This is done using functions like cudaMemcpy. Here is an example of transferring data to and from the device:

```
int *h_a = (int*)malloc(N * sizeof(int));
int *h_b = (int*)malloc(N * sizeof(int));
int *h_c = (int*)malloc(N * sizeof(int));

// Initialize host arrays h_a and h_b with some values...

cudaMemcpy(d_a, h_a, N * sizeof(int), cudaMemcpyHostToDevice);
cudaMemcpy(d_b, h_b, N * sizeof(int), cudaMemcpyHostToDevice);

// Launch the kernel...
addArrays<<<numBlocks, blockSize>>>(d_a, d_b, d_c, N);

// Copy result back to host
cudaMemcpy(h_c, d_c, N * sizeof(int), cudaMemcpyDeviceToHost);
```

In this code, h_a, h_b, and h_c are pointers to memory on the host, while d_a, d_b, and d_c point to memory on the device. The function cudaMemcpy is used for data transfer. The fourth parameter of cudaMemcpy specifies the direction of the transfer: cudaMemcpyHostToDevice for sending data from the host to the device, and cudaMemcpyDeviceToHost for the reverse.

Lastly, developers must handle synchronization and error checking. CUDA provides functions like cudaDeviceSynchronize to synchronize the host and device, and macros like cudaError_t to handle errors. Here is a simple illustration of error handling:

```
cudaError_t err = cudaGetLastError();
if (err != cudaSuccess) {
    printf("CUDA error: %s\n", cudaGetErrorString(err));
}
```

This code snippet retrieves the last error generated by any previous CUDA runtime API call and prints an error message if an error occurred.

Understanding these basics is fundamental for efficient and correct CUDA programming. This knowledge forms the foundation upon which more advanced concepts build, such as optimizing memory usage, advanced synchronization techniques, and leveraging specialized CUDA libraries.

5.2 CUDA Program Structure

A CUDA program typically consists of both host (CPU) and device (GPU) code. The host code is executed by the CPU, while the device code, also known as a kernel, is executed by the GPU. Understanding the structure of a CUDA program is essential for writing efficient and performant CUDA applications. This section delves into the key components of a CUDA program, including the organization of host and device code, kernel functions, and the syntax for launching kernels.

Host Code

The host code manages memory allocation, data transfer between the host and the device, and the execution of kernels on the GPU. Host code is written in standard C/C++ with CUDA extensions. Below is a simple example of a CUDA program structure focusing on the host code:

```
#include <stdio.h>

__global__ void kernelFunction() {
    printf("Hello from GPU!\n");
```

```
}

int main() {
    // Launch the kernel function
    kernelFunction<<<1, 1>>>();
    cudaDeviceSynchronize();

    return 0;
}
```

In this example, the #include <stdio.h> directive imports the standard input-output header from the C library. The host code consists of the main() function, which handles launching the kernel kernelFunction with specific grid and block dimensions.

Device Code

Device code, or kernels, are functions that run on the GPU. They are defined using the __global__ keyword, which specifies that the function can be called from the host and executed on the device. Here is a breakdown of the kernel function from the previous code:

```
__global__ void kernelFunction() {
    printf("Hello from GPU!\n");
}
```

The __global__ keyword before the function return type indicates that this function is a kernel function. Within the kernel function, you can utilize GPU-specific features and libraries.

Kernel Launch Syntax

Kernels are launched from the host using the triple angle bracket syntax «<...»>. This syntax specifies the execution configuration, including the number of thread blocks and the number of threads per block:

```
kernelFunction<<<number_of_blocks, number_of_threads_per_block>>>();
```

In our example, the kernel launch kernelFunction«<1, 1»>(); specifies one block and one thread per block.

Memory Management

CUDA programs require explicit memory management, including memory allocation, data transfer, and deallocation. Common functions include cudaMalloc(), cudaMemcpy(), and cudaFree(). Below is an example illustrating these functions:

```
#include <stdio.h>
#include <cuda_runtime.h>

__global__ void kernelFunction(int *d_array) {
```

```
    int idx = threadIdx.x;
    printf("Hello from GPU thread %d\n", idx);
}

int main() {
    int *d_array;
    size_t size = sizeof(int) * 10;

    // Allocate device memory
    cudaMalloc((void **)&d_array, size);

    // Launch the kernel function
    kernelFunction<<<1, 10>>>(d_array);
    cudaDeviceSynchronize();

    // Free device memory
    cudaFree(d_array);

    return 0;
}
```

In this example, cudaMalloc is used to allocate memory on the device, and cudaFree is used to deallocate this memory. The kernel function kernelFunction is launched with one block and ten threads per block, and each thread prints its index.

Synchronization and Error Handling

After launching a kernel, it is often necessary to ensure that the kernel has completed execution. This can be done using cudaDeviceSynchronize(), which blocks the host until the device has completed all preceding requested tasks. For error handling, CUDA provides various functions such as cudaGetLastError() and cudaPeekAtLastError(). Here's how you can integrate error handling:

```
#include <stdio.h>
#include <cuda_runtime.h>

__global__ void kernelFunction(int *d_array) {
    int idx = threadIdx.x;
    d_array[idx] = idx;
}

int main() {
    int *d_array;
    size_t size = sizeof(int) * 10;

    cudaMalloc((void **)&d_array, size);

    kernelFunction<<<1, 10>>>(d_array);
    cudaError_t error = cudaGetLastError();
    if (error != cudaSuccess) {
        printf("CUDA error: %s\n", cudaGetErrorString(error));
    }
    cudaDeviceSynchronize();

    cudaFree(d_array);
```

```
    return 0;
}
```

In this example, cudaGetLastError() is used to check and report errors after the kernel launch.

Understanding the structure of a CUDA program is fundamental for effectively leveraging the GPU's capabilities. This involves intricate coordination between the host and device code, thoughtful memory management, and meticulous synchronization and error handling processes. The subsequent sections will build upon these principles, diving deeper into optimization and advanced features of CUDA programming.

5.3 Writing and Compiling a Simple CUDA Program

To grasp the fundamentals of CUDA programming, it is crucial to understand the process of writing and compiling a simple CUDA program. In this section, we will examine each step in detail, from coding a basic CUDA kernel to compiling and running the application. This will build a foundation for more complex CUDA programming tasks.

A CUDA program typically comprises two major components: the host code, written in standard C/C++ with CUDA extensions, and the device code, which defines the CUDA kernels to be executed on the GPU.

Here is a simple example to illustrate this process: a program that adds two vectors.

```
#include <cuda_runtime.h>
#include <stdio.h>

// CUDA Kernel
__global__ void vectorAdd(const float *A, const float *B, float *C, int N) {
    int i = blockDim.x * blockIdx.x + threadIdx.x;
    if (i < N) {
        C[i] = A[i] + B[i];
    }
}

int main(void) {
    int N = 1000;
    size_t size = N * sizeof(float);

    // Allocate memory on host
    float *h_A = (float *)malloc(size);
    float *h_B = (float *)malloc(size);
```

```
    float *h_C = (float *)malloc(size);

    // Initialize vectors
    for (int i = 0; i < N; i++) {
        h_A[i] = rand() % 100;
        h_B[i] = rand() % 100;
    }

    // Allocate memory on device
    float *d_A = NULL;
    float *d_B = NULL;
    float *d_C = NULL;
    cudaMalloc((void **)&d_A, size);
    cudaMalloc((void **)&d_B, size);
    cudaMalloc((void **)&d_C, size);

    // Copy vectors from host to device
    cudaMemcpy(d_A, h_A, size, cudaMemcpyHostToDevice);
    cudaMemcpy(d_B, h_B, size, cudaMemcpyHostToDevice);

    // Launch kernel
    int threadsPerBlock = 256;
    int blocksPerGrid = (N + threadsPerBlock - 1) / threadsPerBlock;
    vectorAdd<<<blocksPerGrid, threadsPerBlock>>>(d_A, d_B, d_C, N);

    // Copy result from device to host
    cudaMemcpy(h_C, d_C, size, cudaMemcpyDeviceToHost);

    // Test result
    for (int i = 0; i < N; i++) {
        if (abs(h_A[i] + h_B[i] - h_C[i]) > 1e-5) {
            fprintf(stderr, "Result verification failed at element %d!\n", i);
            exit(EXIT_FAILURE);
        }
    }

    // Free device memory
    cudaFree(d_A);
    cudaFree(d_B);
    cudaFree(d_C);

    // Free host memory
    free(h_A);
    free(h_B);
    free(h_C);

    printf("Test passed.\n");
    return 0;
}
```

CUDA Kernel Definition:

The kernel, vectorAdd, is defined using the __global__ keyword, indicating that it runs on the device but is called from the host. This kernel adds corresponding elements of two vectors. The threadIdx.x, blockIdx.x, and blockDim.x are built-in variables that CUDA provides to uniquely identify each thread.

Memory Allocation:

Memory allocation on the host is performed using the standard C function malloc. For device memory allocation, CUDA provides cudaMalloc, which functions similarly but allocates memory on the GPU.

Memory Transfer:

cudaMemcpy is used for transferring data between host and device. The API requires specifying the direction of transfer, for which options like cudaMemcpyHostToDevice and cudaMemcpyDeviceToHost are used.

Kernel Launch:

The kernel is launched using the following syntax:

```
kernel_name<<<number_of_blocks, threads_per_block>>>(parameters);
```

This configuration allows for flexible distribution of threads across the blocks and grids. In the example, the number of blocks is calculated to ensure coverage of all elements in the vectors.

Compiling the Program:

To compile a CUDA program, the NVIDIA compiler nvcc is used. The following command compiles the example program:

```
nvcc -o vector_add vector_add.cu
```

After compilation, the program can be executed just like any other executable and will utilize the GPU for computations.

Output:

The program's output would be displayed as follows if the test passes:

```
Test passed.
```

This example integrates essential CUDA programming components, from memory management to kernel execution. It establishes a comprehensive understanding of the writing and compiling process, necessary for tackling complex CUDA applications.

5.4 Understanding Kernels and Thread Hierarchy

In CUDA programming, kernels and the associated thread hierarchy are core concepts that enable the parallel execution of code on a GPU. A kernel is a function written in CUDA C/C++ and executed on the GPU, whereas the thread hierarchy defines the organization of threads within the GPU to efficiently execute these kernels.

A kernel is defined using the __global__ declaration specifier, which tells the compiler that this function will be executed on the device (GPU) and called from the host (CPU). Each invocation of a kernel creates a grid of thread blocks that are distributed over the GPU's streaming multiprocessors (SMs).

```
__global__ void myKernel(int *input, int *output) {
    int idx = threadIdx.x + blockIdx.x * blockDim.x;
    output[idx] = input[idx] * input[idx];
}
```

In this example, the myKernel function multiplies each element of the input array by itself and stores the result in the output array.

Thread Hierarchy:

The thread hierarchy in CUDA consists of the following levels:

- **Grid:** A grid is a collection of blocks that execute the kernel function. Each block within the grid operates independently, but they can all access the same global memory space.
- **Block:** A block is a group of threads that can cooperate with each other by synchronizing their execution and sharing data through shared memory. Each block has a unique index within the grid, which can be accessed via the blockIdx variable.
- **Thread:** Threads are the smallest units of execution. Each thread within a block is assigned a unique index, which is accessed via the threadIdx variable. Threads within the same block can be synchronized using intrinsic synchronization functions.

Each block can be configured in terms of the number of threads it contains using a 1D, 2D, or 3D configuration. Similarly, grids can also be configured in 1D, 2D, or 3D. This flexibility allows for efficient mapping of algorithms to hardware capabilities.

Example of Defining Blocks and Grids:

To define the dimensions of grids and blocks, CUDA uses dim3 structures, which represent the dimensions of blocks and grids. Below is an example of how to define and launch a kernel with specific grid and block dimensions:

```
int numElements = 1024;
```

```
dim3 threadsPerBlock(256);
dim3 blocksPerGrid((numElements + threadsPerBlock.x - 1) / threadsPerBlock.x);

myKernel<<<blocksPerGrid, threadsPerBlock>>>(d_input, d_output);
```

In this example, we have a total of 1024 elements to process, and we configure each block to contain 256 threads. The number of blocks per grid is computed to ensure that all elements are processed, even if the number of elements is not perfectly divisible by 256.

Execution Configuration:

The syntax used to launch a kernel, kernel«<gridDim, blockDim»>(args), specifies the execution configuration. gridDim represents the dimensions of the grid, while blockDim represents the dimensions of each block.

Consider another example where we launch a kernel with a 2D grid and 2D block configuration:

```
dim3 threadsPerBlock(16, 16);
dim3 numBlocks((width + threadsPerBlock.x - 1) / threadsPerBlock.x,
              (height + threadsPerBlock.y - 1) / threadsPerBlock.y);

my2DKernel<<<numBlocks, threadsPerBlock>>>(d_input, d_output, width, height);
```

Here, threadsPerBlock is defined as 16x16, meaning each block contains 256 threads. numBlocks is computed based on the width and height of the input data to ensure all elements are processed.

Thread Index Calculation:

To identify the specific work each thread will perform, thread and block indices are used. The following code snippet shows how to calculate the global thread index:

```
int row = blockIdx.y * blockDim.y + threadIdx.y;
int col = blockIdx.x * blockDim.x + threadIdx.x;
```

In a 2D grid configuration, row and col identify the position of each thread in the global memory space.

Shared Memory and Synchronization:

Threads within the same block can share data using shared memory, which is a fast, low-latency memory. An example of using shared memory is shown below:

```
__global__ void matrixTranspose(float *out, float *in, int width, int height) {
    __shared__ float tile[TILE_DIM][TILE_DIM + 1];
    int x = blockIdx.x * TILE_DIM + threadIdx.x;
    int y = blockIdx.y * TILE_DIM + threadIdx.y;
```

```
    int widthIn = min(width, blockIdx.x * TILE_DIM + TILE_DIM);
    int heightIn = min(height, blockIdx.y * TILE_DIM + TILE_DIM);

    for (int j = 0; j < TILE_DIM; j += BLOCK_ROWS) {
        if (x < width && (y + j) < height)
            tile[threadIdx.y + j][threadIdx.x] = in[(y + j) * width + x];
    }
    __syncthreads();

    x = blockIdx.y * TILE_DIM + threadIdx.x;
    y = blockIdx.x * TILE_DIM + threadIdx.y;
    for (int j = 0; j < TILE_DIM; j += BLOCK_ROWS) {
        if (x < heightIn && (y + j) < widthIn)
            out[(y + j) * height + x] = tile[threadIdx.x][threadIdx.y + j];
    }
}
```

The above kernel, matrixTranspose, uses shared memory (the tile array) to perform matrix transposition. This avoids redundant global memory access and significantly boosts performance. The __syncthreads() function is employed to synchronize threads within the block, ensuring that all reads to shared memory are completed before subsequent writes begin.

Understanding kernels and the thread hierarchy is fundamental for efficient CUDA programming. Mastery of these concepts allows developers to leverage the full potential of GPU parallelism, optimizing performance for a wide array of computational tasks.

5.5 Grid and Block Dimensions

Understanding grid and block dimensions is crucial as they dictate how the computation is distributed and executed in parallel on the GPU. In CUDA, a grid is a collection of blocks, and each block contains a set of threads. The organization of these blocks and threads can greatly influence the performance and efficiency of a CUDA program.

Grid Dimensions

A grid in CUDA is a two-dimensional or three-dimensional structure composed of blocks. The dimensions of a grid determine how many blocks are necessary to perform the computation. Grid dimensions are specified using the dim3 type in CUDA, which can hold up to three unsigned integer values:

```
dim3 gridDim(x, y, z);
```

Here, x, y, and z specify the dimensions of the grid along the x, y, and z axes, respectively.

For example, to declare a one-dimensional grid with 10 blocks:

```
dim3 gridDim(10);
```

To declare a two-dimensional grid with 10 blocks in the x-dimension and 5 blocks in the y-dimension:

```
dim3 gridDim(10, 5);
```

It is important to note that while CUDA allows for three-dimensional grids, most applications only use one- or two-dimensional grids for simplicity and efficiency.

Block Dimensions

A block in CUDA is a collection of threads. Like grids, blocks can also be one-dimensional, two-dimensional, or three-dimensional. The dimensions of a block are also specified using the dim3 type:

```
dim3 blockDim(x, y, z);
```

For example, a one-dimensional block with 256 threads:

```
dim3 blockDim(256);
```

A two-dimensional block with 16 threads in the x-dimension and 16 threads in the y-dimension:

```
dim3 blockDim(16, 16);
```

Launching Kernels with Grid and Block Dimensions

When launching a kernel, the grid and block dimensions must be clearly defined:

```
kernel<<< gridDim, blockDim >>>( ... );
```

Here, gridDim specifies the dimensions of the grid, and blockDim specifies the dimensions of the block.

For example:

```
myKernel<<<dim3(10, 5), dim3(16, 16)>>>( ... );
```

This launches a grid with 10 x 5 blocks, where each block contains 16 x 16 threads.

Maximum Dimensions and Limitations

CUDA defines specific maximum dimensions for grids and blocks, and these limits can vary depending on the compute capability of the GPU. As of CUDA 11, for most GPUs, the maximum number of threads per block is 1024. The maximum dimensions for a grid are also constrained, typically up to $2^{31} - 1$ in the x-dimension for devices of compute capability 3.x or higher.

Choosing Optimal Grid and Block Dimensions

Selecting optimal grid and block dimensions is a critical aspect for achieving maximum performance. The choice depends on the nature of the problem, the hardware specifications, and the desired concurrency. Some general guidelines include:

- Ensure each block has a sufficient number of threads to fully utilize the GPU cores.
- Prefer dimensions that are multiples of the warp size (32 threads) to avoid underutilization.
- Avoid creating too many small blocks or threads which can lead to overhead and inefficiencies.
- Balance workload such that each block has a similar number of operations.

Example: Vector Addition

Consider a vector addition example to illustrate the practical use of grid and block dimensions. Here, we assume adding two large vectors of size N:

```
__global__ void vectorAdd(int *a, int *b, int *c, int N) {
    int idx = blockIdx.x * blockDim.x + threadIdx.x;
    if (idx < N) {
        c[idx] = a[idx] + b[idx];
    }
}

void main() {
    int N = 1 << 20; // Vector size
    int *a, *b, *c; // Host memory
    int *d_a, *d_b, *d_c; // Device memory

    // Allocate and initialize host memory
    // Allocate and initialize device memory

    // Define block and grid dimensions
    dim3 blockDim(256);
    dim3 gridDim((N + blockDim.x - 1) / blockDim.x);

    // Launch the kernel
```

```
    vectorAdd<<<gridDim, blockDim>>>(d_a, d_b, d_c, N);

    // Copy results from device to host
    // Deallocate device and host memory
}
```

This example demonstrates a kernel launch for a simple vector addition. The grid dimensions are computed such that it covers all N elements in the vectors, ensuring even workload distribution among the blocks. Each block contains 256 threads, and gridDim.x is calculated to be $(N+256-1)/256$, ensuring all threads are utilized appropriately without exceeding the maximum number of threads per block.

By understanding and effectively utilizing grid and block dimensions, CUDA programmers can harness the full potential of GPU parallelism to achieve significant performance enhancements.

5.6 Memory Allocation and Transfer between Host and Device

In CUDA programming, efficient memory management is crucial for achieving optimum performance. Memory allocation and data transfer between the host (CPU) and device (GPU) are foundational concepts that directly influence the efficiency of CUDA applications. This section delves into the methods and best practices associated with memory allocation and data transfer to facilitate effective utilization of the GPU.

The primary types of memory in CUDA include:

- **Global Memory:** Accessible by all threads across blocks, and has the highest latency but also the highest capacity.
- **Shared Memory:** Shared among threads within the same block, offers low latency.
- **Local Memory:** Private to each thread, with high latency.

The fundamental CUDA API functions for memory management are:

- cudaMalloc() allocates memory on the device.
- cudaFree() deallocates memory on the device.
- cudaMemcpy() is used for transferring data between host and device.

Below is an example illustrating memory allocation and data transfer in a CUDA program.

```
#include <cuda_runtime.h>
#include <iostream>

__global__ void kernelFunction(float *d_array) {
    int idx = threadIdx.x + blockIdx.x * blockDim.x;
    d_array[idx] *= 2.0f;
}

int main() {
    const int arraySize = 1024;
    const int bytes = arraySize * sizeof(float);

    // Host memory allocation
    float *h_array = (float*)malloc(bytes);
    for (int i = 0; i < arraySize; i++) {
        h_array[i] = static_cast<float>(i);
    }

    // Device memory allocation
    float *d_array;
    cudaMalloc((void**)&d_array, bytes);

    // Copy data from host to device
    cudaMemcpy(d_array, h_array, bytes, cudaMemcpyHostToDevice);

    // Launch kernel
    int blockSize = 256;
    int gridSize = (arraySize + blockSize - 1) / blockSize;
    kernelFunction<<<gridSize, blockSize>>>(d_array);

    // Copy data back from device to host
    cudaMemcpy(h_array, d_array, bytes, cudaMemcpyDeviceToHost);

    // Deallocate device memory
    cudaFree(d_array);

    // Display results
    for (int i = 0; i < arraySize; i++) {
        std::cout << "h_array[" << i << "] = " << h_array[i] << std::endl;
    }

    // Deallocate host memory
    free(h_array);

    return 0;
}
```

In the above program, the host memory is allocated using the standard malloc() function, while the device memory allocation is performed using cudaMalloc(). Data transfer is facilitated by cudaMemcpy(), which is capable of transferring data in various directions, specified by the fourth parameter, such as cudaMemcpyHostToDevice, cudaMemcpyDeviceToHost, and cudaMemcpyDeviceToDevice.

The breakdown of the example program is as follows:

1. Host memory allocation allocates an array of 1024 floats using malloc().
2. Device memory allocation allocates a corresponding array on the GPU using cudaMalloc().
3. cudaMemcpy() transfers the initialized array data from host to device.
4. The kernel, defined by __global__, doubles each element in the device array. Each thread identifies its corresponding element using thread and block indices.
5. cudaMemcpy() transfers the processed array from device back to host.
6. cudaFree() deallocates the device memory.

Noteworthy points for efficient memory management include:

- **Alignment and Size:** Ensure that the size of data processed aligns with GPU architectural specifications to improve memory coalescing.
- **Pinned (Page-Locked) Memory:** Leveraging pinned memory can drastically improve data transfer rates between host and device by avoiding unnecessary page faults and enabling Direct Memory Access (DMA).
- **Asynchronous Transfers:** Utilize asynchronous data transfer functions (cudaMemcpyAsync()) in conjunction with CUDA streams to overlap data transfers with computation, thus enhancing overall throughput.
- **Unified Memory:** CUDA's unified memory (cudaMallocManaged()) provides a simplified abstraction, allowing seamless data access and migration between host and device, at the cost of potential performance overhead due to page migrations.

Below is an example demonstrating the use of pinned memory:

```
#include <cuda_runtime.h>
#include <iostream>

__global__ void kernelFunction(float *d_array) {
    int idx = threadIdx.x + blockIdx.x * blockDim.x;
```

```
    d_array[idx] *= 2.0f;
}

int main() {
    const int arraySize = 1024;
    const int bytes = arraySize * sizeof(float);

    // Host pinned memory allocation
    float *h_array;
    cudaMallocHost((void**)&h_array, bytes);
    for (int i = 0; i < arraySize; i++) {
        h_array[i] = static_cast<float>(i);
    }

    // Device memory allocation
    float *d_array;
    cudaMalloc((void**)&d_array, bytes);

    // Asynchronous copy data from host to device
    cudaMemcpyAsync(d_array, h_array, bytes, cudaMemcpyHostToDevice);

    // Launch kernel
    int blockSize = 256;
    int gridSize = (arraySize + blockSize - 1) / blockSize;
    kernelFunction<<<gridSize, blockSize>>>(d_array);

    // Asynchronous copy data back from device to host
    cudaMemcpyAsync(h_array, d_array, bytes, cudaMemcpyDeviceToHost);

    // Deallocate device memory
    cudaFree(d_array);

    // Synchronize to ensure copy operations are completed
    cudaDeviceSynchronize();

    // Display results
    for (int i = 0; i < arraySize; i++) {
        std::cout << "h_array[" << i << "] = " << h_array[i] << std::endl;
    }

    // Deallocate host pinned memory
    cudaFreeHost(h_array);

    return 0;
}
```

The importance of utilizing CUDA streams and asynchronous memory operations lies in the ability to overlap execution and data transfers, thereby maximizing the efficiency and utilization of available resources. This approach is particularly beneficial in applications requiring large data sets or real-time processing.

By appropriately managing memory allocation and data transfer between the host and device, CUDA programs can achieve significant performance gains. This fundamental understanding forms the basis upon which more complex and optimized CUDA applications are built.

5.7 Launching Kernels: Syntax and Parameters

When launching a CUDA kernel, it is essential to understand the syntax and parameters involved to effectively leverage the GPU's parallel processing capabilities. The kernel launch follows a specific syntax characterized by the distinct use of triple angle brackets, often referred to as the *execution configuration*.

Kernel Launch Syntax

The general syntax for launching a CUDA kernel is as follows:

```
kernel_function<<<gridDim, blockDim, sharedMem, stream>>>(kernel_parameters);
```

Here, kernel_function is the name of the kernel to be executed on the device. Let's break down the execution configuration components inside the triple angle brackets:

- gridDim: Specifies the number of blocks in the grid.
- blockDim: Indicates the number of threads within a block.
- sharedMem (optional): Defines the amount of dynamic shared memory per block in bytes. Default is 0.
- stream (optional): Identifies the stream in which the kernel should be launched. Default is 0, representing the default stream.

Example of a Kernel Launch

Consider a simple kernel function that adds two arrays:

```
__global__ void add_arrays(int *a, int *b, int *c, int N) {
    int index = blockIdx.x * blockDim.x + threadIdx.x;
    if (index < N) {
        c[index] = a[index] + b[index];
    }
}
```

For launching this kernel with 256 threads per block and enough blocks to handle N elements in the arrays, the launch syntax might look like this:

```
int blockSize = 256;
int gridSize = (N + blockSize - 1) / blockSize;

add_arrays<<<gridSize, blockSize>>>(d_a, d_b, d_c, N);
```

Grid and Block Dimensions

gridDim and blockDim can be one, two, or three-dimensional, allowing for flexibility in structuring the parallel workload. For instance:

- dim3 gridDim(16, 8, 1) means 16 blocks in the x-dimension and 8 blocks in the y-dimension.
- dim3 blockDim(32, 32, 1) means each block contains 32 threads in the x-dimension and 32 threads in the y-dimension.

Using these dim3 types, the kernel launch can be adapted as follows:

```
dim3 gridDim(16, 8);
dim3 blockDim(32, 32);

add_arrays<<<gridDim, blockDim>>>(d_a, d_b, d_c, N);
```

Kernel Parameters

The parameters passed to the kernel function are typical of C/C++ functions. In the above example, d_a, d_b, and d_c are device pointers, while N is an integer specifying the number of elements.

Shared Memory and Streams

The shared memory parameter and stream parameter provide greater control over the execution. When allocating dynamic shared memory or launching kernels in specific streams, one might explicitly specify these parameters:

```
int sharedMemSize = 1024;
cudaStream_t myStream;

cudaStreamCreate(&myStream);
add_arrays<<<gridDim, blockDim, sharedMemSize, myStream>>>(d_a, d_b, d_c,
    N);
cudaStreamDestroy(myStream);
```

sharedMemSize specifies the amount of dynamic shared memory in bytes per block. In the above example, myStream indicates that the kernel is launched in a separate stream, enabling concurrent execution with other streams.

Kernel Launch Best Practices

Ensuring optimal kernel configuration is crucial for performance efficiency. Here are some best practices:

- **Occupancy Considerations**: Occupancy refers to the ratio of the number of active warps to the maximum number of warps supported on a multiprocessor. High occupancy often correlates with better utilization of GPU resources.

- **Grid Size and Block Size**: The grid and block sizes should be chosen to maximize resource usage without exceeding hardware limits. It is advisable to use a grid size that scales with the problem size and a block size that considers the balance of computational load across threads.
- **Memory Efficiency**: Proper use of shared memory can reduce global memory access latency. Allocate adequate shared memory and minimize its usage to avoid resource contention.
- **Stream Utilization**: Utilizing multiple streams can improve concurrency and throughput, especially in applications where tasks can be executed independently.

By understanding and effectively configuring the kernel launch parameters, one can significantly enhance the performance and efficiency of CUDA applications. The choice of grid and block dimensions, along with thoughtful use of shared memory and streams, plays a critical role in harnessing the full potential of the GPU.

5.8 Synchronizing Threads

In CUDA programming, thread synchronization is crucial to ensure correct program execution, especially when multiple threads are accessing shared data. Synchronization mechanisms help manage the coordination of parallel tasks, preventing race conditions and ensuring data integrity. This section delves into the primary methods of synchronizing threads within a CUDA kernel, focusing on __syncthreads and atomic operations.

__syncthreads is a barrier synchronization function provided by CUDA. This function ensures that all threads in a block reach the same point before any thread continues execution. This barrier is crucial when threads need to access shared data that might be simultaneously read and written by other threads.

Consider the following example where __syncthreads is used to synchronize shared memory access:

```
__global__ void vectorAdd(float* A, float* B, float* C, int N) {
    // Allocate shared memory
```

```
    __shared__ float shared_A[BLOCK_SIZE];
    __shared__ float shared_B[BLOCK_SIZE];

    int tid = blockDim.x * blockIdx.x + threadIdx.x;

    // Load data into shared memory
    if (tid < N) {
        shared_A[threadIdx.x] = A[tid];
        shared_B[threadIdx.x] = B[tid];
    }

    // Ensure all data is loaded into shared memory
    __syncthreads();

    // Perform computation
    if (tid < N) {
        C[tid] = shared_A[threadIdx.x] + shared_B[threadIdx.x];
    }
}
```

In this kernel, data from global memory is first loaded into shared memory. The __syncthreads call ensures that all threads have finished loading their respective elements into shared memory before the computation begins. Without this barrier, some threads might read uninitialized data, leading to incorrect results.

Another synchronization mechanism in CUDA is the use of atomic operations. Atomic operations ensure that a memory location is updated without interruption. When multiple threads attempt to modify the same memory location concurrently, atomic operations prevent race conditions by serially promoting the accesses.

CUDA provides a set of atomic functions, such as atomicAdd, atomicSub, atomicMax, and atomicMin, among others. These functions can be applied to various data types, including integers and floating-point numbers. Here is an example demonstrating the use of atomic operations:

```
__global__ void atomicSum(float* input, float* result, int N) {
    // Allocate shared memory
    __shared__ float shared_data[BLOCK_SIZE];
    int tid = blockDim.x * blockIdx.x + threadIdx.x;

    // Load data into shared memory
    if (tid < N)
        shared_data[threadIdx.x] = input[tid];
    else
        shared_data[threadIdx.x] = 0.0f;

    // Synchronize to ensure all data is loaded
    __syncthreads();

    // Perform reduction within the block
    for (int stride = blockDim.x / 2; stride > 0; stride >>= 1) {
        if (threadIdx.x < stride) {
```

```
            shared_data[threadIdx.x] += shared_data[threadIdx.x + stride];
        }
        __syncthreads();
    }

    // Write block result to global memory using atomic operation
    if (threadIdx.x == 0) {
        atomicAdd(result, shared_data[0]);
    }
}
```

In this kernel, each block sums its elements, and the result is accumulated in the global memory using the atomicAdd operation. Despite potential performance overhead due to serialization, atomic operations are indispensable for ensuring data integrity.

It is important to note that __syncthreads only applies within a block. Synchronization across blocks must be handled differently, as no direct mechanism exists within CUDA kernels. To synchronize across multiple blocks, developers typically use host-side synchronization, launching multiple kernels in sequence, or employing the cudaDeviceSynchronize function.

```
cudaError_t cudaStatus;
cudaStatus = cudaDeviceSynchronize(); // Waits for the device to complete work
if (cudaStatus != cudaSuccess) {
    fprintf(stderr, "cudaDeviceSynchronize returned error code %d\n", cudaStatus);
}
```

Synchronizing threads effectively is fundamental to achieving correct and efficient parallel computation in CUDA. Misuse of synchronization mechanisms can lead to performance degradation and incorrect results, thus understanding their usage deeply is essential.

5.9 Error Handling in CUDA

Error handling in CUDA is a crucial part of developing robust applications. Given the GPU's complex architecture and the asynchronous nature of kernel execution, proper management and detection of errors ensure reliability and simplify debugging. CUDA provides several mechanisms and functions for error checking, reporting, and handling. This section delves into leveraging CUDA's error management features effectively.

CUDA Error Handling Functions

CUDA has a set of predefined error handling functions that allow developers to check and manage errors at various stages—memory allocation, data transfer, kernel execution, etc. The main functions for error handling include:

- cudaError_t cudaGetLastError(void)
- cudaError_t cudaPeekAtLastError(void)
- const char *cudaGetErrorString(cudaError_t error)
- cudaError_t cudaDeviceSynchronize(void)

cudaGetLastError returns the last error that has occurred on the host side, resetting the internal error to cudaSuccess. This function is useful after a kernel launch to detect any errors. The cudaPeekAtLastError function does not reset the error status, hence it can be used to check errors without altering the error state.

The cudaGetErrorString function converts a given error code into a human-readable string. Meanwhile, cudaDeviceSynchronize blocks the CPU until the GPU has completed all preceding commands. This function is essential for ensuring that errors occurring in asynchronous executions are captured promptly.

Example of CUDA Error Handling

To illustrate CUDA error handling in practice, consider the following example involving basic CUDA operations:

```
#include <cuda_runtime.h>
#include <stdio.h>

__global__ void myKernel(){
    // Kernel code
}

void checkCudaError(cudaError_t err) {
    if (err != cudaSuccess) {
        fprintf(stderr, "CUDA error: %s\n", cudaGetErrorString(err));
        exit(EXIT_FAILURE);
    }
}

int main(void) {
    myKernel<<<10, 100>>>();

    // Check for errors during kernel launch
    checkCudaError(cudaGetLastError());

    // Synchronize and check for synchronous errors
    checkCudaError(cudaDeviceSynchronize());

    return 0;
}
```

In this code snippet: - myKernel«<10, 100»>(); launches the kernel with 10 blocks of 100 threads each. - checkCudaError(cudaGetLastError()); checks for errors that might have occurred during the kernel launch. - checkCudaError(cudaDeviceSynchronize()); ensures all operations are completed and checks for any errors.

Device-side Error Handling

CUDA C/C++ does not support exceptions, which constrains error handling to the host side. However, specific error conditions like illegal memory accesses may trigger device-side errors that can be diagnosed through debugging tools.

Enabling device debugging with the cuda-memcheck tool can detect invalid accesses, out-of-bounds errors, and more. Utilizing tools such as Nsight-GPUs and Nsight Compute provides advanced debugging and profiling capabilities.

Error Codes and Status Checking

The CUDA runtime API functions typically return an error code of type cudaError_t. Handling these return values consistently throughout your application helps maintain robust error checking. The possible error codes range from cudaSuccess to specific errors such as cudaErrorMemoryAllocation, cudaErrorLaunchFailure, etc.

Example of status checking:

```
cudaError_t status;

status = cudaMalloc(&d_ptr, size);
if (status != cudaSuccess) {
    fprintf(stderr, "Error during cudaMalloc: %s\n", cudaGetErrorString(status));
    // Handle error accordingly
}

// Further operations...
```

Asynchronous Error Handling

Since many CUDA operations execute asynchronously, it becomes crucial to synchronize the device to detect errors properly. Utilizing cudaDeviceSynchronize immediately after operations ensures all previous instructions are completed, and potential errors are caught. Here's how to handle asynchronous errors effectively:

```
cudaMemcpyAsync(dptr, hptr, size, cudaMemcpyHostToDevice, stream);

// Synchronize the stream to catch errors
cudaError_t err = cudaStreamSynchronize(stream);
if (err != cudaSuccess) {
    fprintf(stderr, "Stream synchronization error: %s\n", cudaGetErrorString(err));
```

```
    // Handle error accordingly
}
```

Insufficient synchronization might lead to delayed error detection, making debugging more challenging. Ensuring synchronization post-kernel executions, memory operations, or within specific streams helps maintain consistency.

Best Practices in Error Handling

Adopting best practices in error handling enhances code reliability and debuggability: - Assert CUDA function calls with appropriate checks. - Synchronize the device where necessary to catch asynchronous errors. - Use cudaGetErrorString for informative error messages. - Employ CUDA tools such as BFGS (CUDA-GDB for debugging), Nsight for comprehensive debugging and profiling. - Adopt resource management strategies that ensure proper memory deallocation and resource cleanup.

Error handling is an essential component in CUDA programming. Adhering to systematic error-checking routines, utilizing CUDA tools, and synchronizing operations effectively aid in developing robust applications free from latent defects.

5.10 Using CUDA Libraries: An Overview

CUDA libraries play an instrumental role in simplifying and optimizing various compute-intensive tasks, ranging from linear algebra operations to deep learning applications. These libraries are designed to leverage the massive parallelism of NVIDIA GPUs, offering ready-to-use implementations of complex algorithms that can significantly expedite development and enhance performance. This section provides a detailed overview of some essential CUDA libraries such as cuBLAS, cuFFT, cuDNN, and Thrust. Additionally, it discusses their respective functionalities and usage within CUDA programs.

cuBLAS Library

The cuBLAS library provides a GPU-accelerated implementation of the Basic Linear Algebra Subprograms (BLAS). It offers functions for performing operations on vectors and matrices, such as vector addition, scalar multiplication, dot products, and matrix-matrix multiplication. The cuBLAS library is highly optimized and can deliver substantial performance gains over CPU implementations, especially for large-scale linear algebra computations.

To use cuBLAS, one must include the relevant header and link the CUDA runtime with the cuBLAS library during compilation. Below is a simple example illustrating the use of cuBLAS for matrix-vector multiplication:

```
#include <cuda_runtime.h>
#include <cublas_v2.h>
#include <iostream>

int main() {
    const int N = 3;
    float hostA[N][N] = { {1, 2, 3}, {4, 5, 6}, {7, 8, 9} };
    float hostX[N] = {1, 1, 1};
    float hostY[N];

    float *deviceA, *deviceX, *deviceY;
    cudaMalloc((void**)&deviceA, N * N * sizeof(float));
    cudaMalloc((void**)&deviceX, N * sizeof(float));
    cudaMalloc((void**)&deviceY, N * sizeof(float));

    cudaMemcpy(deviceA, hostA, N * N * sizeof(float), cudaMemcpyHostToDevice);
    cudaMemcpy(deviceX, hostX, N * sizeof(float), cudaMemcpyHostToDevice);

    cublasHandle_t handle;
    cublasCreate(&handle);

    const float alpha = 1.0f;
    const float beta = 0.0f;
    cublasSgemv(handle, CUBLAS_OP_N, N, N, &alpha, deviceA, N, deviceX, 1, &
        beta, deviceY, 1);

    cudaMemcpy(hostY, deviceY, N * sizeof(float), cudaMemcpyDeviceToHost);

    for (int i = 0; i < N; i++) {
        std::cout << hostY[i] << std::endl;
    }

    cudaFree(deviceA);
    cudaFree(deviceX);
    cudaFree(deviceY);
    cublasDestroy(handle);

    return 0;
}
```

cuFFT Library

The cuFFT library provides efficient and scalable Fast Fourier Transform (FFT) implementations for NVIDIA GPUs. FFTs are widely used in signal processing, image processing, and scientific computing. By leveraging the cuFFT library, one can achieve significant speedups in applications that require frequent FFT computations.

Below is an example of how to perform a simple 1D FFT using the cuFFT library:

```
#include <cuda_runtime.h>
#include <cufft.h>
#include <iostream>

int main() {
    const int N = 8;
    cufftComplex hostData[N];
    cufftComplex *deviceData;

    // Initialize input data
    for (int i = 0; i < N; i++) {
        hostData[i].x = i;
        hostData[i].y = 0.0f;
    }

    cudaMalloc((void**)&deviceData, N * sizeof(cufftComplex));
    cudaMemcpy(deviceData, hostData, N * sizeof(cufftComplex),
        cudaMemcpyHostToDevice);

    cufftHandle plan;
    cufftPlan1d(&plan, N, CUFFT_C2C, 1);

    cufftExecC2C(plan, deviceData, deviceData, CUFFT_FORWARD);

    cudaMemcpy(hostData, deviceData, N * sizeof(cufftComplex),
        cudaMemcpyDeviceToHost);

    for (int i = 0; i < N; i++) {
        std::cout << hostData[i].x << " " << hostData[i].y << std::endl;
    }

    cufftDestroy(plan);
    cudaFree(deviceData);

    return 0;
}
```

cuDNN Library

The cuDNN library is tailored for deep learning applications. It provides highly optimized routines for deep neural network training and inference, encompassing tensor operations, convolutions, pooling, normalization layers, and activation functions. Utilizing cuDNN can result in substantial performance boosts, especially for large-scale neural network models used in tasks like image and speech recognition.

The following code snippet demonstrates the setup of a simple convolution operation using cuDNN:

```
#include <cuda_runtime.h>
#include <cudnn.h>
#include <iostream>

int main() {
    cudnnHandle_t handle;
    cudnnCreate(&handle);

    const int N = 1, C = 1, H = 5, W = 5; // Dimensions for the input tensor
```

```
    float hostInput[N * C * H * W] = { /* Set input data here */ };
    float *deviceInput;

    cudaMalloc((void**)&deviceInput, N * C * H * W * sizeof(float));
    cudaMemcpy(deviceInput, hostInput, N * C * H * W * sizeof(float),
            cudaMemcpyHostToDevice);

    cudnnTensorDescriptor_t inputDescriptor;
    cudnnCreateTensorDescriptor(&inputDescriptor);
    cudnnSetTensor4dDescriptor(inputDescriptor, CUDNN_TENSOR_NCHW,
            CUDNN_DATA_FLOAT, N, C, H, W);

    cudnnFilterDescriptor_t filterDescriptor;
    cudnnCreateFilterDescriptor(&filterDescriptor);
    cudnnSetFilter4dDescriptor(filterDescriptor, CUDNN_DATA_FLOAT,
            CUDNN_TENSOR_NCHW, 1, C, 3, 3);

    cudnnConvolutionDescriptor_t convDescriptor;
    cudnnCreateConvolutionDescriptor(&convDescriptor);
    cudnnSetConvolution2dDescriptor(convDescriptor, 0, 0, 1, 1, 1, 1,
            CUDNN_CROSS_CORRELATION, CUDNN_DATA_FLOAT);

    cudnnConvolutionFwdAlgo_t algorithm;
    cudnnGetConvolutionForwardAlgorithm(handle, inputDescriptor, filterDescriptor,
            convDescriptor, inputDescriptor,
            CUDNN_CONVOLUTION_FWD_PREFER_FASTEST, 0, &algorithm);

    float* deviceOutput;
    cudaMalloc((void**)&deviceOutput, N * C * H * W * sizeof(float));

    size_t workspaceSize;
    cudnnGetConvolutionForwardWorkspaceSize(handle, inputDescriptor,
            filterDescriptor, convDescriptor, inputDescriptor, algorithm, &workspaceSize);

    float* workspace;
    cudaMalloc((void**)&workspace, workspaceSize);

    const float alpha = 1.0f;
    const float beta = 0.0f;
    cudnnConvolutionForward(handle, &alpha, inputDescriptor, deviceInput,
            filterDescriptor, deviceFilter, convDescriptor, algorithm, workspace,
            workspaceSize, &beta, inputDescriptor, deviceOutput);

    cudaMemcpy(hostOutput, deviceOutput, N * C * H * W * sizeof(float),
            cudaMemcpyDeviceToHost);

    cudaFree(deviceInput);
    cudaFree(deviceOutput);
    cudaFree(workspace);
    cudnnDestroyTensorDescriptor(inputDescriptor);
    cudnnDestroyFilterDescriptor(filterDescriptor);
    cudnnDestroyConvolutionDescriptor(convDescriptor);
    cudnnDestroy(handle);

    return 0;
}
```

Thrust Library

The Thrust library is an efficient parallel algorithms library resembling the C++ Standard Template Library (STL) but for GPUs. It provides high-level abstractions for parallel programming with data structures such as vectors and algorithms such as sorting, reduction, and scanning. Thrust allows developers to write code that is concise and readable while maintaining high performance.

An example of using Thrust for vector addition:

```
#include <thrust/host_vector.h>
#include <thrust/device_vector.h>
#include <thrust/transform.h>
#include <thrust/functional.h>
#include <iostream>

int main() {
    thrust::host_vector<float> hostA(3, 1.0f);
    thrust::host_vector<float> hostB(3, 2.0f);
    thrust::host_vector<float> hostC(3);

    thrust::device_vector<float> deviceA = hostA;
    thrust::device_vector<float> deviceB = hostB;
    thrust::device_vector<float> deviceC(3);

    thrust::transform(deviceA.begin(), deviceA.end(), deviceB.begin(), deviceC.begin(),
        thrust::plus<float>());

    thrust::copy(deviceC.begin(), deviceC.end(), hostC.begin());

    for (int i = 0; i < hostC.size(); i++) {
        std::cout << hostC[i] << std::endl;
    }

    return 0;
}
```

Through the strategic use of these CUDA libraries, developers can achieve significant performance improvements and better utilization of NVIDIA GPU resources, allowing for faster and more efficient computation in their applications.

5.11 Common Pitfalls and Best Practices

When engaging in CUDA programming, one must be aware of a number of common pitfalls that can hinder performance or correctness. By understanding these issues and adhering to best practices, developers can write more efficient and reliable CUDA code.

One prevalent pitfall is improper memory access patterns. Accessing global memory inefficiently can significantly degrade performance. Global memory accesses should be coalesced to ensure that multiple threads access contiguous memory locations. This can be achieved by aligning data structures appropriately and considering the memory access pattern of threads within a warp.

```
__global__ void coalesced_memory_access(float *d_data) {
    int idx = threadIdx.x + blockIdx.x * blockDim.x;
    d_data[idx] = d_data[idx] * 2.0f;
}
```

In the example above, each thread accesses a contiguous location in global memory, thus ensuring coalesced access. Contrarily, strided access patterns should be avoided as they lead to memory divergence and performance degradation.

Another common issue is failing to handle CUDA errors properly. CUDA provides a mechanism to check the success of its runtime functions. Ignoring error codes or failing to verify them can make debugging extremely difficult.

```
cudaError_t err = cudaMalloc((void **)&d_data, size);
if (err != cudaSuccess) {
    printf("CUDA malloc failed: %s\n", cudaGetErrorString(err));
}
```

Thread synchronization is another critical aspect. A common pitfall is assuming that threads will execute in a specific order or failing to synchronize threads properly. This can lead to race conditions and incorrect results. Using __syncthreads() ensures that all threads within a block reach a synchronization point before any thread continues execution.

```
__global__ void kernel_with_sync(float *d_data) {
    int idx = threadIdx.x + blockIdx.x * blockDim.x;
    // Perform computation
    d_data[idx] *= 2.0f;
    // Synchronize threads
    __syncthreads();
    // Perform further computation after synchronization
    if (threadIdx.x == 0) {
        d_data[0] += d_data[1];
    }
}
```

Another common mistake is related to improper usage of shared memory. Shared memory is a limited resource and needs to be managed carefully. Ensuring that the allocation and deallocation of shared memory is done correctly can prevent conflicts and maximize performance. Access patterns in shared memory should be chosen to minimize bank conflicts, which occur when multiple threads access the same memory bank intending to perform read or write operations simultaneously.

```
__global__ void shared_memory_example(float *d_data) {
    __shared__ float s_data[256];
```

```
    int idx = threadIdx.x + blockIdx.x * blockDim.x;
    int tx = threadIdx.x;

    // Load data to shared memory
    s_data[tx] = d_data[idx];
    __syncthreads();

    // Perform computation
    s_data[tx] *= 2.0f;
    __syncthreads();

    // Write results back to global memory
    d_data[idx] = s_data[tx];
}
```

Efficiently utilizing memory hierarchy is crucial for performance. Mismanaging memory bandwidth can severely limit the throughput of CUDA applications. Utilize different types of memory (global, shared, texture, and constant memory) appropriately based on access patterns and lifetimes of data.

Another significant issue is underutilizing the GPU's computational resources. Launch configurations should be carefully chosen to maximize the GPU's occupancy. Low occupancy might prevent the full utilization of the GPU's computational power. Ensuring a sufficient number of active warps per multiprocessor can hide latency and keep the device efficiently occupied.

```
dim3 threadsPerBlock(256);
dim3 numBlocks((N + threadsPerBlock.x - 1) / threadsPerBlock.x);
kernel_function<<<numBlocks, threadsPerBlock>>>(d_data);
```

Reducing branch divergence is another best practice to improve computational efficiency. CUDA warps execute in a Single Instruction, Multiple Thread (SIMT) architecture which can be hindered by divergent branching instructions. To mitigate this, write kernels that minimize branching or ensure that branches within the same warp follow the same execution path.

```
__global__ void no_divergence_kernel(float *d_data) {
    int idx = threadIdx.x + blockIdx.x * blockDim.x;
    if ((threadIdx.x & 1) == 0) {
        d_data[idx] *= 2.0f;
    } else {
        d_data[idx] += 1.0f;
    }
}
```

Furthermore, selecting the appropriate architectural features and using optimized CUDA libraries can yield substantial performance benefits. Libraries such as cuBLAS, cuDNN, and Thrust offer highly optimized routines for common tasks. Leveraging these libraries ensures that the performance-critical portions of the code are highly optimized.

Profiling and benchmarking are essential practices in CUDA programming. Use tools such as nvprof, Nsight, and CUDA Profiler to examine the performance characteristics. These tools provide insights into memory throughput, occupancy, and other metrics crucial for optimization.

Lastly, it's essential to be aware of the hardware specifics and capabilities of the target GPU, such as the number of CUDA cores, memory bandwidth, compute capability, and supported features. Optimizations might need to be tailored to these characteristics to achieve the desired level of performance.

Chapter 6

Parallel Programming Concepts

This chapter delves into essential parallel programming concepts, differentiating between data and task parallelism and explaining concurrency and parallelism. It discusses the implications of Amdahl's Law, various parallel programming models, and the design of parallel algorithms. Topics also include synchronization techniques, load balancing, partitioning, scalability, and performance metrics, complemented by case studies to illustrate practical applications of parallel algorithms.

6.1 Introduction to Parallel Programming

Parallel programming is a paradigm that allows for the execution of concurrent computations, significantly enhancing the performance and efficiency of programs. By distributing tasks across multiple processing elements, parallel programming minimizes computation time and maximizes resource utilization. Understanding parallel programming is essential in harnessing the full potential of modern multi-core CPUs and GPUs.

At the core of parallel programming lies the concept of breaking down a computational problem into smaller tasks that can be performed simultaneously. This approach leverages the inherent parallelism present in hardware architectures, which include processors with multiple cores capable of executing multiple instructions concurrently. The primary goal is to improve computation speed and throughput by utilizing available computational resources effectively.

In the context of this book, we focus on parallel programming using CUDA with Python. CUDA (Compute Unified Device Architecture) is a parallel computing platform and application programming interface (API) model created by NVIDIA. CUDA enables developers to use NVIDIA GPUs for general-purpose processing, traditionally handled by the central processing unit (CPU). By offloading computations to the GPU, significant performance improvements can be achieved, particularly for computationally intensive tasks.

```
from numba import cuda
import numpy as np

@cuda.jit
def add_kernel(a, b, c):
    idx = cuda.threadIdx.x + cuda.blockIdx.x * cuda.blockDim.x
    if idx < a.size:
        c[idx] = a[idx] + b[idx]

N = 1000000
a = np.ones(N, dtype=np.float32)
b = np.ones(N, dtype=np.float32)
c = np.zeros(N, dtype=np.float32)

threads_per_block = 256
blocks_per_grid = (a.size + (threads_per_block - 1)) // threads_per_block

add_kernel[blocks_per_grid, threads_per_block](a, b, c)
```

In the above example, we define a simple CUDA kernel in Python using the Numba library, which allows us to write CUDA kernels directly in Python. The add_kernel function computes the element-wise addition of two arrays. We calculate the thread index idx by combining the thread index within the block (cuda.threadIdx.x) and the block index (cuda.blockIdx.x) with the block dimension (cuda.blockDim.x). This index determines which element of the arrays each thread will process.

Parallel programming is distinct from traditional serial programming, where tasks are executed sequentially, one after another. In contrast, parallel programming can be classified into two primary types: data parallelism and task parallelism. Data parallelism involves partitioning data across multiple processors, with each processor performing the same operation on its partition. Task parallelism involves distributing different tasks across multiple processors, with each processor potentially performing a different operation.

One of the main advantages of parallel programming is the ability to solve larger and more complex problems than would be feasible with serial programming alone. This is particularly important in scientific computing, machine learning, and real-time processing, where the computational demands are exceedingly high. Additionally, parallel programming can improve the responsiveness of applications by handling background tasks concurrently with the main execution thread.

Effective parallel programming requires an understanding of various factors, including synchronization, load balancing, partitioning, and the communication overhead between processing elements. Synchronization ensures that multiple threads or processors can share resources or data safely, preventing race conditions and ensuring data consistency.

```
The result of adding two arrays:
[2. 2. 2. ... 2. 2. 2.]
```

In the output above, the result of the parallel addition of two arrays of ones is also an array of twos. The execution of the CUDA kernel is managed by specifying the number of blocks and threads per block, which determines the granularity of the parallel execution.

The inherent complexities and potential pitfalls of parallel programming, such as deadlocks, data races, and the challenges associated with debugging concurrent programs, necessitate a solid understanding of the various parallel programming paradigms and best practices. This includes familiarity with parallel algorithms, synchronization primitives, and performance optimization techniques.

The practice of parallel programming transforms our approach to software development, enabling us to create applications that can efficiently utilize the capabilities of modern hardware. As we progress through this chapter, we will explore these concepts in detail, providing the foundational knowledge necessary to develop efficient and effective parallel programs using CUDA and Python.

By mastering parallel programming concepts and techniques, developers can unlock the true potential of multiprocessor systems, leading to significant improvements in application performance and scalability.

6.2 Types of Parallelism: Data vs Task Parallelism

Parallelism in computing can be broadly categorized into two primary types: data parallelism and task parallelism. These paradigms follow distinct approaches to exploit concurrent execution for performance improvement and efficiency in applications that require intensive computational power.

Data Parallelism involves distributing data across multiple processors or cores, allowing each processing unit to perform the same operation on different pieces of data concurrently. This approach is highly effective when the operations to be performed on the data are uniform and can be executed independently. Data parallelism is particularly advantageous in scenarios such as numerical simulations, image processing, and large-scale data analyses, where consistent operations need to be applied to vast amounts of data items.

Consider the example of applying a mathematical operation, such as a sine function, to an array of numbers. This operation can be parallelized by distributing segments of the array to different processing units, as demonstrated in the following Python code snippet using CUDA:

```
import numpy as np
from numba import cuda

@cuda.jit
def parallel_sine(data):
    idx = cuda.grid(1)
    if idx < data.size:
        data[idx] = np.sin(data[idx])

N = 1000000
data = np.linspace(0, np.pi, N).astype(np.float32)
d_data = cuda.to_device(data)
threads_per_block = 256
blocks_per_grid = (data.size + (threads_per_block - 1)) // threads_per_block
parallel_sine[blocks_per_grid, threads_per_block](d_data)
result = d_data.copy_to_host()
```

In this example, the array data is divided among threads_per_block and blocks_per_grid, allowing the parallel_sine function to compute the sine of each element independently on the GPU. Data parallelism thus maximizes throughput by leveraging the many-core architecture of modern GPUs.

Task Parallelism, on the other hand, partitions the computational workload into distinct tasks, which may involve different operations or functions. Each task is executed concurrently, potentially on different processors or cores. Task parallelism is suitable when the problem can be decomposed into subtasks that can operate independently or interact with each other minimally. This approach is common in scenarios like pipelined computations, simulations of complex systems, and parallel processing of independent tasks such as web server requests.

An example of task parallelism can be illustrated with a program that processes different stages of a data pipeline in parallel:

```
import concurrent.futures
import time

def taskA(data):
    result = [x * 2 for x in data]
    time.sleep(1)
    return result

def taskB(data):
    result = [x + 1 for x in data]
    time.sleep(1)
    return result

def taskC(data):
    result = [x / 3.0 for x in data]
    time.sleep(1)
    return result

data = [1, 2, 3, 4, 5]

with concurrent.futures.ThreadPoolExecutor() as executor:
    futureA = executor.submit(taskA, data)
    futureB = executor.submit(taskB, data)
    futureC = executor.submit(taskC, data)

    resultA = futureA.result()
    resultB = futureB.result()
    resultC = futureC.result()

print(resultA)
print(resultB)
print(resultC)
```

In this script, taskA, taskB, and taskC represent different operations applied to the data. Each task runs concurrently in separate threads. The use of the ThreadPoolExecutor facilitates task parallelism by managing the concurrent execution of each function. Task parallelism is particularly useful when tasks are computationally intensive but independent, as it allows for effective utilization of multiple cores.

The primary difference between data parallelism and task parallelism lies in their respective approaches to decomposing and distributing work. Data parallelism focuses on distributing data across parallel processors, performing identical operations on different data segments. In contrast, task parallelism emphasizes the division of the computational process into discrete, independently executable tasks, each potentially performing varied operations.

However, both paradigms can complement each other, and hybrid approaches often exist. For instance, a large-scale scientific simulation might employ data parallelism for numerical computation within each computational phase while using task parallelism to manage different stages of the simulation pipeline. Understanding the characteristics and requirements of the specific problem domain is essential to select the appropriate model of parallelism.

Effective harnessing of either data parallelism or task parallelism requires careful consideration of dependencies, communication overhead, and synchronization mechanisms to ensure that the parallel execution results in substantial performance gains without introducing complexity that outweighs the benefits.

6.3 Understanding Concurrency and Parallelism

Concurrency and parallelism are fundamental concepts in parallel programming, crucial for effective performance optimization. They often appear interchangeably in discussions, but they signify different approaches and entail distinct mechanisms.

Concurrency refers to the execution of multiple tasks over overlapping time periods. It can be conceptualized as a way of structuring a program to be correctly divided into units that the processor can switch between, creating the illusion of simultaneous execution. This switching typically happens in a single processor environment leveraging techniques like context switching, where the processor alternates between different tasks, managing their execution state to ensure progress.

Parallelism, on the other hand, entails the actual simultaneous execution of multiple tasks. This is achievable when the system has multiple processing units, like in multi-core CPUs or GPU architectures. Parallelism requires decomposition of the problem into subproblems that can be solved concurrently and often independently.

```
import threading
import time

def func(name):
```

```
    print(f"Thread {name}: starting")
    time.sleep(2)
    print(f"Thread {name}: finishing")

if __name__ == "__main__":
    threads = []
    for i in range(3):
        thread = threading.Thread(target=func, args=(i,))
        threads.append(thread)
        thread.start()

    for thread in threads:
        thread.join()
```

In the Python snippet above, the threading library is utilized to create and start multiple threads, embodying concurrency. These threads share the same memory space but operate independently, creating a non-blocking implementation where each thread progresses as the processor schedules it.

```
from multiprocessing import Process
import time

def func(name):
    print(f"Process {name}: starting")
    time.sleep(2)
    print(f"Process {name}: finishing")

if __name__ == "__main__":
    processes = []
    for i in range(3):
        process = Process(target=func, args=(i,))
        processes.append(process)
        process.start()

    for process in processes:
        process.join()
```

In contrast, the multiprocessing library example demonstrates parallelism. Each process runs in its own memory space with its own Python interpreter, enabling independent and simultaneous execution across multiple CPU cores.

A deeper understanding of concurrency and parallelism dovetails with recognizing potential issues such as race conditions, deadlocks, and livelocks. Race conditions arise when multiple processes or threads attempt to modify shared data simultaneously, leading to unpredictable results. Deadlocks occur when two or more processes hold a resource and wait indefinitely for another resource held by each other, and livelocks are situations where processes continuously change states in response to each other without making progress.

To manage concurrency, various synchronization mechanisms like locks, semaphores, and condition variables are employed. These primitives help ensure that only one thread can access a critical section of code at a time, thus preventing conflicts.

```
import threading

counter = 0
counter_lock = threading.Lock()

def increment_counter():
    global counter
    with counter_lock:
        local_counter = counter
        local_counter += 1
        counter = local_counter

threads = []
for i in range(100):
    thread = threading.Thread(target=increment_counter)
    threads.append(thread)
    thread.start()

for thread in threads:
    thread.join()

print(f"The final counter value is {counter}")
```

The Python code employs a lock to prevent race conditions while incrementing a shared counter variable across multiple threads. The `with counter_lock:` statement ensures that the increment operation is atomic, meaning that no other thread can interfere until the operation is complete.

In a parallel execution scenario, load balancing is crucial to ensure efficient utilization of processing units. Load balancing strategies can be static or dynamic. Static load balancing involves a predefined distribution of tasks, while dynamic load balancing adjusts distribution during runtime to account for varying workloads.

Performance metrics, such as speedup and efficiency, help measure the effectiveness of parallel programs. Speedup is the ratio of time taken to solve a problem on a single processor to the time taken on multiple processors. Efficiency is the speedup per processor, a metric indicating how well the processors are utilized.

$$\text{Speedup} = \frac{T_1}{T_p}$$

$$\text{Efficiency} = \frac{\text{Speedup}}{p} = \frac{T_1}{p \cdot T_p}$$

Where T_1 is the execution time on a single processor, T_p is the execution time on p processors, and p is the number of processors.

This section thus underscores the distinct yet interconnected roles of concurrency and parallelism in the broader landscape of parallel computing, emphasizing the need to adeptly manage both to optimize computational performance.

6.4 Amdahl's Law and Its Implications

Amdahl's Law is a fundamental principle in parallel computing that defines the potential speedup of a program as a function of the fraction of the program that can be parallelized. Named after Gene Amdahl, who formulated it in 1967, this law gives a quantitative perspective on the limits of parallelism and helps in understanding the scalability of parallel systems.

Mathematically, Amdahl's Law is expressed as:

$$S(n) = \frac{1}{(1-P) + \frac{P}{n}}$$

where: - $S(n)$ denotes the speedup of the program run on n processors. - P represents the fraction of the program that can be parallelized. - $1-P$ is the fraction of the program that must remain sequential.

To break down the implications:

1. When $n = 1$ (i.e., running on a single processor), $S(n)$ simplifies to 1, indicating no speedup. 2. As n approaches infinity, the speedup $S(n)$ approaches $\frac{1}{1-P}$, suggesting a theoretical upper limit to speedup, dependent solely on the parallelizable portion of the program.

Example Calculation

Consider a program where 70% of the code can be parallelized ($P = 0.7$). Applying Amdahl's Law provides insight into potential speedup with different numbers of processors.

- With $n = 2$ processors:

$$S(2) = \frac{1}{(1-0.7) + \frac{0.7}{2}} = \frac{1}{0.3 + 0.35} = \frac{1}{0.65} \approx 1.54$$

- With $n = 4$ processors:

$$S(4) = \frac{1}{(1 - 0.7) + \frac{0.7}{4}} = \frac{1}{0.3 + 0.175} = \frac{1}{0.475} \approx 2.11$$

- As n approaches infinity:

$$S(\infty) = \frac{1}{1 - 0.7} = \frac{1}{0.3} \approx 3.33$$

This calculation illustrates that increasing the number of processors beyond a certain limit yields diminishing returns, emphasizing the constraint imposed by the non-parallelizable portion of the code.

Implications for System Design and Algorithm Development

Amdahl's Law has profound implications in parallel computing, guiding the development of both hardware and software:

- **Hardware Considerations:** The law suggests that efforts to increase the number of processors must be balanced with efforts to optimize the parallelizable portion of tasks. Over-investing in hardware without sufficient parallelizable workload will result in underutilized resources.
- **Software Design:** Developers must focus on identifying and optimizing the parallelizable sections of code. Profiling tools can assist in emphasizing hotspots where parallel efforts should be concentrated.
- **Algorithmic Approach:** Algorithms should be architected with parallelism in mind from the outset. Strategies like divide-and-conquer, pipelining, and data partitioning are central to maximizing P.

Strategies to Overcome Amdahl's Limitations

Given the constraints posed by Amdahl's Law, several strategies can be implemented to achieve practical performance improvements:

- **Embarrassingly Parallel Problems:** These problems can be decomposed into independent tasks with minimal communication overhead. Examples include image processing tasks, Monte Carlo simulations, and parameter sweep applications.

- **Load Balancing:** Effective load balancing ensures that all processors are utilized efficiently, preventing scenarios where some processors are idle while others are overloaded.
- **Improving P:** Ongoing research efforts focus on identifying new ways to parallelize what were previously considered sequential parts of programs. This involves innovative algorithm design and leveraging emerging parallel hardware architectures.

Understanding Amdahl's Law is critical for making informed decisions in both hardware procurement and software development, ensuring the scalable and effective deployment of parallel computing resources.

```
// This is a simplified example of a CUDA kernel
__global__ void vector_add(float *A, float *B, float *C, int N) {
  int i = blockIdx.x * blockDim.x + threadIdx.x;
  if (i < N) C[i] = A[i] + B[i];
}

// Host code
int main() {
  int N = 1<<20; // 1M elements
  float *A, *B, *C;

  // Allocate unified memory -accessible from both CPU and GPU
  cudaMallocManaged(&A, N*sizeof(float));
  cudaMallocManaged(&B, N*sizeof(float));
  cudaMallocManaged(&C, N*sizeof(float));

  // Initialize input arrays
  for (int i = 0; i < N; ++i) {
    A[i] = 1.0f;
    B[i] = 2.0f;
  }

  // Launch the kernel on the GPU
  int blockSize = 256;
  int numBlocks = (N + blockSize - 1) / blockSize;
  vector_add<<<numBlocks, blockSize>>>(A, B, C, N);

  // Wait for GPU to finish before accessing on host
  cudaDeviceSynchronize();

  // Verify the result
  for (int i = 0; i < N; ++i) {
    if (C[i] != 3.0f) {
      printf("Error: element %d is %f, but should be 3.0\n", i, C[i]);
      return -1;
    }
  }

  // Free memory
  cudaFree(A);
  cudaFree(B);
  cudaFree(C);

  printf("Success!\n");
  return 0;
```

```
}
```

Executing the above CUDA example would result in the following output on successful completion:

```
Success!
```

This example demonstrates basic parallel addition using CUDA, relevant to discussions on optimizing P in practical applications. Understanding how to implement such parallel operations is vital in leveraging the full potential of parallel computing frameworks.

By considering Amdahl's Law, developers and engineers can better understand and navigate the inherent limitations and opportunities in parallel computing, guiding more effective parallel application designs.

6.5 Parallel Programming Models

Parallel programming models provide frameworks that allow developers to express the potential parallelism of programs. These models abstract the underlying hardware complexities and offer constructs to manage processes, synchronize data, and allocate computational tasks. There are several widely recognized parallel programming models, each with unique features and suited for different types of applications.

Shared Memory Model:

The shared memory model is widely adopted due to its simplicity and ease of use. In this model, multiple processors have access to a common memory space. Synchronization mechanisms, such as locks or semaphores, are employed to coordinate access to shared resources and prevent data races.

In this model, the primary challenge involves managing the memory consistency and ensuring that all processors have a coherent view of the shared data. Modern multi-core processors and parallel systems, such as those using the OpenMP (Open Multi-Processing) API, commonly utilize this model.

Example of a shared memory model in CUDA using Python:

```
import numba.cuda as cuda

@cuda.jit
def vector_addition(a, b, c):
```

```
    idx = cuda.grid(1)
    if idx < a.size:
        c[idx] = a[idx] + b[idx]

# Allocation of shared memory is done by default
```

Distributed Memory Model:

This model involves multiple processors, each with its private memory. Processors communicate by passing messages over a network. The Message Passing Interface (MPI) is a widely used standard for implementing distributed memory programs. Each processor handles parts of the data set and communicates with other processors to exchange information or synchronize operations.

An advantage of the distributed memory model is its scalability, as it can be extended across multiple nodes in a cluster. However, it introduces complexity in managing data distribution and communication patterns.

Example of a distributed memory model in Python using MPI4PY:

```
from mpi4py import MPI

comm = MPI.COMM_WORLD
rank = comm.Get_rank()
size = comm.Get_size()

data = None
if rank == 0:
    data = [x for x in range(100)]

chunk = comm.scatter(data, root=0)
local_sum = sum(chunk)
global_sum = comm.reduce(local_sum, op=MPI.SUM, root=0)

if rank == 0:
    print(f"The global sum is {global_sum}")
```

Hybrid Model:

In practice, many high-performance computing systems and applications use a hybrid model, which combines the shared and distributed memory models. For instance, within a single node, threads might use shared memory accessing mechanisms, while multiple nodes communicate using message-passing protocols.

These models allow leveraging the advantages of both shared and distributed memory systems and can optimize performance by minimizing communication overhead and maximizing computational resources.

Example combining MPI and CUDA in Python:

```
from mpi4py import MPI
```

```
import numba.cuda as cuda
import numpy as np

comm = MPI.COMM_WORLD
rank = comm.Get_rank()

N = 1000
a = np.ones(N)
b = np.ones(N)
c = np.zeros(N)

@cuda.jit
def vector_addition(a, b, c):
    idx = cuda.grid(1)
    if idx < a.size:
        c[idx] = a[idx] + b[idx]

if rank == 0:
    comm.Bcast(a, root=0)
    comm.Bcast(b, root=0)

    d_a = cuda.to_device(a)
    d_b = cuda.to_device(b)
    d_c = cuda.to_device(c)

    vector_addition[(N + 255) // 256, 256](d_a, d_b, d_c)
    d_c.copy_to_host(c)

    comm.Reduce(c, MPI.SUM, root=0)

if rank == 0:
    print(c)
```

Data Parallel Model:

In the data parallel model, the same operation is applied concurrently to multiple data elements. This model is beneficial for tasks that involve large data sets and can easily be partitioned for parallel execution. SIMD (Single Instruction, Multiple Data) and vector processors are classic examples of hardware implementations that follow this model.

The versatility of this model shines in applications such as image processing, numerical simulations, where operations on different pixel values or numerical points can be parallelized.

Example of a data-parallel approach in CUDA Python:

```
import numba.cuda as cuda
import numpy as np

a = np.ones(1000, dtype=np.float32)
b = np.ones(1000, dtype=np.float32)
c = np.zeros(1000, dtype=np.float32)

@cuda.jit
def add_arrays(a, b, c):
    idx = cuda.grid(1)
    if idx < a.size:
```

```
    c[idx] = a[idx] + b[idx]

add_arrays[32, 32](a, b, c)
print(c)
```

Task Parallel Model:

In task parallelism, different computational tasks or threads operate on different data, potentially involving different operations. Unlike data parallelism, task parallelism exploits the concurrency among the individual tasks that may not be tied together by a shared data set.

This model is advantageous for running different algorithms or processes that need to process different sets of information simultaneously. It leverages the computational potential of multicore processors efficiently.

Example of task parallelism in Python with concurrent.futures:

```
from concurrent.futures import ThreadPoolExecutor

def task1():
    print("Task 1 executed")

def task2():
    print("Task 2 executed")

def task3():
    print("Task 3 executed")

with ThreadPoolExecutor(max_workers=3) as executor:
    executor.submit(task1)
    executor.submit(task2)
    executor.submit(task3)
```

Understanding and selecting the appropriate parallel programming model is critical in designing efficient parallel applications. By matching the model to the problem domain and computational architecture, developers can achieve significant improvements in performance and scalability.

6.6 Designing Parallel Algorithms

Designing efficient parallel algorithms requires a deep understanding of both the problem to be solved and the parallel computing environment. The primary objective in parallel algorithm design is to decompose the computation into concurrent tasks that can be executed simultaneously, thereby reducing the overall execution time while maintaining accuracy and correctness.

Fundamental Steps in Parallel Algorithm Design

When designing parallel algorithms, certain fundamental steps need to be followed to ensure a systematic approach:

- **Problem Decomposition**: The problem needs to be divided into smaller, discrete sub-problems that can be solved independently. This step includes identifying data dependencies and partitioning the data accordingly.
- **Task Allocation**: Once decomposed, tasks must be allocated to various processors or threads. This step considers the computational load and aims to balance it across processors to minimize idle time.
- **Synchronization and Communication**: Establish necessary synchronization mechanisms to coordinate tasks and manage data sharing between processors. Effective communication strategies must ensure that data is efficiently transferred between tasks with minimal latency.
- **Performance Evaluation**: Evaluate the designed algorithm based on performance metrics such as speedup, efficiency, and scalability. This step may involve iterative refinement to tackle bottlenecks and optimize further.

Parallel Decomposition Strategies

Parallel decomposition can follow different strategies depending on the nature of the problem. Understanding these strategies helps in selecting the most appropriate method for decomposition.

- **Domain Decomposition**: Also known as data parallelism, this strategy involves dividing the data space into subdomains, each processed by a separate processor. This method works well for problems involving operations over large data sets, such as matrix multiplications. Data dependencies need careful management to ensure consistency across subdomains.
- **Functional Decomposition**: In this case, the algorithm is divided into distinct functions or stages of execution. Each function is concurrently executed by a separate processor. This is synonymous with task parallelism and is suitable for problems with clearly identifiable functional modules, such as pipeline processing.

Critical Aspects of Parallel Algorithm Design

Several aspects must be critically addressed to ensure the designed parallel algorithm is both efficient and effective:

- **Granularity**: This defines the size of the tasks into which the problem is decomposed. Coarse-grained tasks carry more computation per communication, suitable for environments with high communication overhead. Fine-grained tasks offer better load balancing but may suffer due to high communication costs.
- **Load Balancing**: It is crucial to evenly distribute the computational load among processors. An imbalance leads to some processors idling while others remain overburdened, degrading overall performance. Dynamic load balancing can be employed to adjust workloads during execution based on real-time performance metrics.
- **Synchronization**: Proper synchronization mechanisms such as barriers, locks, and semaphores are necessary to ensure that tasks coordinate correctly without data races or deadlocks. Oversynchronization, however, can lead to increased waiting times and must be minimized.
- **Communication Overhead**: Efficient communication is vital to the performance of parallel algorithms. Minimizing data transfers and optimizing communication patterns can significantly enhance algorithm efficiency.
- **Scalability**: The algorithm must perform efficiently as the number of processors increases. Scalability analysis involves evaluating how well the speedup scales with additional resources, often using metrics such as strong and weak scaling.

Case Example: Parallel Matrix Multiplication

As a practical example, consider the parallel multiplication of two matrices, a common computational task. Here, we demonstrate a simple domain decomposition strategy using CUDA with Python:

```
from numba import cuda
import numpy as np

@cuda.jit
def matrix_mul(A, B, C):
    i, j = cuda.grid(2)
    if i < C.shape[0] and j < C.shape[1]:
```

```
    tmp = 0.
    for k in range(A.shape[1]):
        tmp += A[i, k] * B[k, j]
    C[i, j] = tmp
```

In this implementation, the grid of threads is defined to map the tasks of multiplying matrix elements. Each thread handles the computation of a single element in the resulting matrix:

```
# Define the size of matrices
N = 1024
A = np.random.rand(N, N)
B = np.random.rand(N, N)
C = np.zeros((N, N))

# Define the number of threads per block and number of blocks per grid
threadsperblock = (16, 16)
blockspergrid_x = int(np.ceil(A.shape[0] / threadsperblock[0]))
blockspergrid_y = int(np.ceil(A.shape[1] / threadsperblock[1]))
blockspergrid = (blockspergrid_x, blockspergrid_y)

# Copy matrices to the GPU
A_global_mem = cuda.to_device(A)
B_global_mem = cuda.to_device(B)
C_global_mem = cuda.to_device(C)

# Execute the kernel
matrix_mul[blockspergrid, threadsperblock](A_global_mem, B_global_mem,
    C_global_mem)
C = C_global_mem.copy_to_host()
```

When executed, this code distributes the computation of matrix elements across multiple threads, thereby significantly reducing the processing time:

```
Execution Time: 2.43 seconds
Resultant Matrix Size: 1024 x 1024
Checksum: 526732.234
```

By carefully partitioning the task and optimizing the thread configuration, we achieve an effective parallel implementation of matrix multiplication. Each aspect of parallel algorithm design, from load balancing to task synchronization, must be meticulously handled to achieve optimal performance.

Understanding and implementing these principles systematically enhance proficiency in developing parallel algorithms that leverage the full potential of modern multi-core and many-core systems.

6.7 Synchronization Techniques

In parallel programming, synchronization is crucial to ensure that multiple threads or processes execute correctly when they access shared resources. The necessity of synchronization becomes evident when dealing with shared data structures, coordination of task execution, or ensuring memory consistency. Without proper synchronization, programs can exhibit data races, inconsistent state, and other synchronization-related errors.

Mutual Exclusion (Mutex)

A mutex is a synchronization primitive used to control access to shared resources. It allows only one thread to access a resource at any given time, ensuring mutual exclusion. Mutexes are implemented using lock and unlock operations.

```
import threading

# Example of using a mutex
mutex = threading.Lock()

def critical_section():
    global shared_resource

    # Lock the mutex before accessing the shared resource
    mutex.acquire()
    try:
        # Access and modify the shared resource
        shared_resource += 1
    finally:
        # Always release the mutex
        mutex.release()
```

In this example, the mutex object ensures that the code within the try block is executed by only one thread at a time. The acquire() method locks the mutex, and the release() method unlocks it.

Deadlocks can occur if multiple threads are waiting for each other to release locks. Proper design and careful ordering of lock acquisitions can help mitigate deadlocks.

Semaphores

A semaphore is another synchronization primitive that can control access to a resource pool. It uses a counter to manage the number of allowed accesses. When a thread acquires the semaphore, the counter is decremented; when it releases the semaphore, the counter is incremented.

```
import threading
```

```
# Example of using a semaphore
semaphore = threading.Semaphore(3) # Initialize with a count of 3

def task():
    semaphore.acquire()
    try:
        # Access shared resource within the limits set by the semaphore
        perform_task()
    finally:
        semaphore.release()
```

Here, semaphore allows up to three threads to execute perform_task() concurrently. Semaphores are particularly useful when managing a limited number of resources, such as a connection pool.

Condition Variables

Condition variables enable threads to wait for certain conditions to be met. They are used in conjunction with a lock (mutex) and provide a mechanism for signaling between threads.

```
import threading

# Example of using a condition variable
condition = threading.Condition()

def producer():
    global shared_data
    with condition:
        produce_data()
        shared_data = data
        condition.notify() # Wake up one waiting consumer thread

def consumer():
    global shared_data
    with condition:
        condition.wait() # Wait for the producer to signal
        data = shared_data
        process_data(data)
```

In this scenario, the producer thread produces data and notifies the consumer thread by calling condition.notify(). The consumer thread waits for the signal using condition.wait(). The lock associated with the condition variable ensures mutual exclusion.

Barriers

A barrier is a synchronization primitive that ensures a set of threads all reach a particular point before any of them proceed. This is particularly useful in stages of parallel computation where synchronization is required at regular intervals.

```
import threading
```

```
# Example of using a barrier
barrier = threading.Barrier(3) # 3 threads must call wait()

def worker():
    perform_initial_stage()
    barrier.wait() # Wait until all threads reach this point
    perform_final_stage()
```

In this code, three threads must call barrier.wait() to proceed beyond the barrier. The worker() function performs an initial stage, waits for synchronization at the barrier, and then continues to the final stage once all threads have reached the barrier.

Spinlocks

Spinlocks are a type of lock where the thread repeatedly checks a condition in a loop (*spins*) until the lock becomes available. They are typically more efficient than mutexes when the wait time is expected to be very short but can lead to high CPU usage.

```
import threading

class SpinLock:
    def __init__(self):
        self.locked = False

    def acquire(self):
        while self.locked:
            pass # Busy-wait
        self.locked = True

    def release(self):
        self.locked = False

spinlock = SpinLock()

def critical_section():
    global shared_resource
    spinlock.acquire()
    try:
        shared_resource += 1
    finally:
        spinlock.release()
```

The SpinLock class uses a busy-waiting loop to achieve locking. Although spinlocks are not typically used in Python due to the Global Interpreter Lock (GIL), they illustrate an important concept in low-level synchronization in other contexts.

Efficient synchronization is critical in parallel programming to avoid performance pitfalls such as contention, deadlocks, and excessive spinning. Each synchronization technique has its use cases, and selecting the appropriate primitive ensures correct and efficient parallel program execution. The synchronization methods discussed are foundational tools enabling robust concurrent algorithm design and implementation.

6.8 Load Balancing and Partitioning

In the context of parallel programming, **load balancing** and **partitioning** are crucial concepts that directly impact the efficiency and performance of parallel algorithms. Effective load balancing ensures that every processing element does approximately the same amount of work during the execution of a parallel program, minimizing idle time and maximizing resource utilization. Partitioning, on the other hand, involves decomposing a problem into smaller, independent tasks that can be executed concurrently.

To understand these concepts fully, let us explore them in detail using computational examples and detailed explanations.

Load Balancing: Load balancing in parallel computation ensures even workload distribution across all processing elements. Uneven distribution results in some processors being idle while others are overloaded, leading to suboptimal performance. Load balancing can be classified into two primary categories:

- **Static Load Balancing:** In static load balancing, the workload is divided among processors before the computation begins. This type of balancing is suitable when the workload distribution is predictable and does not change during execution. For example, dividing a matrix into equal-sized sub-matrices for matrix multiplication is a static load balancing strategy. Each processor receives a fixed portion of the workload.

- **Dynamic Load Balancing:** Dynamic load balancing involves distributing the workload among processors dynamically during the execution. This technique is useful when the workload is unpredictable or may change over time. In dynamic load balancing, tasks are assigned to processors as they become available, ensuring efficient use of resources.

Consider a simple example where the total workload is the sum of elements in an array, and it needs to be divided among multiple processors for parallel computation. Static and dynamic load balancing strategies can be demonstrated with the following Python code using CUDA.

```
import numpy as np
from numba import cuda

@cuda.jit
def sum_array(arr, result, start, end):
    i = cuda.grid(1)
    if start <= i < end:
        cuda.atomic.add(result, 0, arr[i])

n = 1024
arr = np.arange(n, dtype=np.float32)
result = np.array([0], dtype=np.float32)

threads_per_block = 128
blocks_per_grid = (n + (threads_per_block - 1)) // threads_per_block

# Static Load Balancing: Manually partition the array evenly
start_1, end_1 = 0, n//2
start_2, end_2 = n//2, n

# Launch kernel for first half
sum_array[blocks_per_grid, threads_per_block](arr, result, start_1, end_1)

# Launch kernel for second half
sum_array[blocks_per_grid, threads_per_block](arr, result, start_2, end_2)

print("Sum of array (static):", result[0])
```

```
Sum of array (static): 523776.0
```

In the above example, the array is divided into two halves $(0, n/2)$ and $(n/2, n)$, respectively. Each kernel launch is responsible for summing one half. This is a simple static load balancing strategy.

```
import numpy as np
from numba import cuda

@cuda.jit
def sum_array_dynamic(arr, result):
    i = cuda.grid(1)
    if i < arr.size:
        cuda.atomic.add(result, 0, arr[i])

n = 1024
arr = np.arange(n, dtype=np.float32)
result = np.array([0], dtype=np.float32)

threads_per_block = 128
blocks_per_grid = (n + (threads_per_block - 1)) // threads_per_block

# Dynamic Load Balancing: No need to manually partition the array
sum_array_dynamic[blocks_per_grid, threads_per_block](arr, result)

print("Sum of array (dynamic):", result[0])
```

```
Sum of array (dynamic): 523776.0
```

In the dynamic load balancing example, the kernel is configured to sum the entire array without manually partitioning it. The tasks are dynamically allocated as threads become available.

Partitioning: Partitioning can be understood as the process of dividing a problem into smaller chunks to facilitate parallel execution. There are several partitioning strategies, including:

- **Domain Decomposition:** The computational domain is divided into smaller subdomains. For example, in a 2D grid, the grid can be divided into smaller rectangular subgrids, each handled by a different processor.

- **Functional Decomposition:** Different functional tasks of a problem are divided among processors. For example, in a web service, one processor might handle parsing, another handles business logic, and another handles database interactions.

Consider a more sophisticated example: matrix multiplication. This problem can be partitioned using domain decomposition, where the matrices are divided into sub-matrices and each processor multiplies its assigned sub-matrices.

```
import numpy as np
from numba import cuda

@cuda.jit
def matmul(A, B, C):
    row, col = cuda.grid(2)
    if row < C.shape[0] and col < C.shape[1]:
        temp = 0
        for k in range(A.shape[1]):
            temp += A[row, k] * B[k, col]
        C[row, col] = temp

N = 16
A = np.random.randn(N, N).astype(np.float32)
B = np.random.randn(N, N).astype(np.float32)
C = np.zeros((N, N), dtype=np.float32)

threads_per_block = (16, 16)
blocks_per_grid_x = int(np.ceil(A.shape[0] / threads_per_block[0]))
blocks_per_grid_y = int(np.ceil(B.shape[1] / threads_per_block[1]))
blocks_per_grid = (blocks_per_grid_x, blocks_per_grid_y)

matmul[blocks_per_grid, threads_per_block](A, B, C)
print("Matrix C after multiplication:\n", C)
```

```
Matrix C after multiplication:
[[ -0.15960543   1.0384753   -0.8812835   -3.2170875   -4.3082657
   -1.3907354    0.90733093   0.45629242  -5.7497544    0.9386241
    4.314327    -5.0552816    1.3801134   -0.47880766    4.172201
   -2.4675777 ]
 [  7.8689785    5.4591503   -0.94982326   5.8815856   -4.988171
    1.1592025   -0.60787773  -1.1131283   -1.1581144   -1.0859002
    5.5809546    5.6426263   -5.403895    -1.4424186   -4.035263
    0.52277166]
 [ -1.8771981   -0.03769224  -0.5118965    1.0499206    4.45741
    3.5947626  -11.566497    -3.8331528   -6.236756    -2.1101263
   17.35983      5.742315    -4.9158163   10.222172    -7.2015142
    0.2253144 ]
 [ -4.141323     8.029545    -1.833539    -8.328278     2.6784952
    2.1767313    2.9144511    2.005334     0.08455596   8.904055
   12.571766    -5.2448573  -11.824073    -1.131273   -13.679329
   -0.74045736]
 [ -3.551891     4.6826315    1.6239944    1.2260802    2.5370953
    0.94189763   6.6064706    3.5198686    7.9608145    3.295659
   11.823048    -4.834922     8.985182   -11.161082     1.1980499
    2.9867404 ]
 [ -7.2861905   -1.4635826    5.0879974    0.67392445   2.3577225
   -5.478533    -1.1755427    3.2659457    4.2877064   -6.048758
  -16.652273    -7.6795754   -2.668287     3.951252    -9.536968
    2.4466758 ]
 [  5.2957315    7.3276763   -0.8680657    2.2677515    0.60479444
    1.6083255   -8.648686    -2.4976017  -12.865567     6.853621
   12.679637     0.13115183   7.6274824   -0.10250026  -5.605231
    2.7580574 ]
 [ -4.985278     8.901336    16.321573   -13.376853    -4.243781
   -0.9155653    1.9164176    1.334847     0.90719354  -2.4827735
   -5.661863    -0.4116288   -2.199013   -15.642537    -0.79709715
    5.779615  ]
 [-14.206835   -10.119773     5.4527464   14.842466     0.87072945
  -10.326925   -11.174684    -4.6812334   -1.5649194  -12.352576
   -0.39608932  -2.069068   -10.249141     4.049646   -10.282386
    1.4462649 ]
 [-14.419481    -2.9365847   -8.942452     4.659711     7.7646337
   -5.9959474    2.8256269   -8.463439    14.718932    -3.7333486
    4.9952455    3.202371     5.3922873    1.6839178    5.9453673
    2.4628985 ]
 [  1.7311012   -2.092128     9.871929     6.1636467   -4.283074
   -7.3935685   11.316124     3.5172446    8.132989     1.1204097
    5.202061    -8.151295     3.9915705   13.308059   -10.6221485
    8.064406  ]
 [  4.145724     0.36973923   9.108181    -2.0796926   -8.129245
   -1.1779011    8.300833    -0.2306492   -5.4948473   -2.4533508
   -0.39693534   1.4264296   -6.4072075    6.639097    -7.399678
   -0.24765125]
 [ -6.046275     0.2760826    7.692955     2.7150896   -5.663489
    2.9603864    0.35567185  -6.007262   -13.561618     6.58446
   -5.858308    -5.4619927   -9.64681     -4.269801     3.22681
   -2.512461  ]
 [-11.65977      1.1674668  -15.14967    -24.350336     3.7625828
   -6.1333613    0.12537649  -5.387973    -1.7333953    4.237864
   41.36957    -16.019009     4.1310654   30.464914    -4.4615455
  -14.849939  ]
 [  7.933734    11.967258    -1.1617595   -3.380225    -4.982406
    3.4397595   20.124144    10.06224     11.132735     2.55352
   11.888219    -9.788948     1.9986942  -22.161688    12.03895
  -17.911755  ]
 [ -5.9078736   -8.158635   -11.337768    13.69804     -3.9563015
   -8.461707    -1.1722858   -0.7957631   -8.142893    -2.485227
   14.480654    -8.076437     5.7967677   15.112836     6.1456738
    1.192112  ]]
```

This code example demonstrates domain decomposition for the matrix multiplication problem, where the matrices are divided into smaller blocks, and each thread computes a portion of the resulting matrix.

The concepts of load balancing and partitioning are essential for maximizing the performance and efficiency of parallel programs. Static load balancing is beneficial for problems with predictable workloads, while dynamic load balancing is suitable for problems with varying workloads. Partitioning strategies such as domain decomposition and functional decomposition enable the efficient parallel execution of complex tasks. Understanding and effectively applying these strategies are crucial steps towards mastering parallel programming with CUDA.

6.9 Scalability and Performance Metrics

The scalability of a parallel application measures its ability to effectively utilize an increasing number of processing elements. In essence, it evaluates how well performance improves as the scale of the computational resources is increased. Good scalability implies that the algorithm can maintain efficiency and performance gains with the addition of more processors.

To analyze and understand scalability, several key concepts and performance metrics are employed. Two primary types of scalability are strong scaling and weak scaling. Strong scaling measures the efficiency of an application when the problem size remains constant as the number of processors increases, while weak scaling assesses efficiency when both the problem size and the number of processors increase proportionally.

Strong Scaling: This scenario evaluates the ability to solve a fixed-size problem faster using an increased number of processors. The performance metric used in strong scaling is speedup, defined as:

$$S_p = \frac{T_1}{T_p}$$

where T_1 is the execution time with one processor, and T_p is the execution time with p processors. The ideal speedup equals p, indicating perfect scalability. However, in practice, factors such as communication overhead and load imbalance diminish the achievable speedup.

Weak Scaling: This scenario assesses the ability to solve proportionally larger problems with increasing numbers of processors. The goal is to maintain a constant runtime as the number of processors and problem size grow. The performance metric for weak scaling is efficiency, defined as:

$$E_p = \frac{S_p}{p} = \frac{T_1}{p \cdot T_p}$$

Efficiency helps determine how well the parallel application utilizes the processors. An efficiency of 1 (or 100

Analyzing these concepts, it becomes important to consider the sources of inefficiencies like:

- **Communication Overhead:** As the number of processors increases, the communication time between them generally increases. Hence, the communication overhead can significantly impact performance, especially in tightly coupled systems.
- **Load Imbalance:** An uneven distribution of computational work among processors leads to some processors waiting idly for others to complete their tasks. This imbalance can be due to algorithmic limitations or dynamic changes in workload.
- **Synchronization Delays:** Frequently needing synchronization between processors can diminish overall performance. As parallelism increases, achieving a synchronized state becomes more complex and time-consuming.

To further understand scalability, we need to delve into practical performance metrics. An essential metric is parallel overhead, which includes all the non-computational activities and delays that occur due to parallelism, such as communication and synchronization. For a robust performance analysis, other metrics such as latency, throughput, and resource utilization should be considered.

Latency: The time it takes to complete a single task from start to finish. In parallel systems, latency can be affected by the initiation time, communication delays, and synchronization points.

Throughput: The amount of work or number of tasks completed in a given period. High throughput indicates that the system can handle many tasks efficiently.

Resource Utilization: Measures the degree to which the processing power of the system is used. High utilization indicates efficient use of available resources, whereas low utilization can signal issues like load imbalance or excessive overheads.

These metrics help to diagnose performance bottlenecks and guide optimization efforts. As parallel applications scale, it is crucial to minimize overhead and balance loads effectively to achieve superior performance.

Analyzing the performance of parallel algorithms involves running benchmarks to measure execution times and applying models such as Karp-Flatt, which considers the impact of serial portions and overhead in parallel execution. The Karp-Flatt metric is defined as:

$$\epsilon = \frac{\frac{T_p}{T_1} - \frac{1}{p}}{1 - \frac{1}{p}}$$

where ϵ represents the overhead fraction that hampers parallel efficiency. A lower value of ϵ signifies better scalability.

As part of performance optimization, techniques such as reducing communication, optimizing synchronization, and improving load balancing can be employed. These techniques aim to enhance the efficiency and scalability of parallel algorithms, leading to better utilization of computational resources.

```
#include <stdio.h>
#include <omp.h>

void parallel_sum(double *a, int n, int num_threads) {
    double total_sum = 0.0;
    #pragma omp parallel for reduction(+:total_sum) num_threads(num_threads)
    for (int i = 0; i < n; i++) {
        total_sum += a[i];
    }
    printf("Total Sum: %f\n", total_sum);
}

int main() {
    int n = 1000000;
    double *a = (double*)malloc(n * sizeof(double));
    for(int i = 0; i < n; i++) a[i] = i * 0.5;

    double start_time = omp_get_wtime();
    parallel_sum(a, n, 4);
    double end_time = omp_get_wtime();
    printf("Execution Time with 4 threads: %f seconds\n", end_time - start_time);

    start_time = omp_get_wtime();
    parallel_sum(a, n, 8);
    end_time = omp_get_wtime();
```

```
    printf("Execution Time with 8 threads: %f seconds\n", end_time - start_time);

    free(a);
    return 0;
}
```

Below is a potential output for the code execution:

```
Total Sum: 249999750000.000000
Execution Time with 4 threads: 0.012345 seconds
Total Sum: 249999750000.000000
Execution Time with 8 threads: 0.008765 seconds
```

By monitoring execution times with different numbers of threads, we can investigate both strong and weak scaling behaviors, thus providing insights into the scalability of our parallel algorithm.

6.10 Case Studies: Parallel Algorithms

This section explores tangible applications of parallel algorithms by presenting detailed case studies. Through these case studies, readers can gain insights into the practical implementation and optimization of parallel algorithms using CUDA with Python.

Consider the problem of matrix multiplication, which is fundamental in many scientific computations. In a conventional sequential approach, each entry in the resultant matrix is computed independently in a nested loop structure. However, this method does not utilize the computational power of modern multi-core GPUs.

We start by examining how matrix multiplication can be parallelized using CUDA. Assume we have two square matrices A and B of size $N \times N$. The resultant matrix C is also of size $N \times N$, where each element $C[i][j]$ is computed as follows:

$$C[i][j] = \sum_{k=0}^{N-1} A[i][k] \times B[k][j]$$

Parallelizing this operation involves distributing the computation of each element to different CUDA threads. Each thread computes a single element of the matrix C.

```
import numpy as np
from numba import cuda

N = 1024 # Example size
```

```
@cuda.jit
def matmul_cuda(A, B, C):
    row, col = cuda.grid(2)
    if row < C.shape[0] and col < C.shape[1]:
        tmp_sum = 0
        for k in range(A.shape[1]):
            tmp_sum += A[row, k] * B[k, col]
        C[row, col] = tmp_sum

# Initialize matrices
A = np.random.rand(N, N).astype(np.float32)
B = np.random.rand(N, N).astype(np.float32)
C = np.zeros((N, N), dtype=np.float32)

# Define grid and block dimensions
threads_per_block = (16, 16)
blocks_per_grid_x = int(np.ceil(A.shape[0] / threads_per_block[0]))
blocks_per_grid_y = int(np.ceil(A.shape[1] / threads_per_block[1]))
blocks_per_grid = (blocks_per_grid_x, blocks_per_grid_y)

# Call the CUDA kernel function
matmul_cuda[blocks_per_grid, threads_per_block](A, B, C)
```

In the given Python code, the matrix multiplication kernel function matmul_cuda is defined using the @cuda.jit decorator. The dimensions of the grid and the blocks are determined by the problem size, ensuring that each element computation is assigned to a separate thread. The kernel function uses cuda.grid(2) to get the row and column index for each thread, and subsequently performs the multiplication and summation.

Another illustrative case study involves image processing, a process that can benefit significantly from parallelism. Consider the application of a Gaussian Blur filter on an image. The Gaussian Blur is achieved through convolution with a Gaussian kernel which smoothens the image by averaging pixel values around the target pixel.

```
import cv2
from numba import cuda, float32

# Gaussian kernel
KERNEL_SIZE = 5
sigma = 1.0

def gaussian_kernel(size, sigma):
    kernel = np.fromfunction(lambda x, y: (1/ (2 * np.pi * sigma**2)) *
                            np.exp(-( (x - (size - 1) / 2)**2 + (y - (size - 1) / 2)**2) / (2
                                * sigma**2)),
                            (size, size), dtype=np.float32)
    return kernel / np.sum(kernel)

kernel = gaussian_kernel(KERNEL_SIZE, sigma)

@cuda.jit
def gaussian_blur_cuda(image, result, kernel, kernel_size):
    x, y = cuda.grid(2)
```

```
    if x < image.shape[0] and y < image.shape[1]:
        k_center = kernel_size // 2
        blur_sum = 0.0

        for i in range(kernel_size):
            for j in range(kernel_size):
                nx = x + i - k_center
                ny = y + j - k_center

                if nx >= 0 and nx < image.shape[0] and ny >= 0 and ny < image.shape
                    [1]:
                    blur_sum += image[nx, ny] * kernel[i, j]

        result[x, y] = blur_sum

# Load grayscale image
image = cv2.imread('example.jpg', 0).astype(np.float32)
result = np.zeros_like(image)

# Define grid and block dimensions
threads_per_block = (16, 16)
blocks_per_grid_x = int(np.ceil(image.shape[0] / threads_per_block[0]))
blocks_per_grid_y = int(np.ceil(image.shape[1] / threads_per_block[1]))
blocks_per_grid = (blocks_per_grid_x, blocks_per_grid_y)

# Call the CUDA kernel function
gaussian_blur_cuda[blocks_per_grid, threads_per_block](image, result, kernel,
    KERNEL_SIZE)

# Save or visualize the result
cv2.imwrite('blurred_image.jpg', result)
```

In this case study, the Gaussian Blur filter application is divided among GPU threads. The gaussian_blur_cuda function performs convolution for each pixel on the image. The center of the kernel is adjusted for boundary conditions, ensuring the kernel does not exceed image dimensions. CUDA's parallel execution feature enables efficient processing of large images, significantly reducing computation time compared to sequential implementations.

Finally, consider the N-Body Simulation problem, crucial in physics and astrophysics for simulating the gravitational forces and motions of a system of particles. The parallelized version of N-Body Simulation updates the position and velocity of each particle concurrently, taking into account the cumulative gravitational influences from all other particles.

```
G = 6.67430e-11 # Gravitational constant

@cuda.jit
def nbody_cuda(pos, vel, mass, dt):
    i = cuda.grid(1)
    if i < pos.shape[0]:
        force = cuda.local.array(3, dtype=float32)
        force[0] = force[1] = force[2] = 0.0

        for j in range(pos.shape[0]):
```

```
            if i != j:
                dist = cuda.local.array(3, dtype=float32)
                for k in range(3):
                    dist[k] = pos[j, k] - pos[i, k]
                distance = math.sqrt(dist[0]**2 + dist[1]**2 + dist[2]**2 + 1e-9)
                force_factor = G * mass[i] * mass[j] / (distance**3 + 1e-9)
                for k in range(3):
                    force[k] += force_factor * dist[k]

        for k in range(3):
            vel[i, k] += force[k] * dt / mass[i]
            pos[i, k] += vel[i, k] * dt

# Number of bodies
num_bodies = 1000

# Initialize positions, velocities, and masses
pos = np.random.rand(num_bodies, 3).astype(np.float32) * 1e3
vel = np.zeros((num_bodies, 3), dtype=np.float32)
mass = np.random.rand(num_bodies).astype(np.float32) * 1e30

# Time step
dt = 1e-3

# Define grid and block dimensions
threads_per_block = 128
blocks_per_grid = int(np.ceil(num_bodies / threads_per_block))

# Call the CUDA kernel function
nbody_cuda[blocks_per_grid, threads_per_block](pos, vel, mass, dt)
```

The nbody_cuda function calculates gravitational forces and updates positions and velocities for each particle. The parallelization of these computations among CUDA threads allows efficient and simultaneous updates, essential for accurate and timely simulations in large-scale systems.

These case studies illustrate parallel implementations of common computational tasks, demonstrating the power and utility of CUDA in leveraging GPUs for significant performance gains.

Chapter 7

CUDA with Python: Numba Basics

This chapter covers the integration of CUDA with Python using Numba. It guides through setting up Numba for CUDA development, writing and running Numba-CUDA kernels, and understanding the CUDA threading model within Numba. Key areas include memory management, code optimization, troubleshooting common issues, and integrating Numba with other Python libraries. Advanced Numba-CUDA techniques are also discussed to enhance performance and efficiency.

7.1 Introduction to Numba for CUDA

Numba is an open-source, Just-In-Time (JIT) compiler that translates a subset of Python and NumPy code into machine code by leveraging the powerful LLVM compiler infrastructure. When combined with CUDA, a parallel computing platform and application programming interface (API) model created by NVIDIA, Numba brings GPU acceleration capabilities to Python code, making it an effective tool for high-performance computing tasks.

Numba's CUDA Support. Numba provides a highly usable Python interface for CUDA-capable GPUs. It allows Python developers to write CUDA kernels and device functions directly in Python. By exploiting the targeting of GPU architecture, computational tasks that require substantial parallelism can achieve significant performance gains.

Integration with Existing Python Ecosystem. One of Numba's key advantages is its seamless integration with the Python ecosystem, particularly with NumPy. It allows transformation of NumPy functions to run on CUDA-enabled GPUs without rewriting the entire codebase. By utilizing decorators such as @cuda.jit, developers can define GPU functions intuitively.

A simple example of writing a basic Numba-CUDA kernel can illustrate how easily one can start working with this powerful combination. Below is a snippet of code demonstrating a simple vector addition using Numba for CUDA:

```
from numba import cuda
import numpy as np

@cuda.jit
def vector_add(a, b, c):
    pos = cuda.grid(1)
    if pos < a.size:
        c[pos] = a[pos] + b[pos]

# Define input vectors
N = 100000
A = np.ones(N, dtype=np.float32)
B = np.ones(N, dtype=np.float32)
C = np.zeros(N, dtype=np.float32)

# Allocate memory on the device
dA = cuda.to_device(A)
dB = cuda.to_device(B)
dC = cuda.device_array_like(C)

# Configure the kernel
threadsperblock = 256
blockspergrid = (A.size + (threadsperblock - 1)) // threadsperblock

# Launch kernel
vector_add[blockspergrid, threadsperblock](dA, dB, dC)

# Copy the result back to the host
dC.copy_to_host(C)
```

Understanding the Code. The decorator @cuda.jit indicates that the function vector_add is a CUDA kernel. This function will be executed on the GPU. It retrieves a unique thread index using cuda.grid(1), a 1-dimensional grid. The condition if pos < a.size ensures that the index is within the bounds of the array. Properly configuring the kernel launch by setting the number of threads per block and the number of blocks per grid allows the computation to be distributed evenly across the GPU resources.

Compilation Mechanism. When the decorated function is first called, Numba compiles it into a CUDA kernel which is then executed on the GPU. This process includes validation and conversion of Python code into an intermediate representation (IR), then into PTX (Parallel Thread Execution) code which is JIT-compiled for the GPU.

Numba's ease of use in developing GPU kernels eliminates much of the boilerplate and complexity traditionally associated with CUDA C++ programming. This democratizes access to GPU computing power, enabling Python developers to leverage parallel processing for computational tasks without delving into low-level programming.

Throughout later sections of this chapter, we will delve deeper into the specifics of setting up the correct environment, optimizing code, managing memory, and troubleshooting to ensure robust, efficient, and high-performance applications. Bringing these facets together will equip you with the requisite knowledge to harness the full potential of CUDA programming with Numba.

7.2 Setting Up Numba for CUDA Development

To effectively utilize Numba for CUDA development, various steps are necessary to ensure that the environment is correctly configured. This process entails verifying hardware compatibility, installing requisite software, and validating the installation. CUDA development with Numba can only be performed on systems equipped with CUDA-capable NVIDIA GPUs. Utilize the following guidelines for precise setup:

First, verify that your system meets the hardware requirements. Ensure the NVIDIA GPU supports CUDA, typically indicated by a Compute Capability of 3.0 or higher. The list of compatible GPUs and their compute capabilities is available on the official NVIDIA website.

Next, install the NVIDIA drivers. On Linux systems, this can be achieved through the package manager. For instance, on Ubuntu, execute:

```
sudo apt update
sudo apt install nvidia-driver-470
```

Reboot the system post-installation:

```
sudo reboot
```

On Windows, download and install the drivers from the NVIDIA website. Follow the installation wizard instructions and reboot the system as required.

CUDA Toolkit installation is the subsequent step, providing the development environment for creating high-performance GPU-accelerated applications. Different versions of the CUDA Toolkit can be obtained from the NVIDIA website, appropriate to the specific operating system and the CUDA version required.

For Linux systems, download the CUDA Toolkit:

```
wget https://developer.download.nvidia.com/compute/cuda/11.4.0/local_installers/
    cuda_11.4.0_470.42.01_linux.run
sudo sh cuda_11.4.0_470.42.01_linux.run
```

Follow the on-screen instructions to complete the installation. For Windows, execute the installer and adhere to the provided guidelines.

Add CUDA to the system's PATH to enable access to its executables. Append the following lines to your ~/.bashrc file on Linux:

```
export PATH=/usr/local/cuda-11.4/bin:${PATH}
export LD_LIBRARY_PATH=/usr/local/cuda-11.4/lib64:${LD_LIBRARY_PATH}
```

For Windows, add C:\Program Files\NVIDIA GPU Computing Toolkit\CUDA\v11.4\bin to your system environment variables.

Next, install the Python package manager pip if it is not already installed. Then use pip to install Numba. Execute:

```
pip install numba
```

Numba depends on several additional libraries, including llvmlite and the CUDA Development Tools. Ensure these dependencies are installed correctly along with Numba.

To verify the installation, it is prudent to execute a small test program. Below is a simple Numba-CUDA program to validate that everything is set up correctly. Create a Python file numba_test.py and insert the following code:

```
from numba import cuda
import numpy as np

@cuda.jit
def add_kernel(x, y, out):
    idx = cuda.grid(1)
```

```
    if idx < out.size:
        out[idx] = x[idx] + y[idx]

N = 1000000
x = np.random.random(N).astype(np.float32)
y = np.random.random(N).astype(np.float32)
out = np.zeros_like(x)

threads_per_block = 128
blocks_per_grid = (x.size + (threads_per_block - 1)) // threads_per_block

add_kernel[blocks_per_grid, threads_per_block](x, y, out)

print(out[:10])
```

This code allocates memory for two input arrays x and y, each of size N, and initializes a kernel to perform element-wise addition. Compile and run the program:

```
python numba_test.py
```

The output will be the sum of the first ten elements of these arrays, verifying that Numba and CUDA are correctly set up:

```
[0.64590204 1.34767687 1.5295459  1.6460155  1.1086726  0.69909203
 0.82711357 1.0129778  0.68554616 0.8531936 ]
```

This process prepares your development environment for Numba-CUDA, enabling the exploration of CUDA programming within Python.

7.3 Writing Your First Numba-CUDA Kernel

In this section, we will focus on writing your initial Numba-CUDA kernel. A kernel is essentially a function that runs on the GPU. Unlike standard Python functions, Numba-CUDA kernels take advantage of the parallel processing capabilities of modern GPUs, leading to significant performance improvements for data-parallel computations.

To begin, we need to import the necessary Numba and CUDA libraries. The primary library we will use is numba.cuda, which provides functions to define and execute kernels on the GPU.

```
from numba import cuda
import numpy as np
```

With the libraries imported, we now define a simple CUDA kernel. A kernel is a special type of function that is decorated with @cuda.jit. This decorator indicates that the function will compile to run on the GPU.

```
@cuda.jit
def vector_add(a, b, c):
    idx = cuda.threadIdx.x + cuda.blockIdx.x * cuda.blockDim.x
    if idx < a.size:
        c[idx] = a[idx] + b[idx]
```

In this example, vector_add is a simple kernel that takes three arrays a, b, and c. The kernel adds the corresponding elements of arrays a and b, and stores the result in array c. The key value here is idx, which calculates the unique index for each thread.

cuda.threadIdx.x, cuda.blockIdx.x, and cuda.blockDim.x are built-in variables provided by the CUDA API:

- cuda.threadIdx.x: The index of the thread within the current block.
- cuda.blockIdx.x: The index of the current block within the grid.
- cuda.blockDim.x: The dimension (or number) of threads in a block.

Combining these variables allows each thread to compute a unique idx, associating each thread with a specific element in the arrays a, b, and c.

Next, we need to allocate memory for our vectors and copy data from the host (CPU) to the device (GPU). This step is essential since the GPU operates on its own memory space, separate from the CPU.

```
N = 1000000
a = np.random.rand(N).astype(np.float32)
b = np.random.rand(N).astype(np.float32)
c = np.zeros(N, dtype=np.float32)

d_a = cuda.to_device(a)
d_b = cuda.to_device(b)
d_c = cuda.device_array_like(c)
```

Here, a and b are initialized with random floating-point numbers, and c is an array of zeros. cuda.to_device transfers the host data to the device memory, while cuda.device_array_like allocates an array on the device similar to the input array.

To launch the kernel, we must specify the grid (number of blocks) and block (number of threads per block) dimensions.

```
threads_per_block = 256
blocks_per_grid = (a.size + (threads_per_block - 1)) // threads_per_block

vector_add[blocks_per_grid, threads_per_block](d_a, d_b, d_c)
```

The threads_per_block is set to 256. This value is commonly used because it matches the typical warp size of modern GPUs, optimizing performance and resource usage. blocks_per_grid is computed by dividing the total number of elements by threads_per_block and rounding up to ensure coverage.

By executing vector_add[blocks_per_grid, threads_per_block](d_a, d_b, d_c), the kernel runs on the GPU. Post execution, the results must be copied back to the host.

```
c = d_c.copy_to_host()
```

The above line transfers data from the GPU memory back to the CPU memory. Optionally, it is good practice to check the results to ensure correctness.

```
np.testing.assert_almost_equal(c, a + b)
```

This assertion verifies that each element in c is almost equal to the corresponding element in $a + b$, accounting for minor floating-point differences.

By following these steps, you have successfully written, executed, and verified your first Numba-CUDA kernel. Understanding this fundamental example sets the foundation for more complex and efficient data-parallel operations on the GPU.

7.4 Compiling and Running Numba-CUDA Kernels

To harness the power of CUDA within the Python ecosystem, leveraging Numba allows for efficient computational performance while simplifying the code development process. This section delineates the steps required to compile and run Numba-CUDA kernels, ensuring a smooth execution conducive to high-performance computing tasks.

To begin, let's consider a simple Numba-CUDA kernel to add two arrays element-wise. Here's a minimal example to get started:

```
from numba import cuda
import numpy as np

@cuda.jit
def add_kernel(a, b, c):
    idx = cuda.grid(1)
    if idx < a.size:
```

```
    c[idx] = a[idx] + b[idx]
```

In this example, the @cuda.jit decorator specifies that add_kernel is a CUDA kernel. The cuda.grid(1) function calculates the thread's unique index based on the grid dimension, which is crucial for parallel execution.

Upon defining the kernel, the next step involves compiling and running it. Numba handles kernel compilation at runtime, converting the Python function into an efficient machine code suitable for GPU execution.

To compile and execute the add_kernel, follow the steps below:

```
# Define array sizes
n = 100000

# Allocate and initialize host arrays
a = np.random.uniform(0, 1, n).astype(np.float32)
b = np.random.uniform(0, 1, n).astype(np.float32)
c = np.zeros(n, dtype=np.float32)

# Allocate device memory and transfer input data to GPU
a_device = cuda.to_device(a)
b_device = cuda.to_device(b)
c_device = cuda.device_array_like(c)

# Define grid and block dimensions
threads_per_block = 256
blocks_per_grid = (a.size + threads_per_block - 1) // threads_per_block

# Launch kernel
add_kernel[blocks_per_grid, threads_per_block](a_device, b_device, c_device)

# Copy result from device to host
c_device.copy_to_host(c)

# Check results
print(np.all(c == a + b))
```

Here, several critical steps are performed:

- **Array Initialization and Memory Allocation**:
  - The arrays a, b, and c are initialized on the host (CPU) using NumPy.
  - The function cuda.to_device transfers a and b to the GPU device memory, whereas cuda.device_array_like allocates memory for c on the GPU.
- **Defining Grid and Block Dimensions**:
  - Grid and block dimensions are defined to manage how many threads are used. Here, threads_per_block defines the

number of threads within each block, and $\mathrm{blocks\_per\_grid}$ calculates the number of blocks needed to cover all elements in the array.

- **Kernel Launch**:
  - The kernel $\mathrm{add\_kernel}$ is launched using the syntax $\mathrm{kernel\_name[blocks\_per\_grid,\ threads\_per\_block](arguments...)}$ which directs the GPU to execute the kernel with the specified configuration.
- **Data Transfer and Verification**:
  - After execution, $\mathrm{c\_device.copy\_to\_host(c)}$ copies the results from the device (GPU) back to the host (CPU) for verification.
  - The final comparison $\mathrm{np.all(c == a + b)}$ ensures that the computation was performed correctly.

Execution outputs the logical result of True, affirming the correctness of the GPU-accelerated addition.

```
True
```

Compiling and executing Numba-CUDA kernels can involve performance optimization techniques, as presented in later sections. Profiling the kernel execution and tuning the grid and block dimensions are essential steps to maximize GPU resource utilization and efficiency.

7.5 Understanding and Using CUDA Threading Model with Numba

In CUDA programming, the paradigm of parallel computing is achieved through the efficient use of the threading model. Understanding this model is crucial for optimizing the performance of your CUDA-enabled Python applications using Numba. In this section, we'll delve into the intricacies of CUDA's threading model and illustrate how Numba leverages this to facilitate parallel computing.

CUDA's threading model is based on a hierarchical structure of threads, blocks, and grids. A kernel, which is essentially a function written to run on the GPU, is executed in a grid of thread blocks. Each thread block contains threads, which are the smallest units of execution.

- **Thread:** The basic unit of execution in CUDA. Each thread has its own set of registers, a program counter, and a local memory space. Threads perform operations based on the instructions specified in the kernel.
- **Block:** A collection of threads that execute a kernel function. Blocks can be one-dimensional, two-dimensional, or three-dimensional. Each block shares a certain amount of shared memory and can synchronize its threads using barriers.
- **Grid:** A collection of blocks that execute a kernel function. Grids are typically one-dimensional or two-dimensional and can scale to include many blocks, making CUDA capable of executing thousands of parallel threads.

The following code demonstrates how to define and launch a Numba-CUDA kernel with a specific grid and block size configuration:

```
from numba import cuda

# Define a simple kernel to illustrate the threading model
@cuda.jit
def simple_kernel(data):
    idx = cuda.grid(1)
    if idx < data.size:
        data[idx] *= 2

# Initialize an array with 1000 elements
data = cuda.to_device(np.arange(1000, dtype=np.float32))

# Configure the blocks and grid dimensions
threads_per_block = 128
blocks_per_grid = (data.size + (threads_per_block - 1)) // threads_per_block

# Launch the kernel
simple_kernel[blocks_per_grid, threads_per_block](data)

# Copy the result back to the host and verify
result = data.copy_to_host()
print(result)
```

In the example above, `cuda.grid(1)` is used to calculate the global thread index in a one-dimensional grid configuration. Each thread processes an element of the array independently. This kernel multiplies each element by two, demonstrating basic manipulation of data using CUDA threads.

To delve deeper, we should understand the significance of synchronization and memory hierarchy in the threading model. Synchronization is essential to ensure that threads within a block operate in harmony, especially when they share data.

```
from numba import cuda
import numpy as np

@cuda.jit
def shared_memory_example(data):
    # Define shared memory array
    shared_array = cuda.shared.array(shape=(128,), dtype=numba.float32)

    # Calculate the thread's unique index within the grid and block
    tid = cuda.threadIdx.x
    bid = cuda.blockIdx.x
    bdim = cuda.blockDim.x
    idx = tid + bid * bdim

    # Load data into shared memory
    if idx < data.size:
        shared_array[tid] = data[idx]

    # Synchronize before proceeding to ensure all threads have loaded their data
    cuda.syncthreads()

    # Perform a computation using shared memory
    if tid < data.size:
        data[idx] = shared_array[tid] ** 2

# Initialize an array with 1000 elements
data = cuda.to_device(np.arange(1000, dtype=np.float32))

# Configure the blocks and grid dimensions
threads_per_block = 128
blocks_per_grid = (data.size + (threads_per_block - 1)) // threads_per_block

# Launch the kernel
shared_memory_example[blocks_per_grid, threads_per_block](data)

# Copy the result back to the host and verify
result = data.copy_to_host()
print(result)
```

In this kernel, `cuda.shared.array` is used to allocate shared memory accessible by all threads within the block. The `cuda.syncthreads()` function ensures that all threads in the block have completed their data loading into shared memory before any thread proceeds to the computation phase. This is crucial for avoiding race conditions and ensuring that computations are based on the correct and complete set of data.

Global memory is slower compared to shared memory. Therefore, effective use of shared memory and ensuring proper synchronization can significantly optimize performance. The size of the shared memory can be configured, but careful consideration is required based on the specific hardware limitations.

Another critical aspect of CUDA's threading model is warp divergence. A warp is a group of 32 threads that execute instructions in lockstep. If threads within a warp take different execution paths (due to conditional branches), this can lead to performance penalties:

```
@cuda.jit
def warp_divergence_example(data, threshold):
    idx = cuda.grid(1)
    if idx < data.size:
        for i in range(100):
            if data[idx] < threshold:
                data[idx] += 1
            else:
                data[idx] -= 1
```

In such cases where divergent branching occurs, threads within a warp must wait for other threads to complete divergent paths before converging back to the next common instruction, reducing overall efficiency.

Understanding the CUDA threading model requires in-depth comprehension of these concepts. Practicing with various kernel configurations, and optimizing the usage of shared memory and synchronization patterns, will lead to more efficient and powerful Numba-CUDA programs. Such optimizations are vital for achieving higher computational throughput on the GPU, fully leveraging the theoretical potential of parallelism in CUDA with Python and Numba.

7.6 Memory Management with Numba

Effective memory management is essential for optimizing CUDA applications as it directly impacts performance. Managing memory allocation, data transfer between host and device, and ensuring efficient memory usage are crucial steps. Numba provides several tools to facilitate these tasks, integrating seamlessly with CUDA's memory management capabilities.

Device Memory Allocation

To allocate memory on the GPU, Numba provides several functions corresponding to CUDA's cudaMalloc and cudaFree. The most common are numba.cuda.device_array and numba.cuda.device_array_like. These functions create arrays on the device, which can be used within your Numba-CUDA kernels.

```
from numba import cuda
import numpy as np

# Define the size of the array
n = 1000000

# Allocate device memory
d_array = cuda.device_array(n, dtype=np.float32)
```

```
# Allocate device memory like a given array
host_array = np.ones(n, dtype=np.float32)
d_array_like = cuda.device_array_like(host_array)
```

In this example, cuda.device_array allocates an array of specified size on the device, while cuda.device_array_like allocates memory similar to an existing NumPy array. These functions ensure that the arrays are contiguous and properly aligned for CUDA operations.

Data Transfer Between Host and Device

Transferring data between the host (CPU) and the device (GPU) is another critical part of memory management. Numba provides to_device and copy_to_host functions for copying data between host and device.

```
# Copy data from host to device
d_array = cuda.to_device(host_array)

# Perform some computation on the device
# ...

# Copy data from device back to host
host_result = d_array.copy_to_host()
```

The to_device function transfers data from a NumPy array on the host to a device array on the GPU. After computations on the GPU are performed, copy_to_host is used to transfer data back to a NumPy array on the host. This operation is crucial for retrieving results from GPU computations.

Unified Memory

Numba also supports Unified Memory, which allows memory to be accessed by both the host and the device, simplifying memory management at the cost of potential performance penalties. Unified Memory can be particularly useful when dealing with large datasets that do not fit entirely in GPU memory.

```
# Allocate managed memory with cuda.malloc_managed
managed_array = cuda.malloc_managed(n * np.dtype(np.float32).itemsize)

# Convert to a numpy array for ease of use
managed_array_np = np.frombuffer(managed_array, dtype=np.float32)
```

In this example, cuda.malloc_managed allocates memory that can be accessed by both host and device. The np.frombuffer function then creates a NumPy array from this managed memory, allowing for easy manipulation.

Pinned Memory

Pinned (or page-locked) memory is another memory type provided by Numba. Pinned memory is allocated on the host but is page-locked, meaning it cannot be swapped to disk. This results in faster data transfer rates between host and device.

```
# Allocate pinned memory
host_pinned_array = cuda.pinned_array(n, dtype=np.float32)

# Initialize pinned memory
host_pinned_array[:] = 1.0

# Copy pinned memory to device
d_pinned_array = cuda.to_device(host_pinned_array)
```

Pinned memory is particularly useful for reducing data transfer latency, as it allows direct memory access (DMA) transfers to the GPU without the overhead of paging.

Context Management

Efficient memory usage in CUDA applications requires careful context management to ensure that memory is allocated and freed appropriately. Numba manages CUDA contexts automatically, but advanced users may need to handle contexts manually using cuda.current_context(), especially when dealing with multiple GPUs.

```
# Get the current CUDA context
context = cuda.current_context()

# Allocate and use memory within this context
buffer = cuda.device_array(1024, dtype=np.float32)
# ...

# Explicitly free memory and destroy context when done
buffer.close()
context.reset()
```

In this example, the current context is retrieved using cuda.current_context(), and memory is then managed within this context. It's a good practice to explicitly free memory and reset contexts in complex applications to avoid memory leaks and ensure optimal performance.

Device Synchronization

Ensuring all computations and memory operations are complete before accessing data is crucial. Device synchronization methods like cuda.synchronize() ensure that all preceding commands on the device are completed.

```
# Launch a kernel
my_kernel[grid_size, block_size](d_array)

# Synchronize device to wait for kernel completion
```

```
cuda.synchronize()
```

In this example, cuda.synchronize() is called after launching a kernel to ensure that all device operations are completed before proceeding. This is particularly important when timing code for performance analysis or when subsequent operations depend on the results of previous computations.

Careful management of memory allocation, data transfers, and synchronization not only ensures correct program execution but also maximizes performance on GPUs. Numba's memory management tools align closely with CUDA's native capabilities, providing a powerful interface for Python developers.

7.7 Optimizing Numba-CUDA Code

Optimization is a crucial phase in CUDA programming, aiming to make the code not only functional but also efficient. The optimization could include minimizing the execution time, maximizing the usage of GPU resources, and reducing data transfer overheads. This section covers strategies to optimize Numba-CUDA code to achieve better performance and efficiency.

Firstly, the execution time of a CUDA kernel may be improved by maximizing the occupancy of the GPU, which involves ensuring a large number of threads are active on the GPU. This can be achieved by optimizing the number of threads per block and the allocation of shared memory.

```
from numba import cuda

@cuda.jit
def optimized_kernel(array):
    shared_array = cuda.shared.array(shape=(32,), dtype=numba.float32)
    idx = cuda.threadIdx.x

    # Load data into shared memory
    shared_array[idx] = array[idx]
    cuda.syncthreads()

    # Perform computation
    shared_array[idx] *= 2
    cuda.syncthreads()

    # Store results back to global memory
    array[idx] = shared_array[idx]
```

In this example, shared memory is used to store intermediate data, reducing the need for repeated global memory access which is slower. The cuda.syncthreads() function ensures that all threads in the block have completed their tasks before any thread accesses shared memory.

Secondly, minimizing data transfers between the host (CPU) and the device (GPU) is essential. Data transfer can be a significant bottleneck if not managed efficiently. Using device arrays defined in Numba can help keep data on the GPU.

```
import numpy as np
from numba import cuda

# Allocate device array
d_array = cuda.to_device(np.random.rand(1024))

@cuda.jit
def compute_kernel(d_array):
    idx = cuda.grid(1)
    if idx < d_array.size:
        d_array[idx] *= 2

# Invoke the kernel
threads_per_block = 128
blocks = (d_array.size + (threads_per_block - 1)) // threads_per_block
compute_kernel[blocks, threads_per_block](d_array)

# Copy result back to host
result = d_array.copy_to_host()
```

This code snippet demonstrates minimizing data transfer by allocating the array directly on the GPU with cuda.to_device() and only transferring back to the host when necessary.

Thirdly, optimizing memory access patterns can dramatically impact performance. Memory coalescing is critical, especially when threads access contiguous memory locations, ensuring that memory transactions are efficient.

```
@cuda.jit
def memory_coalesced_kernel(data):
    tid = cuda.threadIdx.x
    bid = cuda.blockIdx.x
    bdim = cuda.blockDim.x
    gid = tid + bid * bdim

    # Access global memory in a coalesced manner
    for i in range(gid, data.size, bdim * cuda.gridDim.x):
        data[i] += 1
```

Ensuring global memory accesses are coalesced by organizing data access patterns leads to fewer memory transaction requests, greatly improving memory bandwidth usage.

Another optimization technique is using efficient mathematical functions and operations supported by CUDA. For example, utilizing the intrinsic math functions provided by Numba, such as math.expf(), can lead to substantial speedups.

```
from numba import cuda, float32
import math

@cuda.jit
def efficient_math_kernel(data):
    idx = cuda.grid(1)
    if idx < data.size:
        # Use efficient CUDA math functions
        data[idx] = math.expf(data[idx]) + math.sinf(data[idx])
```

Proper use of intrinsics provided ensures maximal use of the GPU's computational capabilities, as these functions are highly optimized for performance on the hardware.

Lastly, profiling and benchmarking are crucial steps in optimization. CUDA provides tools like Nsight Systems and Nsight Compute to profile the kernel execution, exposing bottlenecks and inefficiencies. By iteratively profiling and optimizing, a developer can progressively enhance the performance of the Numba-CUDA code.

A comprehensive optimization process typically involves tuning different parameters, testing various configurations of thread blocks, and continually measuring the impacts of each optimization. Taking advantage of CUDA's powerful profiling tools yields insightful data to guide these optimization efforts, ultimately leading to well-performing CUDA applications written in Python with Numba.

7.8 Troubleshooting and Common Issues

When working with Numba-CUDA, it is not uncommon to encounter a variety of issues that can impede development progress. A thorough understanding of common problems and their resolutions can greatly enhance the debugging process and ensure efficient use of your computational resources. This section outlines prevalent issues and systematic troubleshooting methods.

1. Installation and Environment Issues

- **Incorrect Numba or CUDA Toolkit Version**: Ensure compatibility between Numba, CUDA Toolkit, and the GPU driver. Numba's official documentation provides a compatibility matrix that should be referenced. Use the following command to verify the installed versions:

```
$ numba -s
```

Check the version against the requirements. Mismatched versions often result in import errors or runtime failures.

- **CUDA Toolkit Not Found**: If Numba cannot locate the CUDA Toolkit, verify the installation path. Setting the CUDA_PATH environment variable can resolve this issue.

```
$ export CUDA_PATH=/usr/local/cuda-11.0
```

Ensure that nvcc (NVIDIA's CUDA compiler) is in your PATH.

- **GPU Driver Incompatibility**: After updating the GPU driver, ensure that it is compatible with the installed CUDA Toolkit version. Check driver properties with:

```
$ nvidia-smi
```

2. **Compilation Errors**

- **Syntax Errors**: CUDA kernels in Numba use Python syntax within decorators. Check for typos or misplaced characters. Use brief and clear code snippets that isolate the problematic syntax.

```
@cuda.jit
def add_kernel(a, b, c):
    i = cuda.grid(1)
    if i < a.size:
        c[i] = a[i] + b[i] # Ensure the kernel logic is correct
```

- **Unsupported Features**: Some Python features are not supported within Numba-CUDA kernels, such as certain built-in functions or complex data structures. Refer to the Numba documentation for a list of supported features. Rewrite code to conform to supported constructs.

```
from numba import cuda
@cuda.jit
def unsupported_kernel(a):
    print(a) # Causes an error. Prints are not supported in GPU functions
```

- **Type Inference Problems**: Numba requires explicit type definitions. If type inference fails, specify types within the kernel.

```
@cuda.jit
def typed_kernel(a: int32, b: float64):
    # Correctly inferred types
```

3. Runtime Errors

- **Index Out of Bounds**: Ensure that thread indices do not exceed the array bounds, which will lead to runtime errors.

```
@cuda.jit
def safe_kernel(a, b, c):
    i = cuda.grid(1)
    if i < a.size: # Bound check
        c[i] = a[i] + b[i]
```

- **Memory Access Errors**: Mismanaging memory between host and device can cause access violations. Always ensure proper allocation and data transfer.

```
a_device = cuda.to_device(a) # Transfer data to device
# Ensure corresponding memory is allocated and accessible
```

- **Kernel Launch Failures**: Kernel launch parameters must be appropriately set. Improper dimensions may lead to failures.

```
threadsperblock = 32
blockspergrid = (a.size + (threadsperblock - 1)) // threadsperblock
add_kernel[blockspergrid, threadsperblock](a, b, c)
```

4. Performance Issues

- **Low Throughput**: Suboptimal thread configuration can lead to underutilization of GPU capabilities. Experiment with different threadsperblock and blockspergrid values.

```
threadsperblock = 128
blockspergrid = (a.size + (threadsperblock - 1)) // threadsperblock
add_kernel[blockspergrid, threadsperblock](a, b, c)
```

- **Uncoalesced Memory Access**: Ensure that memory access patterns are coalesced to avoid bottlenecks. Arrange data and threads to align with the memory architecture.

```
@cuda.jit
def coalesced_kernel(a, b, c):
    i = cuda.grid(1)
    if i < a.size:
        c[i] = a[i] + b[i]
# Properly aligned access patterns
```

- **Excessive Data Transfer**: Minimize data transfers between host and device. Transfer data in bulk and only when necessary.

```
# Transfer data once, perform computation on GPU
a_device = cuda.to_device(a)
b_device = cuda.to_device(b)
add_kernel[blockspergrid, threadsperblock](a_device, b_device, c_device)
c = c_device.copy_to_host()
```

5. Logical Errors

- **Incorrect Kernel Logic**: Logical errors in kernels can be challenging to debug. Verify kernel logic independently with a smaller dataset first.

```
@cuda.jit
def logic_kernel(a, b, c):
    i = cuda.grid(1)
    if i < len(a):
        c[i] = a[i] + b[i]
# Test with a small, simplified dataset
```

- **Race Conditions**: When multiple threads access shared data without proper synchronization, race conditions occur. Implement atomic operations or appropriate synchronization mechanisms.

```
@cuda.jit
def race_kernel(a):
    i = cuda.grid(1)
    if i < len(a):
        cuda.atomic.add(a, i, 1)
```

By methodically addressing these issues, substantial improvement in both development experience and code performance can be achieved. Accurate diagnosis is crucial; hence, breaking down the problem systematically will identify the root cause efficiently.

7.9 Integrating Numba with Other Python Libraries

Numba's ability to parallelize code and offload computations to GPUs can significantly enhance the performance of applications that traditionally relied on CPU-bound processes. Nonetheless, a smooth integration of Numba with other Python libraries is crucial for leveraging the full potential of data analysis, machine learning, and scientific computing workflows. This section delves into the integration aspects, discussing how to utilize Numba alongside popular Python libraries such as NumPy, SciPy, and Pandas, enabling seamless performance improvements.

NumPy Integration

NumPy, a cornerstone library for numerical computing in Python, works effectively with Numba. Numba's @vectorize and @guvectorize decorators allow you to independently optimize element-wise and generalized functions, harnessing GPU acceleration. Below is an example demonstrating the integration:

```
import numpy as np
from numba import vectorize

@vectorize(['float32(float32, float32)'], target='cuda')
def add(a, b):
    return a + b

a = np.array([1, 2, 3], dtype=np.float32)
b = np.array([4, 5, 6], dtype=np.float32)
c = add(a, b)

print(c)
```

This vectorized addition operation is executed on the GPU, significantly improving the computation speed, especially for larger arrays. The target='cuda' argument directs Numba to compile the function for CUDA-capable GPUs.

SciPy Integration

SciPy, built on NumPy, offers extensive modules for optimization, interpolation, integration, and other advanced mathematical functions. Integrating Numba with SciPy typically involves transforming computationally intensive parts into Numba-compatible functions. Consider the following example using SciPy's numerical integration capabilities integrated with Numba:

```
import numpy as np
from scipy import integrate
from numba import cuda

@cuda.jit(device=True)
def integrand(x):
    return x ** 2

def quad_numba(a, b, n):
    dx = (b - a) / n
    result = 0.0
    for i in range(n):
```

```
        result += integrand(a + i * dx) * dx
    return result

result = quad_numba(0, 1, 1000)
print(result)
```

In this case, integrand is compiled to run on the GPU, providing an efficient numerical integration using the trapezoidal rule by leveraging CUDA.

Pandas Integration

Pandas, a powerful library for data manipulation and analysis, benefits from Numba's acceleration in operations on DataFrame columns that involve numerical computations. Numba's @jit decorator can be used to optimize specific functions applied to Pandas objects:

```
import pandas as pd
import numpy as np
from numba import jit

@jit(nopython=True)
def calculate_mean(arr):
    return np.mean(arr)

# Create a Pandas DataFrame
df = pd.DataFrame({
    'A': np.random.random(1000000),
    'B': np.random.random(1000000)
})

# Applying Numba-optimized function
df['Mean_A'] = df['A'].apply(calculate_mean)
```

This example demonstrates how the calculate_mean function, optimized by Numba, can be applied to a Pandas DataFrame column, drastically reducing computation time for large datasets by leveraging Numba's JIT compilation.

Interoperability with Machine Learning Libraries

Machine learning libraries like scikit-learn and TensorFlow can also benefit from Numba-accelerated preprocessing steps. While direct integration into core algorithms requires careful consideration due to the complexity of these libraries, Numba provides performance boosts for pre and post-processing tasks. Here is an example of how Numba can accelerate a custom preprocessing function used with scikit-learn's pipeline:

```
from sklearn.preprocessing import StandardScaler
from sklearn.pipeline import Pipeline
from numba import jit
import numpy as np
```

```
@jit(nopython=True)
def custom_transform(arr):
    return (arr - np.mean(arr)) / np.std(arr)

data = np.random.random((1000, 20))

pipeline = Pipeline([
    ('scaler', StandardScaler()),
    ('custom', FunctionTransformer(custom_transform))
])

transformed_data = pipeline.fit_transform(data)
```

The custom_transform function is optimized by Numba, ensuring that intensive computations are executed more efficiently, seamlessly integrating with scikit-learn's pipeline.

Visualization Libraries

Visualization libraries such as Matplotlib and Seaborn can also be used in conjunction with Numba. Although Numba itself doesn't directly accelerate the visualization rendering process, it speeds up the data preparation and transformation steps necessary for generating plots. An example illustrating the integration with Matplotlib:

```
import matplotlib.pyplot as plt
import numpy as np
from numba import jit

@jit(nopython=True)
def generate_data(n):
    x = np.random.random(n)
    y = np.sin(2 * np.pi * x) + np.random.normal(0, 0.1, n)
    return x, y

x, y = generate_data(100000)

plt.scatter(x, y, alpha=0.5)
plt.title("Scatter plot of Numba-generated data")
plt.xlabel("X values")
plt.ylabel("Y values")
plt.show()
```

In this case, Numba accelerates the data generation step, which is particularly useful when dealing with large datasets, feeding the processed data directly into Matplotlib for visualization.

By effectively integrating Numba with these core Python libraries, we capitalize on the improved computational performance, enabling more efficient data manipulation, processing, and analysis workflows.

7.10 Advanced Techniques with Numba-CUDA

To fully leverage the capabilities of Numba-CUDA, it is imperative to delve into advanced techniques that push the boundaries of performance and efficiency. This section covers intricate details of memory management, performance tuning, multi-GPU programming, and techniques for implementing parallel algorithms.

Optimizing memory usage and transfer between host and device is crucial for achieving maximum performance. Numba-CUDA provides several mechanisms for efficient memory management, such as the use of pinned memory and streams. Pinned memory allows faster transfer rates by preventing the operating system from swapping memory pages to disk. To allocate pinned memory in Numba, use the cuda.pinned_array function:

```
import numpy as np
from numba import cuda

# Allocate pinned memory on the host
pinned_memory = cuda.pinned_array(shape=(1024,), dtype=np.float32)

# Initialize data
pinned_memory[:] = np.random.randn(1024).astype(np.float32)

# Allocate device memory
device_memory = cuda.device_array_like(pinned_memory)

# Copy data from host to device
cuda.to_device(pinned_memory, to=device_memory)
```

Using streams allows overlapping computation with data transfer, which can hide latency and improve overall throughput. A stream is a sequence of operations that execute in order on the GPU. Operations in different streams can execute concurrently. In Numba, streams are created with the cuda.stream function:

```
# Create a stream
stream = cuda.stream()

# Asynchronously copy data from host to device
cuda.to_device(pinned_memory, to=device_memory, stream=stream)

# Launch kernel asynchronously
my_kernel[blocks, threads_per_block, stream](device_memory)

# Perform computations on the host while the GPU is busy
result = some_host_computation()

# Synchronize the stream to ensure completion
```

```
stream.synchronize()
```

For multi-GPU programming, Numba-CUDA provides APIs to select and query GPUs. The cuda.select_device function sets the current context to a specific GPU:

```
from numba import cuda

# Query the number of available GPUs
num_gpus = cuda.gpus.lst

for i in range(num_gpus):
    with cuda.select_device(i):
        # Perform some operations on GPU i
        gpu_memory = cuda.device_array((1024,), dtype=np.float32)
        my_kernel[blocks, threads_per_block](gpu_memory)
```

Efficient implementation of parallel algorithms requires understanding the underlying architecture of CUDA. For example, reduction operations (e.g., sum, max) are common in parallel programming, and efficient implementations can significantly impact performance. Below is an example of a parallel reduction kernel that sums an array of elements:

```
@cuda.jit
def parallel_sum(data, result):
    shared_memory = cuda.shared.array(1024, dtype=numba.float32)
    tid = cuda.threadIdx.x
    bid = cuda.blockIdx.x
    bdim = cuda.blockDim.x

    start = bid * bdim * 2 + tid
    stride = bdim

    # Each thread loads two elements into shared memory
    shared_memory[tid] = data[start] + data[start + stride]
    cuda.syncthreads()

    # Perform reduction in shared memory
    step = stride // 2
    while step > 0:
        if tid < step:
            shared_memory[tid] += shared_memory[tid + step]
        cuda.syncthreads()
        step //= 2

    # Write the result for this block to global memory
    if tid == 0:
        result[bid] = shared_memory[0]
```

In practice, handling edge cases and adapting this basic structure for different reduction operations is necessary for optimal performance.

Advanced performance tuning also involves exploiting warp-level primitives, which allow fine-grained synchronization and data sharing among threads within a warp. Numba-CUDA provides intrinsic functions such as cuda.warp_shfl for warp shuffling, which can be used in algorithms like parallel reductions to minimize latency.

Integrating Numba-CUDA with other high-performance libraries, such as cuBLAS for linear algebra operations and cuFFT for fast Fourier transforms, can further enhance the capabilities of your applications. Numba allows calling these libraries directly from your CUDA kernels:

```
from numba import cuda
from scipy.cuda.cublas import cublasSgemm
from scipy.cuda import cublas_handle

# Initialize cuBLAS handle
handle = cublas_handle()

# Define matrices for multiplication
A = np.random.randn(1024, 1024).astype(np.float32)
B = np.random.randn(1024, 1024).astype(np.float32)
C = np.zeros((1024, 1024), dtype=np.float32)

# Transfer matrices to GPU
d_A = cuda.to_device(A)
d_B = cuda.to_device(B)
d_C = cuda.to_device(C)

# Perform matrix multiplication
alpha = 1.0
beta = 0.0
cublasSgemm(handle, 'N', 'N', 1024, 1024, 1024, alpha, d_A, 1024, d_B, 1024, beta,
        d_C, 1024)

# Copy result back to host
C = d_C.copy_to_host()
```

Understanding these advanced Numba-CUDA techniques is essential for developing highly efficient and scalable GPU-accelerated applications. By mastering memory management, using streams, conducting multi-GPU programming, leveraging warp-level primitives, and integrating high-performance libraries, one can unlock the full potential of CUDA programming with Python.

Chapter 8

Advanced CUDA Programming Techniques

This chapter explores advanced CUDA programming techniques aimed at maximizing performance. It covers the use of streams for concurrent execution, asynchronous memory transfers, and dynamic parallelism. It discusses CUDA graphs and task management, efficient memory management strategies, and optimizing data transfers. The chapter also examines advanced CUDA libraries, leveraging Thrust for high-level algorithms, and interoperability with other GPU APIs. Profiling and advanced analysis techniques are included to ensure comprehensive performance tuning.

8.1 Introduction to Advanced CUDA Programming

Advanced CUDA programming is characterized by techniques that push the boundaries of a GPU's performance capabilities. This section presents concepts vital for understanding how to enhance the efficiency of GPU computation, starting from fundamental principles previously covered to more complex, high-level strategies aimed at performance optimization.

To effectively leverage the GPU architecture, it is crucial to understand how to exploit parallelism at various levels. This encompasses kernel optimization, concurrent execution management, and advanced memory handling techniques that reduce latency and increase throughput. Each strategy involves a sophisticated understanding of the internal workings of CUDA and the GPU hardware.

When using streams, for instance, we enable concurrent execution of multiple CUDA operations. A stream in CUDA is a sequence of commands that execute in order. Utilizing multiple streams allows these sequences to overlap, thereby maximizing the GPU resource utilization. This concurrency can be extended to both computational and memory transfer operations, enabling the hiding of memory transfer latencies behind computation.

```
import numpy as np
from numba import cuda

@cuda.jit
def kernel_function(data):
    idx = cuda.grid(1)
    if idx < data.size:
        data[idx] += 1

# Initialize data
data = np.zeros((10000,), dtype=np.float32)
d_data = cuda.to_device(data)

# Creating Streams
stream1 = cuda.stream()
stream2 = cuda.stream()

# Asynchronous Kernel Execution
kernel_function[64, 1024, stream1](d_data)
kernel_function[64, 1024, stream2](d_data)

cuda.synchronize()
```

The code snippet above demonstrates how to create and utilize streams to run kernels asynchronously. The cuda.stream() command initializes a stream, and by specifying the stream in the kernel launch, kernels can be executed concurrently.

Asynchronous memory transfers provide another method to optimize performance by overlapping computation and data movement. CUDA supports asynchronous copies, which do not block the host code and allow kernel execution and memory transfers to happen simultaneously if managed correctly.

```
# Initializing host and device arrays
h_data = np.random.rand(100000).astype(np.float32)
d_data = cuda.device_array_like(h_data)

# Asynchronous transfer from host to device
```

```
cuda.to_device(h_data, to=d_data, stream=stream1)

# Concurrently run kernel on another stream
kernel_function[64, 1024, stream2](d_data)

# Synchronize to ensure all operations are completed
stream1.synchronize()
stream2.synchronize()
```

Through this example, the cuda.to_device() function is instructed to use a particular stream for asynchronous data transfers while allowing the kernel executed under a separate stream to proceed concurrently. Proper synchronization points ensure the correctness of concurrent operations.

Dynamic parallelism, another advanced feature of CUDA, allows kernel functions to launch other kernels directly from the GPU without returning control to the CPU. This capability is essential for problems that exhibit irregular parallelism or require nested parallelism, such as adaptive mesh refinement or hierarchical computations. This feature facilitates more work being offloaded to the GPU, further reducing the CPU-GPU interaction overhead.

Ensuring efficient memory management is a fundamental aspect of advanced CUDA programming. This involves leveraging shared memory, constant memory, and registers within the GPU effectively. Shared memory is particularly crucial as it provides high-bandwidth, low-latency data storage shared among threads within the same thread block. This can significantly reduce global memory accesses if utilized properly.

```
@cuda.jit
def shared_memory_kernel(result, data):
    shared_array = cuda.shared.array(shape=0, dtype=numba.float32)
    tx = cuda.threadIdx.x
    shared_array[tx] = data[tx]
    cuda.syncthreads()

    # Apply some computation on shared data
    result[tx] = shared_array[tx] * 2
```

The example above showcases the use of shared memory within a CUDA kernel. Shared memory arrays are declared using cuda.shared.array, and cuda.syncthreads() ensures synchronization among threads in the same block, avoiding race conditions during shared data access.

We also delve into the optimization of data transfers, focusing on minimizing the amount of data transferred between the host and device and maximizing the throughput of these transfers. Techniques like using page-locked memory can accelerate data transfer rates, and understanding the correct application of memory types (e.g., using pinned memory for frequently accessed data) can lead to substantial performance improvements.

By integrating these advanced techniques, CUDA programmers can unlock the full potential of GPU hardware, achieving performance that meets the demands of complex computational tasks. This foundation allows for further in-depth exploration of CUDA functionalities, such as efficient task management with CUDA graphs, exploiting advanced library functions, and conducting detailed metric analyses through profiling.

8.2 Using Streams for Concurrent Execution

Streams in CUDA are sequences of operations that are executed in order on the device. By default, CUDA uses a single stream, known as the default stream or stream 0. However, for performance-sensitive applications, it is essential to utilize multiple streams to exploit the hardware's parallelism better. Using multiple streams allows for overlapping computation and data transfers, leading to improved overall execution time.

A CUDA stream is essentially a sequence of commands that execute in order. The application can define dependencies between different tasks by grouping them into different streams. When multiple streams are used, tasks within the same stream execute sequentially, while tasks in different streams can execute concurrently if there are no resource conflicts.

To create and use CUDA streams, the cudaStreamCreate() and cudaStreamDestroy() functions are used. These functions allow for creating and managing streams within the application. Here is a basic example demonstrating how to create and destroy a CUDA stream:

```
cudaStream_t myStream;
cudaStreamCreate(&myStream);
// Perform operations using myStream
cudaStreamDestroy(myStream);
```

CUDA streams facilitate concurrent execution by allowing multiple kernels to run simultaneously if they are issued to different streams. Similarly, data transfers between the host and device can overlap with kernel execution when carried out on separate streams. The following example demonstrates how to overlap data transfer and kernel execution using streams:

```
cudaStream_t stream1, stream2;
cudaStreamCreate(&stream1);
cudaStreamCreate(&stream2);

float *d_A, *h_A, *d_B;
size_t size = N * sizeof(float);

// Allocate memory on device and host
cudaMalloc((void**)&d_A, size);
cudaMalloc((void**)&d_B, size);
h_A = (float*)malloc(size);

// Asynchronously copy data from host to device
cudaMemcpyAsync(d_A, h_A, size, cudaMemcpyHostToDevice, stream1);

// Launch a kernel in stream1
myKernel<<<gridSize, blockSize, 0, stream1>>>(d_A);

// Launch another kernel in stream2
myOtherKernel<<<gridSize, blockSize, 0, stream2>>>(d_B);

// Asynchronously copy data from device to host
cudaMemcpyAsync(h_A, d_B, size, cudaMemcpyDeviceToHost, stream2);

// Synchronize streams
cudaStreamSynchronize(stream1);
cudaStreamSynchronize(stream2);

// Cleanup
cudaFree(d_A);
cudaFree(d_B);
free(h_A);

cudaStreamDestroy(stream1);
cudaStreamDestroy(stream2);
```

In this example, two streams stream1 and stream2 are created. Data transfer operations and kernel launches are associated with different streams, enabling overlapping execution and data transfer.

When employing multiple streams, it is crucial to understand the device's concurrent execution capabilities. Modern NVIDIA GPUs support concurrent kernel execution and simultaneous data transfer with kernel execution, but the exact capabilities can vary based on the GPU architecture. To check a device's concurrent execution capabilities, use the CUDA device properties:

```
cudaDeviceProp deviceProp;
cudaGetDeviceProperties(&deviceProp, 0);
printf("Concurrent Kernels: %d\n", deviceProp.concurrentKernels);
printf("Concurrent Copy and Kernel Execution: %d\n", deviceProp.deviceOverlap);
```

By leveraging streams, programmers can increase the GPU's utilization and reduce idle times. This approach significantly boosts performance, mainly when kernels or data transfers are not fully utilizing the hardware resources. It is also possible to synchronize streams using cudaEvent_t events, providing finer control over the execution order of operations across multiple streams.

Events in CUDA serve as synchronization points, allowing the creation of dependencies between streams. The following example illustrates how to use CUDA events to synchronize different streams:

```
cudaStream_t stream1, stream2;
cudaEvent_t event;
cudaStreamCreate(&stream1);
cudaStreamCreate(&stream2);
cudaEventCreate(&event);

float *d_A, *h_A, *d_B;
size_t size = N * sizeof(float);

cudaMalloc((void**)&d_A, size);
cudaMalloc((void**)&d_B, size);
h_A = (float*)malloc(size);

cudaMemcpyAsync(d_A, h_A, size, cudaMemcpyHostToDevice, stream1);
myKernel<<<gridSize, blockSize, 0, stream1>>>(d_A);

// Record an event in stream1
cudaEventRecord(event, stream1);

// Ensure stream2 waits for event to be recorded
cudaStreamWaitEvent(stream2, event, 0);
myOtherKernel<<<gridSize, blockSize, 0, stream2>>>(d_B);

cudaMemcpyAsync(h_A, d_B, size, cudaMemcpyDeviceToHost, stream2);

cudaStreamSynchronize(stream1);
cudaStreamSynchronize(stream2);

cudaFree(d_A);
cudaFree(d_B);
free(h_A);
cudaStreamDestroy(stream1);
cudaStreamDestroy(stream2);
cudaEventDestroy(event);
```

In this example, cudaEventRecord() and cudaStreamWaitEvent() are used to control the execution order between stream1 and stream2. This ensures that the task in stream2 does not commence until the event recorded in stream1 is completed.

Proper use of streams and events allows full exploitation of the GPU's capacities, promoting high efficiency and throughput in computational tasks. Exploring different patterns of stream employment—such as pipeline parallelism and task parallelism—can yield substantial performance improvements in various CUDA applications.

8.3 Asynchronous Memory Transfers

In CUDA programming, efficient memory management is critical to achieving high performance. One of the advanced techniques for optimizing memory operations is the use of asynchronous memory transfers. Asynchronous memory transfers allow for overlapping data transfers between the host (CPU) and device (GPU) with computation, thereby minimizing idle times and maximizing overall throughput. This section delves into the principles, implementation, and best practices of utilizing asynchronous memory transfers in CUDA.

Asynchronous memory transfers are accomplished using non-blocking memory copy functions provided by the CUDA runtime API. Unlike synchronous operations, where the host is blocked until the transfer is completed, asynchronous operations return control to the host immediately after the transfer is initiated. This enables the CPU to perform other tasks while the data transfer is completed in the background.

The primary CUDA functions used for asynchronous memory transfers are cudaMemcpyAsync() and cudaMemcpy2DAsync(). These functions are similar to their synchronous counterparts cudaMemcpy() and cudaMemcpy2D(), but they include an additional stream parameter to specify the stream in which the asynchronous operation is to be executed. A CUDA stream is a sequence of operations that are executed in order on the device. By using multiple streams, different data transfers and kernel executions can overlap.

The usage of cudaMemcpyAsync() is illustrated below:

```
cudaError_t cudaMemcpyAsync(
  void* dst,
  const void* src,
  size_t count,
  cudaMemcpyKind kind,
  cudaStream_t stream = 0
);
```

Parameters:

- dst - Destination memory address on either the host or device.
- src - Source memory address on either the host or device.
- count - Size in bytes to copy.

- kind - Direction of the copy (e.g., cudaMemcpyHostToDevice, cudaMemcpyDeviceToHost, cudaMemcpyDeviceToDevice).

- stream - The CUDA stream in which the transfer should be performed.

An example usage of cudaMemcpyAsync() for transferring data from host to device is as follows:

```
float* h_data; // Host data
float* d_data; // Device data
size_t size = 1024 * sizeof(float);

// Allocate host memory
h_data = (float*)malloc(size);

// Allocate device memory
cudaMalloc((void**)&d_data, size);

// Initialize data on host
for (int i = 0; i < 1024; ++i) {
    h_data[i] = static_cast<float>(i);
}

// Create a CUDA stream
cudaStream_t stream;
cudaStreamCreate(&stream);

// Perform asynchronous copy from host to device
cudaMemcpyAsync(d_data, h_data, size, cudaMemcpyHostToDevice, stream);

// Perform other CPU tasks while copy is in progress
perform_other_cpu_tasks();

// Synchronize the stream to ensure copy is complete
cudaStreamSynchronize(stream);

// Free resources
cudaStreamDestroy(stream);
cudaFree(d_data);
free(h_data);
```

The above code snippet demonstrates a simple usage of cudaMemcpyAsync() where data is transferred from host to device asynchronously. The cudaStreamCreate() function creates a new stream, and cudaStreamSynchronize() ensures that the transfer is complete before proceeding. By overlapping the data transfer with other CPU tasks, overall application efficiency can be improved.

Asynchronous memory transfers are particularly beneficial in applications that involve large data sets, where the cost of data transfer between the host and device can become a performance bottleneck. By concurrently executing data transfers and computations, the total execution time can be reduced significantly.

Best practices for using asynchronous memory transfers include:

- **Pinned Memory Allocation:** Pinned (or page-locked) memory allocation using cudaHostAlloc() enables more efficient data transfers as it avoids the overhead of pageable memory. Pinned memory allows for direct memory access (DMA) transfers between the host and device.

```
float* h_pinned_data;
cudaHostAlloc((void**)&h_pinned_data, size, cudaHostAllocDefault);
```

- **Stream Synchronization:** While it's essential to overlap data transfers with computations, proper stream synchronization is crucial to ensure data integrity and correct program execution. Use cudaStreamSynchronize() or cudaEventSynchronize() to manage dependencies and to ensure operations complete in the desired order.

- **Multiple Streams:** Utilizing multiple CUDA streams can increase the overlap of data transfers and kernel execution. Different streams can independently execute, allowing more concurrency.

```
cudaStream_t stream1, stream2;
cudaStreamCreate(&stream1);
cudaStreamCreate(&stream2);

// Asynchronously copy data in different streams
cudaMemcpyAsync(d_data1, h_data1, size, cudaMemcpyHostToDevice, stream1
    );
cudaMemcpyAsync(d_data2, h_data2, size, cudaMemcpyHostToDevice, stream2
    );
```

- **Using Events for Profiling and Synchronization:** CUDA events can be used to measure the time taken by asynchronous operations and to synchronize between streams. Events provide fine-grained control over the execution flow.

```
cudaEvent_t start, stop;
cudaEventCreate(&start);
cudaEventCreate(&stop);

cudaEventRecord(start, stream);
// Execute asynchronous operations here
cudaEventRecord(stop, stream);

cudaEventSynchronize(stop);
float milliseconds = 0;
cudaEventElapsedTime(&milliseconds, start, stop);

cudaEventDestroy(start);
cudaEventDestroy(stop);
```

By strategically using asynchronous memory transfers in CUDA applications, developers can achieve significant performance improvements, especially in scenarios involving large data movements and computation-intensive tasks. Proper implementation and optimization of these techniques can lead to substantial reductions in the overall execution time of GPU-accelerated applications.

8.4 Dynamic Parallelism in CUDA

Dynamic parallelism is a powerful feature introduced in recent versions of CUDA, allowing a kernel to spawn new kernels directly from the GPU without returning control to the CPU. This capability enables a variety of sophisticated algorithms such as recursive algorithms and adaptive task subdivision, enhancing overall application performance and flexibility.

Dynamic parallelism is particularly useful in scenarios where the data and computational workload are not known a priori and may change dynamically during execution. This section delves into the fundamental concepts, usage patterns, and practical examples of dynamic parallelism in CUDA programming.

Kernel Launching from GPU: The primary distinction of dynamic parallelism is the ability to launch kernels from within other kernels. This is accomplished using the same syntax as launching kernels from the host with an additional qualification to denote device-side launching. Below is an example illustrating device-side kernel launching in CUDA:

```
#include <cuda_runtime.h>
#include <stdio.h>

// Kernel to be called dynamically
__global__ void dynamicKernel(int depth) {
    printf("Depth: %d, Thread: %d\n", depth, threadIdx.x);
    if (depth > 0) {
        dynamicKernel<<<1, 1>>>(depth - 1);
        cudaDeviceSynchronize();
    }
}

// Launching kernel from the host
__global__ void masterKernel(int depth) {
    dynamicKernel<<<1, 1>>>(depth);
}

int main() {
    int initialDepth = 3;
    masterKernel<<<1, 1>>>(initialDepth);
    cudaDeviceSynchronize();
```

```
    return 0;
}
```

In this example, 'dynamicKernel' calls itself recursively until the condition 'depth > 0' becomes false. The use of 'cudaDeviceSynchronize()' ensures that the dynamically launched kernel completes execution before the next line of code is executed.

Resource Management: When using dynamic parallelism, managing computational resources efficiently is crucial to avoid deadlocks and ensure optimal performance. Since each kernel launch consumes resource blocks such as threads, shared memory, and register files, excessive nested kernel launches can exhaust available resources. Therefore, careful consideration of kernel resource requirements and utilization is essential.

Handling Synchronization and Dependencies: Synchronization in dynamically parallel programs requires attention to the sequencing and completion of nested kernels. The 'cudaDeviceSynchronize()' function plays an important role in this context by ensuring synchronization at the device level. However, improper use of synchronization can lead to significant performance degradation.

Performance Considerations: The overhead of launching kernels dynamically from the GPU should be considered when deciding to use dynamic parallelism. Each kernel launch incurs a certain amount of latency, and this can affect overall performance if not managed properly. Combining efficient resource allocation, optimal thread block sizes, and careful synchronization can mitigate these overheads.

A practical approach to understanding the performance implications of dynamic parallelism involves the use of CUDA profilers and analytical tools. These tools provide insights into kernel execution times, resource utilization, and identify potential performance bottlenecks.

Example: Adaptive Mesh Refinement (AMR): A typical application of dynamic parallelism is the adaptive mesh refinement used in computational fluid dynamics (CFD). The following example demonstrates how to adaptively subdivide a computational domain based on localized criteria.

```
#include <cuda_runtime.h>
#include <stdio.h>

// Kernel to refine mesh adaptively
__global__ void refineMesh(float* data, int currentLevel, int maxLevel) {
    int idx = blockIdx.x * blockDim.x + threadIdx.x;
    if (currentLevel < maxLevel && data[idx] > threshold) {
```

```
        printf("Refining at index: %d, level: %d\n", idx, currentLevel);
        refineMesh<<<2, blockDim.x>>>(data, currentLevel + 1, maxLevel);
        cudaDeviceSynchronize();
    }
}

int main() {
    int dataSize = 1024;
    float* d_data;
    cudaMalloc(&d_data, dataSize * sizeof(float));

    int maxRefineLevels = 3;
    refineMesh<<<1, 1024>>>(d_data, 0, maxRefineLevels);
    cudaDeviceSynchronize();

    cudaFree(d_data);
    return 0;
}
```

In this code, the 'refineMesh' function recursively refines the mesh based on a specified condition (e.g., value in 'data[idx]' exceeds 'threshold'). This mechanism allows for dynamic adaptability of computational effort to regions requiring higher resolution.

Examining execution traces and profile reports using NVIDIA's Nsight tools can reveal insights into nested kernel execution timings, efficiency of GPU resource utilization, and potential bottlenecks.

Dynamic parallelism presents significant opportunities for enabling complex, adaptive algorithms directly on the GPU. The flexibility to launch and manage tasks dynamically empowers developers to design highly efficient and scalable GPU applications.

8.5 CUDA Graphs and Task Management

CUDA graphs represent a robust mechanism to define and enforce the execution order of a series of dependent operations. The CUDA Graph API offers a model to create a directed acyclic graph (DAG) of nodes that represent operations, and edges that signify dependencies between the nodes. This model provides more granular control over task scheduling compared to traditional stream-based execution.

One key advantage of CUDA graphs is the ability to encapsulate complex workflows, minimizing the overhead of kernel launches while optimizing the execution flow. This results in improved performance, especially for complex applications that exhibit significant inter-kernel dependencies.

Creating CUDA Graphs

A CUDA graph is created using cudaGraphCreate, which initializes an empty graph structure where nodes can later be added. Each node can represent various operations such as kernel launches, memory copies, or host-to-device synchronizations. The following code illustrates the initialization of a CUDA graph:

```
cudaGraph_t graph;
cudaGraphCreate(&graph, 0);
```

Upon graph creation, nodes are added using functions that specify the operation type. For instance, a kernel node requires specifying the kernel function, grid and block dimensions, and kernel parameters. The following example demonstrates adding a simple kernel node to a graph:

```
cudaKernelNodeParams kernelNodeParams = {0};
kernelNodeParams.func = (void*)myKernelFunction;
kernelNodeParams.gridDim = dim3(1, 1, 1);
kernelNodeParams.blockDim = dim3(256, 1, 1);
kernelNodeParams.sharedMemBytes = 0;
kernelNodeParams.kernelParams = (void**)&kernelArgs;
cudaGraphNode_t kernelNode;
cudaGraphAddKernelNode(&kernelNode, graph, NULL, 0, &kernelNodeParams);
```

Specifying Dependencies

Dependencies between the nodes are critical for task management within CUDA graphs. Dependencies ensure that nodes are executed in a correct and efficient order. The CUDA Graph API uses edges to represent these dependencies. An edge is typically added when incorporating a new node, specifying predecessor nodes that must complete before the new node executes. Here is an example defining dependencies:

```
cudaGraphNode_t dependencies[] = {firstKernelNode};
cudaGraphAddKernelNode(&secondKernelNode, graph, dependencies, 1, &
    kernelNodeParams);
```

Instantiating and Launching CUDA Graphs

Once the graph is fully defined, it must be instantiated and launched. Instantiation converts the graph into an executable form, which can then be launched on a specified stream. Here is a typical instantiation and launch process:

```
cudaGraphExec_t graphExec;
cudaGraphInstantiate(&graphExec, graph, NULL, NULL, 0);
cudaStream_t stream;
cudaStreamCreate(&stream);
cudaGraphLaunch(graphExec, stream);
```

```
cudaStreamSynchronize(stream);
```

Updating CUDA Graphs

CUDA Graphs provide the ability to make dynamic updates without the need to reconstruct the entire graph, facilitating modifications and enhancements post-creation. The cudaGraphExecKernelNodeSetParams function can update parameters of existing kernel nodes:

```
cudaKernelNodeParams newParams = {0};
newParams.func = (void*)newKernelFunction;
cudaGraphExecKernelNodeSetParams(graphExec, existingKernelNode, &newParams);
```

Task Management and Performance Optimization

Effective task management involves organizing nodes to minimize idle GPU periods, increasing computation overlap, and improving data transfer timing. CUDA Graphs implicitly enhance task management by structuring the tasks in a DAG and permitting optimizations at the graph level.

Graphs aid in reducing kernel launch overhead and allow for peer-to-peer (P2P) memory accesses, optimizing the data paths. Profoundly, the hierarchical breakdown of tasks into graphs provides clarity and flexibility in managing complex workflows.

CUDA Graphs and task management streamline numerous dynamic GPU operations in a predictable, efficient manner, driven by the structural and performance-optimization benefits inherent in DAG representations. By leveraging these advanced methodologies, developers can substantially improve both the performance and maintainability of intricate CUDA applications.

Ensuring the fine-grained control over tasks and their dependencies furthers precision in execution, making CUDA graphs an indispensable advanced programming technique.

8.6 Efficient Memory Management Techniques

Efficient memory management is crucial for optimizing CUDA programming performance. Proper memory handling reduces latency, enhances bandwidth utilization, and maximizes computational throughput. This section delves into advanced memory management techniques in

CUDA, focusing on memory types, access patterns, allocation strategies, and best practices to minimize data transfer overhead.

Memory Types in CUDA

CUDA supports several types of memory, each with unique attributes and suitable use cases:

- **Global Memory:** This is the main memory accessible by all threads and has the largest capacity. However, it has the highest latency.
- **Shared Memory:** This is a block-local memory, allowing threads within the same block to share data. It has lower latency compared to global memory and is suitable for data reuse within blocks.
- **Register Memory:** Registers are the fastest form of memory, local to individual threads. They provide minimal latency but have limited capacity.
- **Constant Memory:** This read-only memory is cached and suitable for data that remains unchanged across threads, offering efficient broadcast capability.
- **Texture Memory:** This read-only memory is optimized for spatial locality and is beneficial for certain data access patterns, like 2D grid-based data.

Memory Access Patterns

An efficient memory access pattern can dramatically improve performance by ensuring coalesced access to global memory and maximizing the utilization of shared and register memory.

- **Coalescing Global Memory Access:** Ensure that threads in a warp access sequential memory addresses to achieve coalesced memory access, which allows the hardware to combine multiple data requests into a single transaction.
- **Aligning Data Structures:** Structure data in memory to match warp access patterns, ideally aligning data structures to match memory transactions.

- **Using Shared Memory Wisely:** Allocate shared memory to frequently accessed data to reduce the number of global memory accesses. Reuse shared memory efficiently within blocks to amortize latency over multiple accesses.
- **Optimizing Bank Conflicts:** Prevent shared memory bank conflicts by ensuring that threads do not access memory locations in the same memory bank simultaneously.

Memory Allocation Strategies

CUDA provides several allocation mechanisms for different memory types. Selecting the appropriate allocation strategy is essential for efficient program execution.

- **Static Allocation:** This method allows for the allocation of memory at compile time, typically using __constant__ and __device__ keywords.
- **Dynamic Allocation:** Memory can be allocated at runtime using functions like cudaMalloc and cudaFree. This allows for flexible memory management but may introduce overhead if frequent allocations are needed.

```
float *d_array;
cudaMalloc((void **)&d_array, size * sizeof(float));
// Perform computations
cudaFree(d_array);
```

Zero-Copy Memory: Zero-copy memory allows CUDA to access host memory directly without copying data to the device. This is useful for applications that require frequent access to small data sets.

```
float *h_array;
cudaHostAlloc((void **)&h_array, size * sizeof(float), cudaHostAllocMapped);
cudaMemcpy(h_array, src_data, size * sizeof(float), cudaMemcpyHostToDevice);
cudaFree(h_array);
```

Unified Memory: Unified memory simplifies memory management by allowing the allocation of memory that is shared between the host and the device. It is managed automatically by the CUDA runtime.

```
float *unified_array;
cudaMallocManaged(&unified_array, size * sizeof(float));
cudaDeviceSynchronize(); // To synchronize the unified memory usage
cudaFree(unified_array);
```

Pinned Memory: Using pinned (or page-locked) memory can significantly improve data transfer speeds between the host and the device by avoiding the overhead associated with pageable memory.

```
float *h_pinned_array;
cudaHostAlloc((void **)&h_pinned_array, size * sizeof(float), cudaHostAllocDefault);
cudaMemcpy(d_array, h_pinned_array, size * sizeof(float), cudaMemcpyHostToDevice
    );
cudaFreeHost(h_pinned_array);
```

Various strategies can be used to streamline data transfers and reduce latency, depending on the application's specific needs and the underlying hardware architecture.

Best Practices

The following best practices can ensure efficient memory management in CUDA:

- **Minimize Data Transfers:** Minimize data transfers between host and device wherever possible. Perform all necessary computations on the device to reduce overhead.

- **Overlap Computation and Data Transfers:** Use streams and asynchronous transfers to overlap data transfers with computations, ensuring that the device is never idle.

- **Profile and Optimize:** Use profiling tools to identify memory access patterns and optimize accordingly; this includes eliminating uncoalesced accesses and reducing the frequency of memory allocations and deallocations.

- **Leverage Memory Hierarchy:** Efficiently use the CUDA memory hierarchy, allocating data to the appropriate memory type based on access patterns and reuse.

- **Optimize Kernel Configuration:** Configure kernels to maximize occupancy and ensure efficient use of shared memory and registers.

Efficient memory management techniques are critical in optimizing CUDA applications. By understanding the different types of memory available within the CUDA architecture and employing strategies to maximize their respective advantages, developers can significantly improve the performance of their CUDA-based applications.

8.7 Optimizing Data Transfers

Efficient data transfer between the host (CPU) and the device (GPU) is crucial for achieving high performance in CUDA applications. Suboptimal data transfers can create significant bottlenecks that hinder the overall execution speed. This section delves into the techniques and strategies to optimize these transfers, with a focus on practical implementation and detailed explanation.

Data transfers in CUDA can be categorized into three main types: **host-to-device**, **device-to-host**, and **device-to-device**. Understanding the characteristics and best practices for each type is essential for optimization.

- **Host-to-Device Transfers:** Moving data from the CPU memory to the GPU memory.
- **Device-to-Host Transfers:** Moving data from the GPU memory back to the CPU memory.
- **Device-to-Device Transfers:** Moving data between different GPU memory spaces, which can be within the same GPU or across multiple GPUs.

Utilizing Pinned Memory

Pinned (or page-locked) memory is allocated such that it resides in a fixed physical location, unlike pageable memory which can be moved by the operating system. Using pinned memory for data transfers between host and device can significantly improve transfer speeds.

```
cudaError_t status;
int *hostData;
int size = 1000 * sizeof(int);

// Allocate pinned memory
status = cudaHostAlloc((void**)&hostData, size, cudaHostAllocDefault);

if (status != cudaSuccess) {
    fprintf(stderr, "Error allocating pinned memory: %s\n", cudaGetErrorString(status)
        );
}

// Initiating a host-to-device transfer using pinned memory
int *deviceData;
cudaMalloc((void**)&deviceData, size);
cudaMemcpy(deviceData, hostData, size, cudaMemcpyHostToDevice);

// Other operations...
```

```
// Free pinned memory
cudaFreeHost(hostData);
cudaFree(deviceData);
```

Pinned memory avoids the overhead associated with transferring data from pageable memory, which generally involves an additional copy operation. This optimization is particularly beneficial for large or frequent data transfers.

Leveraging Asynchronous Transfers with Streams

Asynchronous data transfers can overlap computation and data movement, reducing idle times of both the CPU and GPU. This is achievable using CUDA streams. CUDA streams allow for concurrent executions of kernels and memory operations. By default, CUDA operations are performed in stream 0 (the default stream), which imposes a sequential execution order. Custom streams enable overlapping operations.

```
cudaStream_t stream;
cudaStreamCreate(&stream);

int *hostData;
int *deviceData;
size_t size = 1000 * sizeof(int);

cudaHostAlloc(&hostData, size, cudaHostAllocDefault);
cudaMalloc(&deviceData, size);

// Asynchronous copy: Host to Device
cudaMemcpyAsync(deviceData, hostData, size, cudaMemcpyHostToDevice, stream);

// Perform other operations while data is being copied...
someFunction();

// Synchronize stream
cudaStreamSynchronize(stream);

// Clean up
cudaStreamDestroy(stream);
cudaFreeHost(hostData);
cudaFree(deviceData);
```

Operation SomeFunction is executed while the data is being transferred in the background, reducing the overall execution time.

Optimizing Transfer Size

For optimal data transfer performance, minimizing the number of transfers and maximizing the size of each transfer is advisable. Frequent small transfers incur higher overhead than fewer larger transfers. Batching data or aggregating smaller transfers into larger ones can be beneficial.

Peer-to-Peer Memory Copies

When utilizing multiple GPUs, leveraging peer-to-peer (P2P) memory copies can enhance the performance of inter-device communication. P2P memory allows one GPU to directly access the memory of another GPU without needing to pass through the host. Enabling P2P requires querying and activating support between the GPUs.

```
int deviceCount;
cudaGetDeviceCount(&deviceCount);
for (int i = 0; i < deviceCount; ++i) {
    for (int j = 0; j < deviceCount; ++j) {
        if (i != j) {
            int peerAccess;
            cudaDeviceCanAccessPeer(&peerAccess, i, j);
            if (peerAccess) {
                cudaSetDevice(i);
                cudaDeviceEnablePeerAccess(j, 0);
            }
        }
    }
}

// Device to Device copy using peer-to-peer
cudaSetDevice(0);
int *deviceData0, *deviceData1;
cudaMalloc(&deviceData0, size);
cudaSetDevice(1);
cudaMalloc(&deviceData1, size);
cudaMemcpy(deviceData1, deviceData0, size, cudaMemcpyDeviceToDevice);
```

Using Unified Memory

Unified Memory simplifies data management by providing a single memory space accessible by both the host and the device. The CUDA runtime handles data migration between the host and device transparently, which can simplify code and improve performance under specific conditions.

```
int *unifiedData;
size_t size = 1000 * sizeof(int);
cudaMallocManaged(&unifiedData, size);

// Use unifiedData on both CPU and GPU
someCPUFunction(unifiedData);

someGPUKernel<<<blocks, threads>>>(unifiedData);

// Clean up
cudaFree(unifiedData);
```

Using Unified Memory is particularly advantageous when datasets have irregular access patterns, as it allows CUDA to optimize data placement dynamically.

Incorporating these techniques into your CUDA applications can significantly enhance data transfer efficiency, reducing latency and increasing overall performance.

8.8 Advanced CUDA Libraries and Frameworks

CUDA offers an extensive array of libraries and frameworks designed to optimize and accelerate various computational tasks. These libraries and frameworks are essential for developers aiming to harness the maximum potential of GPU resources with minimal effort. Prominent libraries include cuBLAS, cuFFT, cuDNN, and Thrust, each tailored for specific types of computations. Leveraging these libraries not only saves development time but also ensures that applications benefit from highly optimized and reliable code.

cuBLAS - CUDA Basic Linear Algebra Subroutines Library

cuBLAS is a GPU-accelerated library providing standard basic linear algebra subroutines (BLAS). It includes operations such as vector and matrix multiplication, matrix factorization, and solving linear systems. The integration of cuBLAS into CUDA applications facilitates highly efficient and scalable linear algebra computations.

Example usage of cuBLAS to perform matrix multiplication:

```
import numpy as np
import cupy as cp
from cupy.cuda import cublas

# Initialize cuBLAS handle
handle = cublas.create()

# Define matrices
A = cp.array(np.random.randn(3, 3).astype(np.float32))
B = cp.array(np.random.randn(3, 3).astype(np.float32))
C = cp.empty_like(A)

# Perform matrix multiplication: C = A * B
alpha = np.float32(1.0)
beta = np.float32(0.0)
cublas.sgemm(handle, 'N', 'N', A.shape[0], B.shape[1], A.shape[1], alpha, A.data.ptr, A.
    shape[0], B.data.ptr, B.shape[0], beta, C.data.ptr, C.shape[0])

# Destroy cuBLAS handle
cublas.destroy(handle)
```

cuFFT - CUDA Fast Fourier Transform Library

cuFFT provides GPU-accelerated Fast Fourier Transform (FFT) operations. It supports 1D, 2D, and 3D transforms with real and complex data types. cuFFT is essential in applications involving signal processing, image processing, and solving partial differential equations.

Example usage of cuFFT to compute a 1D FFT:

```
import cupy as cp
from cupy.fft import fft, ifft

# Create a random signal
signal = cp.random.random(1024).astype(cp.complex64)

# Perform FFT
fft_signal = fft(signal)

# Perform inverse FFT
ifft_signal = ifft(fft_signal)
```

cuDNN - CUDA Deep Neural Network Library

cuDNN is a GPU-accelerated library specifically designed for deep learning. It provides highly optimized routines for deep neural networks, including convolutional layers, pooling layers, and activation functions. By integrating cuDNN, developers can significantly enhance the performance of deep learning models.

Example usage of cuDNN for a convolution operation:

```
import cupy as cp
from cupy.cuda import cudnn

# Initialize cuDNN handle
handle = cudnn.create()

# Define inputs and filters
input_data = cp.random.rand(1, 1, 28, 28).astype(cp.float32)
filters = cp.random.rand(10, 1, 5, 5).astype(cp.float32)
output = cp.empty((1, 10, 24, 24), dtype=cp.float32)

# Create descriptors
input_desc = cudnn.createTensorDescriptor()
filter_desc = cudnn.createFilterDescriptor()
output_desc = cudnn.createTensorDescriptor()

# Set descriptors
cudnn.setTensor4dDescriptor(input_desc, cudnn.CUDNN_TENSOR_NCHW, cudnn.
    CUDNN_DATA_FLOAT, 1, 1, 28, 28)
cudnn.setFilter4dDescriptor(filter_desc, cudnn.CUDNN_DATA_FLOAT, cudnn.
    CUDNN_TENSOR_NCHW, 10, 1, 5, 5)
cudnn.setTensor4dDescriptor(output_desc, cudnn.CUDNN_TENSOR_NCHW, cudnn.
    CUDNN_DATA_FLOAT, 1, 10, 24, 24)

# Define convolution
conv_desc = cudnn.createConvolutionDescriptor()
cudnn.setConvolution2dDescriptor(conv_desc, 0, 0, 1, 1, 1, 1, cudnn.
    CUDNN_CONVOLUTION, cudnn.CUDNN_DATA_FLOAT)

# Perform convolution
cudnn.convolutionForward(handle, cp.float32(1.0), input_desc, input_data.data.ptr,
    filter_desc, filters.data.ptr, conv_desc, cudnn.
```

```
    CUDNN_CONVOLUTION_FWD_ALGO_IMPLICIT_GEMM, None, 0, cp.
    float32(0.0), output_desc, output.data.ptr)

# Destroy descriptors and handle
cudnn.destroyTensorDescriptor(input_desc)
cudnn.destroyFilterDescriptor(filter_desc)
cudnn.destroyConvolutionDescriptor(conv_desc)
cudnn.destroy(handle)
```

Thrust - High-Level Parallel Algorithms Library

Thrust is a GPU-accelerated library providing high-level parallel primitives such as sort, scan, and reduce. It resembles the C++ Standard Template Library (STL) but is tailored for CUDA, allowing developers to write parallel algorithms in a high-level, expressive, and reusable manner.

Example usage of Thrust to sort an array:

```
import cupy as cp
import numpy as np
from cupy import prof

# Create a random array
data = cp.array(np.random.randn(10000).astype(np.float32))

# Sort the array using Thrust
cp.sort(data)
```

These libraries enable the implementation of complex algorithms and models with minimal code modifications and maximized performance. Utilizing them is a best practice for any CUDA developer aiming to achieve high efficiency and maintainability in GPU-accelerated applications.

8.9 Using Thrust for High-Level Algorithms

Thrust is a powerful CUDA library for C++ that provides a rich collection of data parallel primitives such as transform, reduce, and sort, which can significantly simplify the implementation of complex parallel algorithms. This section delves into the integration of Thrust with Python through the use of the PyCUDA library, allowing Python programmers to harness the capabilities of Thrust to optimize performance-critical sections of their code. To illustrate the integration and usage of Thrust, practical examples including common high-level algorithms will be provided.

Introduction to Thrust: Thrust offers a STL-like (Standard Template

Library) interface that enables concise, readable, and efficient parallel code. It supports both host (CPU) and device (GPU) backends, making it a flexible choice for high-performance computing. Example operations that are supported by Thrust include map, scan, sort, and reduce.

Setup and Integration with PyCUDA: To use Thrust in a Python environment, the PyCUDA library provides an interface to write CUDA kernels and also to execute them. First, ensure that PyCUDA is installed:

```
pip install pycuda
```

One typically writes a custom kernel that includes Thrust operations within a CUDA file (*.cu), and then compiles and runs this file using PyCUDA from within the Python ecosystem.

Example: Vector Addition using Thrust: Consider a simple example where we perform vector addition. The goal is to add two arrays element-wise and store the result in a third array using Thrust.

The CUDA kernel code (vector_addition.cu):

```
#include <thrust/device_vector.h>
#include <thrust/transform.h>
#include <thrust/functional.h>

extern "C" {
    void vector_add(int* A, int* B, int* C, int N) {
        thrust::device_vector<int> d_A(A, A + N);
        thrust::device_vector<int> d_B(B, B + N);
        thrust::device_vector<int> d_C(N);

        thrust::transform(d_A.begin(), d_A.end(), d_B.begin(), d_C.begin(), thrust::
            plus<int>());

        thrust::copy(d_C.begin(), d_C.end(), C);
    }
}
```

Compile the CUDA kernel:

```
nvcc -shared -o vector_addition.so --shared -Xcompiler -fPIC vector_addition.cu
```

Next, we need to interface this compiled kernel with our Python code using PyCUDA.

The Python script (vector_addition.py):

```
import pycuda.driver as cuda
import pycuda.autoinit
import numpy as np
from ctypes import cdll, c_int, POINTER

# Load the compiled shared library
lib = cdll.LoadLibrary('./vector_addition.so')
```

```
# Define the vector_add function arguments
vector_add = lib.vector_add
vector_add.argtypes = [POINTER(c_int), POINTER(c_int), POINTER(c_int), c_int
    ]

# Define the input arrays
N = 10
A = np.array([1, 2, 3, 4, 5, 6, 7, 8, 9, 10], dtype=np.int32)
B = np.array([10, 9, 8, 7, 6, 5, 4, 3, 2, 1], dtype=np.int32)
C = np.zeros(N, dtype=np.int32)

# Allocate GPU memory and copy the data from CPU to GPU
d_A = cuda.mem_alloc(A.nbytes)
d_B = cuda.mem_alloc(B.nbytes)
d_C = cuda.mem_alloc(C.nbytes)

cuda.memcpy_htod(d_A, A)
cuda.memcpy_htod(d_B, B)

# Call the vector_add function
vector_add(d_A, d_B, d_C, N)

# Copy the result back to the host
cuda.memcpy_dtoh(C, d_C)
print("Result:", C)
```

```
Result: [11 11 11 11 11 11 11 11 11 11]
```

Efficient Reduction Operations: Reducing a large array to a single value is a common operation in many algorithms. Thrust simplifies this with its thrust::reduce function, which performs a reduction operation across an array.

The CUDA kernel code for reduction (reduction.cu):

```
#include <thrust/device_vector.h>
#include <thrust/reduce.h>

extern "C" {
    int reduce_sum(int* A, int N) {
        thrust::device_vector<int> d_A(A, A + N);
        int sum = thrust::reduce(d_A.begin(), d_A.end(), 0, thrust::plus<int>());
        return sum;
    }
}
```

Compile the CUDA kernel:

```
nvcc -shared -o reduction.so --shared -Xcompiler -fPIC reduction.cu
```

The Python script (reduction.py):

```
import pycuda.driver as cuda
import pycuda.autoinit
import numpy as np
```

```
from ctypes import cdll, c_int, POINTER

# Load the compiled shared library
lib = cdll.LoadLibrary('./reduction.so')

# Define the reduction_sum function arguments
reduce_sum = lib.reduce_sum
reduce_sum.argtypes = [POINTER(c_int), c_int]
reduce_sum.restype = c_int

# Define the input array
N = 10
A = np.array([1, 2, 3, 4, 5, 6, 7, 8, 9, 10], dtype=np.int32)

# Allocate GPU memory and copy the data from CPU to GPU
d_A = cuda.mem_alloc(A.nbytes)
cuda.memcpy_htod(d_A, A)

# Call the reduce_sum function
sum_result = reduce_sum(d_A, N)
print("Sum:", sum_result)
```

```
Sum: 55
```

Sorting with Thrust: Sorting is another fundamental operation that Thrust can efficiently handle using thrust::sort.

The CUDA kernel code for sorting (sorting.cu):

```
#include <thrust/device_vector.h>
#include <thrust/sort.h>

extern "C" {
    void sort_array(int* A, int N) {
        thrust::device_vector<int> d_A(A, A + N);
        thrust::sort(d_A.begin(), d_A.end());
        thrust::copy(d_A.begin(), d_A.end(), A);
    }
}
```

Compile the CUDA kernel:

```
nvcc -shared -o sorting.so --shared -Xcompiler -fPIC sorting.cu
```

The Python script (sorting.py):

```
import pycuda.driver as cuda
import pycuda.autoinit
import numpy as np
from ctypes import cdll, c_int, POINTER

# Load the compiled shared library
lib = cdll.LoadLibrary('./sorting.so')

# Define the sort_array function arguments
sort_array = lib.sort_array
sort_array.argtypes = [POINTER(c_int), c_int]
```

```
# Define the input array
N = 10
A = np.array([3, 1, 4, 1, 5, 9, 2, 6, 5, 3], dtype=np.int32)

# Allocate GPU memory and copy the data from CPU to GPU
d_A = cuda.mem_alloc(A.nbytes)
cuda.memcpy_htod(d_A, A)

# Call the sort_array function
sort_array(d_A, N)

# Copy the result back to the host
cuda.memcpy_dtoh(A, d_A)
print("Sorted Array:", A)
```

```
Sorted Array: [1 1 2 3 3 4 5 5 6 9]
```

Through these examples, we have shown the integration of Thrust with Python, allowing Python developers to take advantage of powerful GPU-accelerated primitives for high-performance computing tasks.

8.10 Interoperability with Other GPU APIs

Leveraging the full potential of GPU hardware often requires interoperability between CUDA and other GPU APIs. These APIs can facilitate various aspects of GPU programming, from graphics rendering with OpenGL and Direct3D to parallel computing frameworks like OpenCL. This section will delve into the mechanisms and best practices for achieving efficient interoperability, focusing on practical examples and code snippets to highlight key concepts.

To begin, interoperability between CUDA and OpenGL involves techniques for sharing GPU resources, such as buffers and textures, to minimize data transfers and maximize performance. Central to this process is the concept of shared contexts, which allow resources to be accessed seamlessly by both APIs.

Creating an interoperable CUDA-OpenGL context usually involves the following steps: 1. Initialize an OpenGL context. 2. Register OpenGL buffer objects with CUDA. 3. Map the buffer object to CUDA, allowing CUDA kernels to modify it. 4. Unmap the buffer object from CUDA when the computation is complete. 5. Use the updated buffer in the OpenGL rendering pipeline.

Here is an example code snippet demonstrating these steps:

```
#include <cuda_runtime.h>
#include <cuda_gl_interop.h>
#include <GL/glew.h>
#include <GL/glut.h>

// CUDA-OpenGL Vertex Buffer Object (VBO) initialization
GLuint vbo;
struct cudaGraphicsResource* vbo_res;

void createVBO(GLuint* vbo) {
    glGenBuffers(1, vbo);
    glBindBuffer(GL_ARRAY_BUFFER, *vbo);
    glBufferData(GL_ARRAY_BUFFER, sizeof(float) * 3 * 256, 0,
          GL_DYNAMIC_DRAW);
    glBindBuffer(GL_ARRAY_BUFFER, 0);

    // Register VBO with CUDA
    cudaGraphicsGLRegisterBuffer(&vbo_res, *vbo, cudaGraphicsMapFlagsNone);
}

void display() {
    // Map OpenGL VBO for CUDA access
    float3* dev_ptr;
    size_t num_bytes;
    cudaGraphicsMapResources(1, &vbo_res, 0);
    cudaGraphicsResourceGetMappedPointer((void**)&dev_ptr, &num_bytes, vbo_res
          );

    // Perform CUDA computation to modify VBO data
    launch_cuda_kernel(dev_ptr);

    // Unmap the VBO, making it available to OpenGL
    cudaGraphicsUnmapResources(1, &vbo_res, 0);

    // Proceed with OpenGL rendering
    glBindBuffer(GL_ARRAY_BUFFER, vbo);
    glVertexPointer(3, GL_FLOAT, 0, 0);
    glEnableClientState(GL_VERTEX_ARRAY);
    glDrawArrays(GL_POINTS, 0, 256);
    glDisableClientState(GL_VERTEX_ARRAY);
    glBindBuffer(GL_ARRAY_BUFFER, 0);

    glutSwapBuffers();
}
```

For interoperability with Direct3D, a similar approach is taken. The primary difference involves Direct3D-specific resource management functions. Below is an example illustrating CUDA and Direct3D interoperability:

```
#include <cuda_runtime.h>
#include <cuda_d3d11_interop.h>
#include <d3d11.h>

// Direct3D buffer
ID3D11Buffer* pBuffer;
struct cudaGraphicsResource* cudaResource;

void initializeD3DResource(ID3D11Device* pd3dDevice) {
```

```
    // Create D3D buffer
    D3D11_BUFFER_DESC desc = {};
    desc.Usage = D3D11_USAGE_DEFAULT;
    desc.ByteWidth = sizeof(float) * 3 * 256;
    desc.BindFlags = D3D11_BIND_VERTEX_BUFFER;
    pd3dDevice->CreateBuffer(&desc, NULL, &pBuffer);

    // Register D3D buffer with CUDA
    cudaGraphicsD3D11RegisterResource(&cudaResource, pBuffer,
            cudaGraphicsRegisterFlagsNone);
}

void executeKernel(ID3D11DeviceContext* pContext) {
    // Map D3D resource for CUDA access
    float* dev_ptr;
    size_t size;
    cudaGraphicsMapResources(1, &cudaResource, 0);
    cudaGraphicsResourceGetMappedPointer((void**)&dev_ptr, &size, cudaResource);

    // Perform CUDA computation
    launch_cuda_kernel(dev_ptr);

    // Unmap the resource, making it available to Direct3D
    cudaGraphicsUnmapResources(1, &cudaResource, 0);

    // Use the buffer in Direct3D pipeline
    UINT stride = sizeof(float) * 3;
    UINT offset = 0;
    pContext->IASetVertexBuffers(0, 1, &pBuffer, &stride, &offset);
    pContext->Draw(256, 0);
}
```

Interoperability with OpenCL is achieved using the CUDA 'cudaInterop' namespace functions to share resources between the two. These functions handle resource mapping between CUDA and OpenCL contexts, facilitating efficient data exchange.

An example of CUDA-OpenCL interoperability:

```
#include <cuda_runtime.h>
#include <CL/cl.h>
#include <cuda_interop.h>

// OpenCL buffer
cl_mem clBuffer;
struct cudaGraphicsResource* cudaResource;

void createCLBuffer(cl_context context, size_t size) {
    clBuffer = clCreateBuffer(context, CL_MEM_READ_WRITE, size, NULL, NULL)
        ;

    // Register OpenCL buffer with CUDA
    cudaGraphicsRegisterOCLBuffer(&cudaResource, clBuffer,
            cudaGraphicsRegisterFlagsNone);
}

void executeWithOpenCL(cl_command_queue queue, cl_kernel kernel) {
    // Map the resource to CUDA
    float* devPtr;
    size_t size;
```

```
    cudaGraphicsMapResources(1, &cudaResource, 0);
    cudaGraphicsResourceGetMappedPointer((void**)&devPtr, &size, cudaResource);

    // Perform CUDA computation
    launch_cuda_kernel(devPtr);

    // Unmap the resource, making it available to OpenCL
    cudaGraphicsUnmapResources(1, &cudaResource, 0);

    // Use the buffer in OpenCL kernel
    clSetKernelArg(kernel, 0, sizeof(cl_mem), &clBuffer);
    size_t globalWorkSize = 256;
    clEnqueueNDRangeKernel(queue, kernel, 1, NULL, &globalWorkSize, NULL, 0,
         NULL, NULL);
}
```

Throughout these examples, effective resource management ensures that data is not unnecessarily copied between the host and the GPU, promoting optimal performance. Integrating CUDA with other GPU APIs facilitates sophisticated workflows, harnessing the unique strengths of each API for diverse computing tasks.

8.11 Advanced Profiling and Analysis Techniques

CUDA programming for performance requires detailed profiling and analysis to pinpoint bottlenecks and inefficiencies. Advanced profiling and analysis techniques enable developers to optimize complex CUDA applications effectively. This section delves into the tools and methodologies necessary to achieve fine-grained performance tuning, focusing on the use of NVIDIA's profiling tools, such as nvprof, NVIDIA Visual Profiler, and Nsight Systems and Nsight Compute.

The nvprof command-line profiler provides detailed information about how CUDA applications utilize the GPU. It measures a wide range of metrics, including kernel execution time, memory throughput, and occupancy. Understanding the output of nvprof allows developers to identify performance issues at a granular level.

```
// Profiling a CUDA application using nvprof
$ nvprof --metrics all ./my_cuda_application
```

The output of nvprof includes data on thread execution, memory access patterns, and more. The following is a sample output:

```
==4769== Profiling application: ./my_cuda_application
==4769== Profiling result:
Time(%)      Time     Calls      Avg       Min       Max  Name
 50.00%  30.0ms           3  10.0ms   9.8ms   10.2ms  kernel1
 30.00%  18.0ms           2   9.0ms   8.8ms    9.2ms  kernel2
 20.00%  12.0ms           1  12.0ms  12.0ms   12.0ms  memcpyHtoD
```

NVIDIA Visual Profiler provides a graphical interface complementing nvprof. It allows for visual inspection of kernel execution timelines, memory transfer operations, and computational efficiency. Using Visual Profiler, developers can observe the correlation between CPU and GPU activities and identify opportunities for concurrency.

Nsight Systems offers a comprehensive view of the whole system performance, including both CPU and GPU timelines. It provides insights into how the application utilizes both CPUs and GPUs and reveals inefficiencies in task scheduling and synchronization. Nsight Systems is particularly useful for applications with complex interdependencies between CPU and GPU operations.

Nsight Compute is a detailed tool for kernel analysis, offering insights into various performance metrics such as warp execution efficiency, shared memory utilization, and instruction throughput. It allows users to perform detailed kernel profiling and compare performance across multiple kernel launches.

Utilizing these tools effectively requires understanding key performance metrics in CUDA. Some of the critical metrics include:

- **Instruction Throughput:** Measures the number of instructions executed per clock cycle. High throughput indicates efficient use of GPU resources.
- **Warp Occupancy:** Indicates the percentage of active warps per multiprocessor. Higher occupancy generally denotes better utilization of streaming multiprocessors.
- **Memory Bandwidth Utilization:** Assesses the effective use of memory bandwidth. Ensuring high memory bandwidth utilization is crucial for performance, especially for memory-bound kernels.
- **Branch Efficiency:** Evaluates the effectiveness of branch prediction and execution. Divergent branches can reduce efficiency and should be minimized.
- **L2 Cache Hit Rate:** Examines the hit rate of the L2 cache. High hit rates reduce the demand on global memory, thereby improving performance.

The process of optimizing a CUDA application typically involves identifying the slowest components (kernels or memory operations) and iteratively refining them. Analysis tools like Nsight Compute facilitate a detailed examination of kernel execution. For instance, profiling a kernel with Nsight Compute might reveal that memory coalescing issues are impeding performance. Addressing these issues could involve rearranging data structures or modifying memory access patterns to ensure better memory alignment.

```
// Profiling a kernel with Nsight Compute
$ nsys profile -o analysis_report ./my_cuda_application
```

Post-profiling, the detailed report generated by Nsight Compute helps pinpoint specific performance bottlenecks. Here is an example of such a detailed output:

```
==PROF== Profiling result:
Metric Name                          Metric Value      Unit
sm___cycles_elapsed.avg.per_second   1.20e+12          cycle/s
sm___inst_executed.avg.per_second    3.60e+12          inst/s
dram___throughput.avg                330.43            GB/s
l2___read_throughput.avg             120.56            GB/s
l2___write_throughput.avg            45.12             GB/s
```

Kernel optimization should also consider hardware limitations and architectural features. For instance, ensuring that kernel code adheres to warp-based execution (32 threads per warp) can avoid warp divergence. Additionally, managing register and shared memory usage carefully can prevent excess spilling to local memory, which significantly degrades performance. Strategically minimizing global memory access and maximizing shared memory usage often yields considerable speedups.

Adopting a methodical approach that combines the use of nvprof, NVIDIA Visual Profiler, Nsight Systems, and Nsight Compute establishes a robust profiling and analysis framework. This comprehensive strategy provides an in-depth understanding of application behavior on the GPU and informs necessary adjustments to optimize performance. Through this refined process, CUDA developers can achieve significant performance enhancements, harnessing the full computational power of modern GPUs.

8.12 Leveraging Peer-to-Peer Memory Access

Peer-to-Peer (P2P) memory access in CUDA enables direct communication between GPUs, bypassing the host system's memory. This technique is critical for multi-GPU systems where minimizing data transfer latency and maximizing bandwidth are essential for achieving optimal performance. By enabling P2P memory access, one GPU can directly read from or write to the memory of another GPU, facilitating efficient data exchange in multi-GPU applications.

To leverage P2P memory access, it is necessary first to ensure that the GPUs in the system support P2P communication. This can be checked using the CUDA 'cudaDeviceCanAccessPeer' function. Suppose two GPUs with IDs 'device1' and 'device2' respectively; the following code snippet demonstrates how to ascertain their P2P capability:

```
int canAccessPeer = 0;
cudaDeviceCanAccessPeer(&canAccessPeer, device1, device2);

if (canAccessPeer) {
    printf("GPU %d can access GPU %d's memory.\n", device1, device2);
} else {
    printf("GPU %d cannot access GPU %d's memory.\n", device1, device2);
}
```

If the GPUs support P2P access, the next step is to enable it using 'cudaDeviceEnablePeerAccess'. This function must be called for each pair of devices requiring P2P communication:

```
cudaSetDevice(device1);
cudaDeviceEnablePeerAccess(device2, 0);

cudaSetDevice(device2);
cudaDeviceEnablePeerAccess(device1, 0);
```

Once enabled, one GPU can access the memory of another directly. Consider the following example where 'device1' writes to an array in 'device2''s memory:

```
float *d_A;
size_t size = N * sizeof(float);

// Allocate memory on device2
cudaSetDevice(device2);
cudaMalloc((void**)&d_A, size);

// Write to device2 memory from device1
cudaSetDevice(device1);
cudaMemcpyPeer(d_A, device2, d_A, device1, size);
```

The 'cudaMemcpyPeer' function facilitates copying data directly between the memories of different GPUs. This eliminates the need for intermediate data transfers through the host memory, significantly reducing transfer times.

It is essential also to disable P2P access when it is no longer needed, which can be done using 'cudaDeviceDisablePeerAccess':

```
cudaSetDevice(device1);
cudaDeviceDisablePeerAccess(device2);

cudaSetDevice(device2);
cudaDeviceDisablePeerAccess(device1);
```

To elucidate the effect of P2P memory access on performance, consider the example where data is being transferred between two GPUs:

```
cudaEvent_t start, stop;
float time;
cudaEventCreate(&start);
cudaEventCreate(&stop);

// Allocate and initialize host memory
float *h_A = (float*)malloc(size);
for (int i = 0; i < N; i++) {
    h_A[i] = (float)i;
}

// Allocate memory on GPUs
cudaSetDevice(device1);
cudaMalloc((void**)&d_A, size);

cudaSetDevice(device2);
cudaMalloc((void**)&d_B, size);

// Copy data from host to device1
cudaSetDevice(device1);
cudaMemcpy(d_A, h_A, size, cudaMemcpyHostToDevice);

// Enable Peer-to-Peer access
cudaDeviceEnablePeerAccess(device2, 0);
cudaSetDevice(device2);

// Measure time for Peer-to-Peer transfer
cudaEventRecord(start, 0);
cudaMemcpyPeer(d_B, device2, d_A, device1, size);
cudaEventRecord(stop, 0);
cudaEventSynchronize(stop);
cudaEventElapsedTime(&time, start, stop);

printf("P2P transfer time: %f ms\n", time);

// Disable Peer-to-Peer access
cudaDeviceDisablePeerAccess(device2);

cudaFree(d_A);
cudaFree(d_B);
free(h_A);
```

```
cudaEventDestroy(start);
cudaEventDestroy(stop);
```

The code above measures the transfer time for a P2P copy operation. By comparing these timings with traditional methods that use host-memory as an intermediate buffer, the performance advantages of direct P2P communication can be empirically observed.

Practical applications of P2P memory access include complex simulations, neural network training, and tasks requiring frequent inter-GPU data exchange. P2P enhances scalability and performance by providing high-bandwidth and low-latency communication channels across multiple GPUs.

Understanding the capabilities and limitations of different GPU architectures, along with the appropriate use of P2P memory access, forms a cornerstone of advanced CUDA programming. This knowledge empowers developers to design and implement high-performance multi-GPU applications adeptly.

Chapter 9

Debugging and Profiling CUDA Applications

This chapter addresses the critical aspects of debugging and profiling CUDA applications. It covers common debugging challenges and the use of tools like NVIDIA Nsight and CUDA-GDB for effective debugging. The chapter introduces profiling tools such as the NVIDIA Visual Profiler, detailing how to interpret profiling reports and optimize performance based on profiling data. Special attention is given to debugging and profiling within Jupyter Notebooks and best practices to ensure efficient and error-free CUDA applications.

9.1 Introduction to Debugging and Profiling CUDA Applications

Debugging and profiling CUDA applications are essential skills for developers to ensure the correctness, performance, and efficiency of their code. As CUDA applications often run on massively parallel architectures, traditional debugging and profiling techniques may not be sufficient. This section introduces fundamental concepts and specialized tools necessary for debugging and profiling CUDA applications effectively.

At its core, debugging involves identifying and rectifying errors or bugs in code. In CUDA applications, this process is complicated by parallel execution, which can introduce unique challenges such as race conditions, deadlocks, incorrect memory accesses, and synchronization issues. Debugging these issues requires a thorough understanding of parallel programming constructs and the CUDA programming model.

Profiling, on the other hand, is the process of measuring the performance characteristics of a program, such as execution time, memory usage, and computational efficiency. Profiling CUDA applications is crucial for identifying performance bottlenecks and optimizing code to achieve maximum efficiency on NVIDIA GPUs. Proper profiling can reveal insights into how well the application utilizes the GPU's resources, such as the number of active threads, warps, and memory bandwidth.

Consider the following simple CUDA kernel as a starting point for discussing debugging and profiling:

```
__global__ void vectorAdd(const float *A, const float *B, float *C, int N) {
    int i = blockDim.x * blockIdx.x + threadIdx.x;
    if (i < N) {
        C[i] = A[i] + B[i];
    }
}
```

This kernel adds two vectors, A and B, storing the result in C. Understanding how to debug and profile such a kernel provides valuable insights into more complex CUDA applications.

To effectively debug and profile CUDA applications, developers can use NVIDIA's suite of tools, such as Nsight and CUDA-GDB for debugging, and the NVIDIA Visual Profiler for profiling. Nsight offers an integrated development environment (IDE) with robust debugging capabilities, while CUDA-GDB is a command-line debugger specifically designed for CUDA applications. Both tools help in setting breakpoints, examining variables, and stepping through code.

The NVIDIA Visual Profiler provides a comprehensive environment for analyzing the performance of CUDA applications. It collects detailed metrics and visualizes them to help developers pinpoint performance bottlenecks. This profiler supports features such as timeline views, which illustrate how kernels are executed over time, and metric views, which provide insights into memory throughput and utilization.

Consider a scenario where a vector addition program runs slower than expected. Profiling the program might reveal that the memory bandwidth is not fully utilized, suggesting a possibility of optimizing memory access patterns. Simple changes, such as ensuring coalesced memory accesses, can significantly enhance performance:

```
__global__ void vectorAddOptimized(const float *A, const float *B, float *C, int N) {
    int i = blockIdx.x * blockDim.x + threadIdx.x;
    if (i < N) {
        C[i] = __ldg(&A[i]) + __ldg(&B[i]);
    }
}
```

In this optimized version, the __ldg function ensures that the accesses are cached, potentially resulting in a significant performance boost if data reusability is high enough.

Another vital aspect includes analyzing memory errors and race conditions. These issues are often subtle and challenging to detect but can be efficiently handled with CUDA-Memcheck, a runtime analysis tool that intercepts and analyzes memory access patterns in CUDA applications. Consider the following code that intentionally triggers a memory error:

```
__global__ void faultyKernel(int *A) {
    int idx = threadIdx.x + blockIdx.x * blockDim.x;
    A[idx] = A[idx] + 1; // Potential out-of-bounds write
}

int main() {
    int *d_A;
    int N = 1024;
    cudaMalloc(&d_A, N * sizeof(int));
    faultyKernel<<<1, 1024>>>(d_A);
    cudaFree(d_A);
    return 0;
}
```

By using CUDA-Memcheck, developers can identify out-of-bounds access and other memory-related errors, ensuring that the application handles memory safely and correctly.

Furthermore, profiling helps in understanding how well an application scales with the available hardware. For instance, developers can experiment with different grid and block dimensions to find the optimal configuration for their specific hardware. Efficient utilization of shared memory, constant memory, and texture memory also falls under the scope of profiling efforts to enhance performance.

Debugging and profiling CUDA applications require a mindful approach that integrates fundamental knowledge of parallel computing, an understanding of CUDA-specific challenges, and the proficient use of NVIDIA's tools. These practices contribute significantly to developing high-performance, reliable CUDA applications.

9.2 Common Debugging Challenges in CUDA

CUDA programming introduces unique debugging challenges that arise primarily from the parallel and heterogeneous nature of GPU computing. These challenges can lead to complex and sometimes non-deterministic behavior in applications, making debugging an indispensable skill for CUDA developers. This section delves into the most common issues encountered and provides insights into identifying and addressing them.

1. Memory Allocation Failures

Memory management is a critical aspect of CUDA programming. The dynamic allocation and deallocation of memory on the GPU can lead to failures if not handled correctly. Memory allocation failures often arise due to insufficient memory on the GPU or incorrect usage of allocation functions. For example, using cudaMalloc() improperly can result in allocation errors that might not be immediately obvious.

```
cudaError_t err = cudaMalloc((void**)&d_A, size);
if (err != cudaSuccess) {
    printf("CUDA error: %s\n", cudaGetErrorString(err));
    // Handle error appropriately
}
```

Debugging these issues requires careful attention to memory allocation functions and checking the returned error codes. Ensuring that allocations and deallocations are balanced and verifying that adequate memory is available can mitigate these problems.

2. Kernel Launch Failures

Another significant challenge is kernel launch failures, which can occur due to incorrect configurations of grid and block dimensions or due to resource constraints. For instance, launching a kernel with more threads than the GPU can support will result in a launch failure.

```
dim3 blockDim(BLOCK_SIZE_X, BLOCK_SIZE_Y);
dim3 gridDim(GRID_SIZE_X, GRID_SIZE_Y);
kernel_function<<<gridDim, blockDim>>>(params);
cudaError_t err = cudaGetLastError();
if (err != cudaSuccess) {
    printf("Kernel launch error: %s\n", cudaGetErrorString(err));
    // Execute corrective action
}
```

To debug kernel launch issues, it is essential to check the return status of kernel launches using cudaGetLastError(). This function returns the last error that has been created by any of the runtime API calls and can help pinpoint failures resulting from incorrect kernel configurations.

3. Memory Access Violations

Memory access violations are common and can cause crashes or invalid results. These violations often result from out-of-bounds accesses, illegal memory accesses (such as dereferencing a null or uninitialized pointer), and shared memory conflicts. Debugging these issues typically involves checking array indices, ensuring pointers are correctly initialized, and using tools like cuda-memcheck to detect illegal accesses.

```
__global__ void kernel_function(int* d_A, int size) {
    int idx = threadIdx.x + blockIdx.x * blockDim.x;
    if (idx < size) {
        d_A[idx] = idx;
    }
}
```

The above kernel function ensures that accesses are within bounds by checking the index against the array size. Such bounds checks are crucial in preventing memory access violations.

4. Race Conditions and Synchronization Issues

Race conditions are a substantial challenge in parallel programming. They occur when multiple threads concurrently access shared data, and the outcome depends on the order of execution. Synchronization mechanisms, such as __syncthreads() within a block and atomic operations, are essential to ensure correct results. Misuse or lack of synchronization can result in erratic behavior and incorrect computations.

```
__shared__ float shared_data[BLOCK_SIZE];
__global__ void kernel_function(float* d_A) {
    int idx = threadIdx.x + blockIdx.x * blockDim.x;
    shared_data[threadIdx.x] = d_A[idx];
    __syncthreads();
    // Perform operations on shared_data
    d_A[idx] = shared_data[threadIdx.x];
}
```

Using __syncthreads() ensures that all threads within a block reach the synchronization point before proceeding, thereby preventing race conditions. Properly identifying points in the code where synchronization is required and verifying the use of atomic operations where necessary helps mitigate these issues.

5. Divergent Branches

Warp divergence occurs when threads of the same warp take different execution paths due to conditional branching. This divergence can lead to performance degradation since divergent paths are serialized, reducing the parallel efficiency of the program. Detecting and minimizing divergent branches is critical for optimizing performance.

```
__global__ void kernel_function(int* d_A) {
    int idx = threadIdx.x;
    if (idx % 2 == 0) {
        // Do something for even threads
    } else {
        // Do something for odd threads
    }
}
```

Optimization involves restructuring code to reduce divergence. For instance, separating threads into different kernels based on their execution paths can minimize divergence and improve performance.

Understanding these common debugging challenges in CUDA programming is essential for developing efficient and reliable GPU applications. Employing systematic debugging techniques and leveraging CUDA debugging tools can significantly reduce the complexity and time required to identify and resolve issues.

9.3 Using NVIDIA Nsight for Debugging

NVIDIA Nsight is an integrated development environment (IDE) that provides powerful debugging and profiling tools specific to CUDA applications. It includes features for source-level debugging, performance analysis, and real-time inspection of variable states. It supports both host and device code, enabling a thorough examination of applications running on NVIDIA GPUs.

NVIDIA Nsight allows developers to visually track the flow of their CUDA code, set breakpoints, and monitor variables across different kernel executions and memory states. This section will delve into configuring and utilizing NVIDIA Nsight for debugging CUDA applications.

To start debugging with NVIDIA Nsight, ensure that the Nsight IDE is correctly installed and that the necessary components are appropriately configured. The prerequisites include the NVIDIA driver, CUDA Toolkit, and a compatible version of the Nsight Eclipse Edition or Visual Studio Edition. Once the setup is complete, follow these steps to create a debugging session:

1. Open the Nsight IDE and create a new CUDA project.

2. Import existing CUDA source files into the project, ensuring that the project configuration matches the target environment.

3. Enable kernel debugging features by setting appropriate project properties. In Nsight Eclipse Edition, this can be done via **Project Properties** → **Build** → **Settings** → **CUDA C/C++** → **Debugging**.

4. Configure the debugging session by setting target settings in **Run** → **Debug Configurations**. Here, specify the executable, communication method (e.g., shared memory or TCP/IP), and target platform.

Once the project is set up for debugging, you can start a debugging session. Follow these steps to leverage the debugging features effectively:

Setting Breakpoints: Breakpoints are essential to pause the execution of your program at specified lines of code to inspect variable states and memory. To set a breakpoint, open the source file in the editor, right-click on the line number where the breakpoint is desired, and select **Toggle Breakpoint**. Breakpoints can be conditional or unconditional:

```
__global__ void vectorAdd(float *A, float *B, float *C, int N) {
    int i = threadIdx.x + blockIdx.x * blockDim.x;
    if (i < N) {
        C[i] = A[i] + B[i]; // Set breakpoint here
    }
}
```

Launching the Debugger: To start the debugging session, go to **Run** → **Debug**. The debugger will launch and pause at any set breakpoints. If breakpoints are not hit, ensure that the code path genuinely reaches them.

Inspecting Variables: While the application is paused at a breakpoint, the **Variables** window displays the values of local, global, and shared variables. For instance, suppose the breakpoint is hit in the example above. In this case, you can inspect the values of A, B, C, and i to verify the correctness of the computation.

Step Actions: Use step actions to navigate through the code:

- **Step Into**: Dive into function calls or kernel launches.

- **Step Over**: Execute the next line of code without descending into functions or kernels.
- **Step Out**: Exit the current function or kernel.
- **Resume**: Continue execution until the next breakpoint or program termination.

These actions are accessible via the toolbar or by right-clicking within the editor.

Analyzing Memory States: Nsight provides comprehensive tools for examining memory states, including local, global, shared, and constant memory. Monitoring memory can reveal alignment issues, out-of-bounds accesses, and ensure that data is correctly transferred between host and device. The **Memory** window displays the memory contents and allows you to navigate through different memory spaces.

CUDA Thread and Warp Details: Nsight enables viewing detailed thread and warp information. The **CUDA Threads** window shows the current status (e.g., active, suspended) and execution scopes of individual threads and warps. This feature is invaluable for identifying synchronization issues and ensuring thread-level correctness:

```
Thread 1: Suspended at line 20
Thread 2: Active, executing line 22
...
Warp 1: Active
Warp 2: Suspended
```

Examining Kernel Launches: In the **CUDA Kernels** window, inspect kernel launch parameters, execution configurations (blocks, grids, threads), and launch outcomes. This window lists all kernel launches with the ability to further analyze in-flight kernels:

```
Kernel: vectorAdd<<<1,256>>>()
Launch Parameters:
  Blocks: 1
  Threads per Block: 256
  Shared Memory: 0 bytes
  Execution: Completed
```

Call Stack and Performance Metrics: The **Call Stack** window provides the current call hierarchy, allowing backtracing through the function calls leading to the breakpoint. Additionally, performance metrics such as execution time, memory throughput, and computational efficiency are accessible. These metrics guide optimization by highlighting performance bottlenecks and underutilized resources.

The combination of these features in NVIDIA Nsight enables a robust and detailed debugging workflow for CUDA applications, enhancing the ability to identify, understand, and resolve issues efficiently.

9.4 Debugging with CUDA-GDB

CUDA-GDB is an extension of the GNU Debugger (GDB) designed specifically for debugging CUDA applications. It allows the developer to control the execution of CUDA kernels, inspect and modify GPU memory, and track down bugs that occur within GPU code. Understanding and effectively using CUDA-GDB can significantly aid in resolving complex issues in CUDA applications.

To start debugging a CUDA application with CUDA-GDB, it is essential first to compile the application with debugging information. This is achieved by adding the -g and -G flags to the nvcc compiler command. The -g flag includes debugging information for the host code, while -G adds debugging information for the device code.

```
nvcc -g -G -o my_cuda_application my_cuda_application.cu
```

Once the program is compiled with the necessary debugging information, CUDA-GDB can be started by invoking it from the command line with the executable name:

```
cuda-gdb ./my_cuda_application
```

After launching CUDA-GDB, the first step is typically to set breakpoints. Breakpoints can be set in both host and device code. Setting a breakpoint in host code is straightforward and similar to the usual GDB commands:

```
(gdb) break main
```

Setting a breakpoint in device code, however, requires a precise syntax. Since CUDA C++ functions (kernels) and device functions can have the same name as host functions, it is crucial to specify the unique identifier for the kernel. The identifier includes the module name, function name, and any template parameters. The following command sets a breakpoint in a kernel function named myKernel in the kernel.cu file:

```
(gdb) break kernel.cu::myKernel
```

With the breakpoints set, the program can be started using the run command. Once execution hits a breakpoint, CUDA-GDB enters an interactive debugging session. During this session, various commands can be utilized to inspect variables, step through code, and modify GPU or CPU memory.

To inspect variables in CUDA-GDB, the print command is used, similar to GDB. However, it's essential to specify whether the variable resides in host or device memory. For instance, to print a host variable hVar:

```
(gdb) print hVar
```

Inspecting device variables involves dereferencing GPU pointers. Assume dVar is a device pointer to an array of integers on the GPU. To print the first element of this array, the command would be:

```
(gdb) print dVar[0]
```

CUDA-GDB also provides commands to manage the execution of GPU threads. The thread command switches between different threads, allowing the developer to view the state of each one. For example, to switch to thread 2:

```
(gdb) thread 2
```

Specific GPU thread IDs can be identified using the info cuda threads command, which lists all active GPU threads along with their unique IDs.

```
(gdb) info cuda threads
```

Stepping through device code in CUDA-GDB follows the same principle as in standard GDB. The step and next commands allow single-stepping through the code, with step entering functions and next stepping over functions.

```
(gdb) step
(gdb) next
```

CUDA-GDB offers specialized commands for managing GPU-specific operations. For instance, the cuda kernel command lists all the active kernel launches, providing their grid and block dimensions.

```
(gdb) cuda kernel
```

Debugging race conditions and memory errors is a common task when working with CUDA applications. CUDA-GDB can help analyze race conditions by allowing breakpoints on specific memory accesses. Using data breakpoints, developers can halt execution when certain memory locations are read or written.

```
(gdb) watch *(dVar + 10)
```

The command above sets a watchpoint on the memory location pointed to by dVar + 10. The program will pause whenever this memory location is accessed, aiding in identifying race conditions or improper memory access.

Identifying and correcting race conditions also involves examining the state of multiple threads when a watchpoint is triggered. The info threads command helps list all threads, and the thread apply all command can execute a command across all threads to gather their state.

```
(gdb) info threads
(gdb) thread apply all bt
```

Handling the debugging of complex CUDA applications where multiple kernels execute concurrently requires understanding and using CUDA-GDB's advanced features. CUDA-GDB's ability to control thread and block execution and examine GPU memory contents makes it an indispensable tool for CUDA developers.

9.5 Analyzing Memory Errors and Race Conditions

Memory errors and race conditions are frequent sources of bugs in CUDA applications. These issues can lead to unpredictable behavior, making debugging a critical step in the development process. This section delves into methods for identifying and resolving these problems to ensure stable and efficient CUDA applications.

Memory errors typically arise from incorrect memory allocations, out-of-bounds accesses, or illegal memory operations. CUDA provides several tools to assist in the identification and correction of these errors. One of the most effective is the CUDA-MEMCHECK toolset, which is designed to detect various memory errors, including misaligned memory access, out-of-bounds memory access, and illegal memory access.

```
cuda-memcheck ./myCUDAapp
```

The output of the above tool can be essential for pinpointing memory access violations.

```
========= Invalid __global__ read of size 4
```

```
=========     at 0x00000050 in file.cu:100
=========     by thread (0,0,0) in block (0,0,0)
=========     Address 0x7fe80000000 is out of bounds
========= ERROR SUMMARY: 1 error
```

In the example output above, CUDA-MEMCHECK reports an invalid global memory read occurring at a specific line in the source file and identifies the offending thread and memory address. This information can be instrumental in diagnosing and fixing the memory error.

Race conditions occur when multiple threads simultaneously execute code that accesses shared resources without proper synchronization, leading to inconsistent results. They are particularly challenging to debug due to their non-deterministic nature. An effective strategy to identify race conditions in CUDA involves using the cuda-memcheck –tool racecheck command. This tool detects data access hazards in GPU kernels.

```
cuda-memcheck --tool racecheck ./myCUDAapp
```

The tool yields results that help locate conflicts between threads accessing shared variables, which need to be synchronized properly.

```
========= Hazardous read 0x7fc0034b0060 in thread (0,0,0)
=========     Write 0x7fc0034b0060 first observed
=========     Kernel code.cu: line 200
=========     Variable: my_shared_array[4]
=========     Hazard location: file.cu line 205
=========     Last accessed by thread (1,0,0)
========= ERROR SUMMARY: 1 data race
```

This output clearly points out the hazardous read/write operations leading to the race condition and the locations in the code where these conflicts arise. Developers can address such issues by implementing proper synchronization mechanisms, such as __syncthreads(), which synchronizes all threads in a block:

```
__global__ void myKernel(int* data) {
    int idx = threadIdx.x + blockIdx.x * blockDim.x;
    __shared__ int shared_data[256];
    // Some operations
    __syncthreads();
    // Access shared_data with synchronized threads
    shared_data[threadIdx.x] = data[idx];
    __syncthreads();
}
```

In the kernel above, __syncthreads() ensures that all threads reach the same point of execution before proceeding. This prevents race conditions by ensuring that shared memory operations are completed by all threads.

Another effective approach to handling race conditions is using atomic operations, which are guaranteed to be executed without interference from other threads. CUDA provides atomic functions for various arithmetic and bitwise operations, helping maintain data consistency.

```
__global__ void atomicKernel(int* data) {
    int idx = threadIdx.x + blockIdx.x * blockDim.x;
    atomicAdd(&data[0], data[idx]);
}
```

In the atomicKernel example, atomicAdd ensures that the addition operation on data[0] is atomic, preventing simultaneous conflicting updates by multiple threads.

Furthermore, analyzing runtime output with tools like NVIDIA Nsight Systems can offer insights into synchronization issues. This tool provides a timeline of kernel executions, highlighting stalls and identifying concurrency issues. By visualizing thread activities and barriers, developers can optimize their code and eliminate race conditions.

Developers should also be meticulous about kernel launch configurations. Appropriate grid and block dimensions can significantly impact performance and correctness. If kernels heavily depend on shared resources or high inter-thread communication, selecting block sizes that align with the hardware's multiprocessor design can reduce potential synchronization issues.

Proper error handling in CUDA is essential. The use of cudaGetLastError and cudaDeviceSynchronize functions helps catch errors early and offers debugging insights.

```
myKernel<<<grid, block>>>(data);
cudaError_t err = cudaGetLastError();
if (err != cudaSuccess) {
    printf("CUDA Error: %s\n", cudaGetErrorString(err));
}
cudaDeviceSynchronize();
```

In this example, cudaGetLastError checks for any errors after the kernel launch, while cudaDeviceSynchronize ensures the CPU waits for the GPU to finish.

Understanding how to analyze memory errors and race conditions in CUDA applications is crucial for developing robust and reliable software. By leveraging CUDA-MEMCHECK, appropriate synchronization techniques, and vigilant kernel configurations, developers can significantly reduce these common issues, ensuring their applications run efficiently on CUDA-enabled devices.

9.6 Introduction to Profiling Tools

Profiling tools are indispensable in the realm of CUDA programming as they offer insights into the performance and efficiency of GPU applications. These tools enable developers to understand where their application spends the most time, identify bottlenecks, and ascertain which parts of the code are the most computationally expensive. By providing detailed metrics, profiling tools allow fine-tuning of the CUDA kernels and overall application to achieve optimal performance.

To elucidate their utility, let us consider a simple CUDA program where we perform element-wise addition of two large vectors. Profiling such a program will help us determine if there are inefficiencies in memory usage, unoptimized kernel configurations, or other latent performance issues.

```
import numpy as np
from numba import cuda

# Kernel function to add two vectors
@cuda.jit
def vector_add(a, b, c):
    idx = cuda.grid(1)
    if idx < a.size:
        c[idx] = a[idx] + b[idx]

# Initialize vectors with large size
N = 1000000
A = np.ones(N, dtype=np.float32)
B = np.ones(N, dtype=np.float32)
C = np.zeros(N, dtype=np.float32)

# Allocate device memory and transfer data
d_A = cuda.to_device(A)
d_B = cuda.to_device(B)
d_C = cuda.device_array_like(C)

# Configure the blocks and grids
threads_per_block = 256
blocks_per_grid = (A.size + (threads_per_block - 1)) // threads_per_block

# Launch the kernel
vector_add[blocks_per_grid, threads_per_block](d_A, d_B, d_C)

# Copy the result back to the host
C = d_C.copy_to_host()
```

When profiling the above code, tools like nvprof, NVIDIA Visual Profiler (nvvp), and Nsight Systems will provide statistics such as execution time, memory transfer rates, compute utilization, and more. Firstly, let's execute the program under nvprof to collect some preliminary profiling data.

```
nvprof python vector_add.py
```

The output will provide a timeline of kernel execution and memory operations, including metrics like elapsed time and throughput.

```
==12345== NVPROF is profiling process 12345, command: python vector_add.py
==12345== Profiling application: python vector_add.py
==12345== Profiling result:
Time(%)      Time     Calls       Avg       Min       Max  Name
 50.00%  500.00ms         1  500.00ms  500.00ms  500.00ms  vector_add(float *, float *, float *)
 50.00%  500.00ms         3  166.67ms  100.00ms  200.00ms  [CUDA memcpy HtoD]
==12345== API calls:
Time(%)      Time     Calls       Avg       Min       Max  Name
 50.00%  500.00ms         1  500.00ms  500.00ms  500.00ms  cudaDeviceSynchronize
 50.00%  500.00ms         3  166.67ms  100.00ms  200.00ms  cudaMemcpy
```

From the preliminary data, developers can note the distribution of time between kernel execution and memory operations. Profiling tools also allow the examination of other performance-impacting factors such as memory access patterns and computational efficiency.

NVIDIA Visual Profiler (nvvp) is a GUI-based tool that provides a more intuitive representation of profiling data. It facilitates the collection and visualization of performance metrics over time, and users can explore various aspects like latency, throughput, and resource utilization. To profile the same application with nvvp, use the command:

```
nvvp python vector_add.py
```

Nsight Systems and Nsight Compute offer advanced ways to profile and analyze CUDA applications. Nsight Systems provides a system-wide overview and helps identify higher-level bottlenecks, while Nsight Compute offers detailed insights into individual CUDA kernels, including metrics such as instruction throughput, memory access patterns, and potential warp serialization issues.

When using Nsight Systems, one gains the ability to see interactions between CPU and GPU, inspect API calls, synchronize events, and identify long CPU or GPU tasks impacting performance. Profiling with Nsight Systems involves launching it as follows:

```
nsys profile python vector_add.py
```

The graphical outputs from these tools can be analyzed to detect inefficiencies such as sub-optimal grid configurations, insufficient memory bandwidth utilization, or memory contention among other issues. These observations can then inform modifications to both kernel codes and overall program structure, thus achieving improved performance.

Conclusively, utilizing profiling tools effectively allows pinpointing precise areas for optimization and ensuring the development of high-performance CUDA applications. Critically analyzing metrics and visualizations provided by these tools leads to performance enhancements and a deeper understanding of GPU computing paradigms.

9.7 Using NVIDIA Visual Profiler

NVIDIA Visual Profiler (NVVP), a performance analysis tool, allows developers to analyze the performance of their CUDA applications meticulously. By visualizing the application's behavior, identifying bottlenecks, and suggesting optimization techniques, NVVP enhances the efficiency and performance of CUDA code.

To initiate NVVP, ensure proper installation and configuration of CUDA Toolkit. NVVP is integrated into the Toolkit and can be invoked either through a GUI interface or command line. Below are the essential steps to launch NVVP:

```
$ nvvp
```

For analysis, the CUDA application must be compiled with debugging symbols. The debugging symbols enable NVVP to map the binary code back to the source code, facilitating a more insightful analysis. Use the -G switch in the compilation command for this purpose:

```
$ nvcc -G -o myCUDAapp myCUDAapp.cu
```

Once the application is profiled, NVVP collects various performance metrics. These metrics are categorized under different analyses like Memory, Compute, and Latency Analysis. The following describes the key components and their interpretations within the NVVP:

Timeline View: The timeline view provides a chronological representation of the kernel executions, data transfers, and other CUDA-related events. This visualization helps in understanding the concurrency and overlap between compute and data transfer operations.

CUDA Kernels: Kernels are color-coded and their execution periods are shown on the timeline. By examining the start and end times, developers can determine which kernels are the most time-consuming and may require optimization.

Memory Operations: The data transfer between host and device memory is displayed, allowing developers to observe any potential inefficiencies in memory access patterns. For instance, lengthy or frequent memory transfers can be pinpointed and reduced to enhance the application's performance.

Occupancy Analysis: Occupancy is a critical factor determining how well the GPU resources are utilized. NVVP reports the occupancy rates, helping developers understand if the kernels are making maximum use of the GPU's capabilities. Enhancing occupancy often involves adjusting the number of active warps and reducing resource usage per thread block.

The following code snippet illustrates a typical CUDA kernel invocation which can be profiled using NVVP:

```
__global__ void vectorAdd(float *A, float *B, float *C, int N) {
    int i = threadIdx.x + blockIdx.x * blockDim.x;
    if (i < N)
        C[i] = A[i] + B[i];
}

int main() {
    int N = 1<<20;
    size_t size = N * sizeof(float);

    float *h_A = (float*)malloc(size);
    float *h_B = (float*)malloc(size);
    float *h_C = (float*)malloc(size);

    float *d_A, *d_B, *d_C;
    cudaMalloc(&d_A, size);
    cudaMalloc(&d_B, size);
    cudaMalloc(&d_C, size);

    cudaMemcpy(d_A, h_A, size, cudaMemcpyHostToDevice);
    cudaMemcpy(d_B, h_B, size, cudaMemcpyHostToDevice);

    int threadsPerBlock = 256;
    int blocksPerGrid = (N + threadsPerBlock - 1) / threadsPerBlock;
    vectorAdd<<<blocksPerGrid, threadsPerBlock>>>(d_A, d_B, d_C, N);

    cudaMemcpy(h_C, d_C, size, cudaMemcpyDeviceToHost);

    cudaFree(d_A);
    cudaFree(d_B);
    cudaFree(d_C);
    free(h_A);
    free(h_B);
    free(h_C);

    return 0;
}
```

By profiling this kernel with NVVP, the timeline view will display the kernel execution period, allowing detailed assessments of the kernel's performance across different contexts.

Event and Metric Collection: NVVP supports the collection of both events and metrics from GPU execution: - **Events**: Discrete occurrences such as kernel launches or data transfers. - **Metrics**: Quantitative data such as memory throughput or compute utilization.

Analysis and Recommendations: Based on the collected data, NVVP provides detailed performance analysis along with recommendations. These suggestions might include optimizing memory access patterns, increasing kernel occupancy, or leveraging specific hardware features.

Below is an example of command to collect metrics via command line:

```
$ nvprof --metrics achieved_occupancy ./myCUDAapp
```

The output is generally detailed, providing insights into how effectively the GPU resources are utilized:

```
==21905== Profiling application: ./myCUDAapp
==21905== Profiling result:
        Type  Metric Name         Metric Description                         Value
  Device "Tesla K80 (0)"
  Kernel: vectorAdd(float*, float*, float*, int)
        Metric Achieved Occupancy  Ratio of active warps to max warps on a multiprocessor    0.625000
```

NVVP's ability to pinpoint inefficiencies and provide actionable recommendations transforms the performance tuning process into an empirical and data-driven task. Proper use of this tool significantly elevates a CUDA developer's capability to optimize and debug high-performance applications efficiently.

9.8 Understanding and Interpreting Profiling Reports

Profiling reports in CUDA provide insights into the performance of your applications by highlighting bottlenecks and inefficiencies. The primary goal of interpreting these reports is to identify areas for optimization which can lead to enhanced performance and resource utilization. Profiling reports typically include metrics on execution time, memory usage, and computational intensity. This section will delineate the key components of profiling reports, discuss how to read them, and illustrate how to apply the insights gained towards optimizing your CUDA applications.

A typical profiling tool such as the NVIDIA Visual Profiler or Nsight Systems generates detailed reports that include several important sections: timeline views, kernel execution summaries, memory bandwidth utilization, and occupancy analysis. Understanding each of these sections is crucial for effective optimization.

Timeline Views

Timeline views provide a visual representation of the execution of your application over time. This includes the sequence of kernel launches, memory transfers, and CPU activity. In CUDA programming, observing the timeline is essential to identify issues such as serialization of tasks that should ideally be overlapped.

```
cudaMemcpyAsync(hostData, deviceData, size, cudaMemcpyDeviceToHost, stream1);
kernel<<<blocks, threads, 0, stream2>>>(deviceData);
// Assuming stream1 and stream2 are created and passed to these functions
```

In the above example, the use of asynchronous memory transfer ('cudaMemcpyAsync') and kernel execution in separate streams should, in theory, allow these operations to overlap. The timeline view can help confirm whether this overlap is occurring. If the operations are serialized, the timeline will indicate a dependency or a stream synchronization issue.

Kernel Execution Summaries

The kernel execution summary provides statistics on each kernel's execution, including the average execution time, the number of executions, and the variance in execution time. These data points are critical for identifying which kernels are taking more time and may need optimization.

```
Kernel Execution Summary:
Kernel Name    Avg Execution Time (ms)    Total Executions    Total Time (ms)
myKernel              1.5                      50                  75
otherKernel           2.0                      30                  60
```

The above summary indicates that 'myKernel' has an average execution time of 1.5 ms and has been executed 50 times, contributing a total of 75 ms to the application's runtime. Identifying such frequently executed and time-consuming kernels is the first step toward performance improvement.

Memory Bandwidth Utilization

High memory utilization and bandwidth are often indicators of potential performance bottlenecks. Profiling reports include metrics like achieved bandwidth versus theoretical bandwidth, memory throughput (both read and write), and cache hit rates.

```
Memory Bandwidth Utilization:
Achieved Bandwidth (GB/s)   Theoretical Bandwidth (GB/s)   Utilization (%)
150                         250                            60
```

In the above report, the achieved bandwidth is 150 GB/s, while the theoretical bandwidth is 250 GB/s, indicating 60% utilization. An important optimization could be to improve memory access patterns or to reduce memory transfers between the host and device.

Occupancy Analysis

Occupancy is the ratio of active warps to the maximum number of warps supported on a multiprocessor. Higher occupancy typically implies more efficient utilization of the GPU resources, though this is not always directly correlated with performance.

```
Occupancy Analysis:
Kernel Name   Achieved Occupancy (%)   Theoretical Occupancy (%)
myKernel      70                       75
otherKernel   80                       85
```

Though 'myKernel' has a high occupancy (70%), it does not reach the theoretical maximum (75%) due to constraints like register usage or shared memory. Techniques to improve occupancy include reducing register usage per thread or adjusting the block size of kernels.

To interpret these metrics effectively:

1. **Identify Critical Paths**: In timeline views, locate sequences of dependent operations that take the most time. 2. **Check for Underutilization**: Areas with low memory bandwidth or low occupancy might indicate inefficiencies. 3. **Focus on Hotspots**: Kernels with high execution times or high variance indicate potential areas for code optimization. 4. **Evaluate Asynchrony**: Ensure that asynchronous operations are truly overlapping to maximize parallelism.

By understanding and interpreting the various metrics and visualizations in profiling reports, one can take informed steps to optimize CUDA applications. For example, if a kernel shows low occupancy, experiments can be conducted to adjust its resource utilization and monitor the effects in subsequent profiling sessions. Similarly, if memory bandwidth is underutilized, strategies such as coalescing memory accesses or leveraging shared memory can be employed to enhance performance.

Profiling is an iterative process. Each modification to your CUDA code should be followed by profiling to measure its impact and to ensure that optimization attempts are leading to the desired performance improvements without introducing new bottlenecks. This approach fosters a deeper understanding of the interplay between various components of your application and the underlying CUDA architecture, ultimately resulting in more efficient and performant CUDA programs.

9.9 Optimizing Performance Based on Profiling Data

Profiling data provides crucial insights into the behavior of CUDA applications, identifying bottlenecks and inefficiencies. Understanding how to interpret this data enables targeted optimization efforts, leading to significant performance improvements.

The primary objective of profiling is to identify parts of the code that consume the most time or resources. Once these parts are identified, optimizations can be applied to reduce their impact on overall performance. The key metrics to focus on include kernel execution time, memory transfer rates, and utilization of computational resources.

When analyzing profiling data, it is useful to start by examining the kernel execution time. Kernels that consume disproportionate amounts of time are prime candidates for optimization. Profile tools such as NVIDIA Visual Profiler provide detailed timing information for each kernel execution, which aids in pinpointing inefficiencies.

Consider the following CUDA kernel for matrix multiplication:

```
__global__ void matrixMul(float* C, float* A, float* B, int N) {
    int row = blockIdx.y * blockDim.y + threadIdx.y;
    int col = blockIdx.x * blockDim.x + threadIdx.x;
    float value = 0.0;
    for (int e = 0; e < N; ++e) {
        value += A[row * N + e] * B[e * N + col];
    }
    C[row * N + col] = value;
}
```

Profiling this kernel may reveal that it is memory bound due to inefficient global memory accesses. One common optimization is to use shared memory, which is much faster than global memory. Shared memory can be used to store sub-matrices of A and B, reducing the number of global memory accesses.

Here is an optimized version of the matrix multiplication kernel using shared memory:

```
__global__ void matrixMulShared(float* C, float* A, float* B, int N) {
    __shared__ float As[TILE_SIZE][TILE_SIZE];
    __shared__ float Bs[TILE_SIZE][TILE_SIZE];
    int row = blockIdx.y * blockDim.y + threadIdx.y;
    int col = blockIdx.x * blockDim.x + threadIdx.x;
    float value = 0.0;

    for (int m = 0; m < N / TILE_SIZE; ++m) {
        As[threadIdx.y][threadIdx.x] = A[row * N + (m * TILE_SIZE + threadIdx.x)];
        Bs[threadIdx.y][threadIdx.x] = B[(m * TILE_SIZE + threadIdx.y) * N + col];
        __syncthreads();

        for (int e = 0; e < TILE_SIZE; ++e) {
            value += As[threadIdx.y][e] * Bs[e][threadIdx.x];
        }
        __syncthreads();
    }
    C[row * N + col] = value;
}
```

By utilizing shared memory, the number of accesses to global memory is significantly reduced, allowing the kernel to run more efficiently.

Memory transfer rates between the host and device is another critical area for optimization. If large amounts of data are being transferred frequently, it can create a bottleneck. Employing techniques such as asynchronous memory transfers and overlapping computation with communication helps mitigate this issue. CUDA streams enable concurrent execution of memory transfers and kernel executions.

Here is an example of using CUDA streams to overlap data transfer and kernel computation:

```
cudaStream_t stream1, stream2;
cudaStreamCreate(&stream1);
cudaStreamCreate(&stream2);

cudaMemcpyAsync(d_A, h_A, size, cudaMemcpyHostToDevice, stream1);
cudaMemcpyAsync(d_B, h_B, size, cudaMemcpyHostToDevice, stream2);

matrixMulShared<<<gridDim, blockDim, 0, stream1>>>(d_C, d_A, d_B, N);

cudaMemcpyAsync(h_C, d_C, size, cudaMemcpyDeviceToHost, stream1);

cudaStreamSynchronize(stream1);
cudaStreamSynchronize(stream2);

cudaStreamDestroy(stream1);
cudaStreamDestroy(stream2);
```

This approach reduces idle time by performing memory transfers while the GPU is executing computations, thus improving the overall throughput of the application.

Finally, an aspect often overlooked is the efficient utilization of computational resources. Profiling data can highlight imbalances in workload distribution across threads and blocks. Ensuring that each thread block has enough work to perform, without being under or over-utilized, can lead to better performance. Adjusting block and grid sizes, as well as maximizing the occupancy of the GPU, are strategies to consider.

It is also important to leverage intrinsic functions provided by CUDA. These functions can execute much faster than an equivalent piece of code written using standard operations. For example, using __mul24 for 24-bit integer multiplication can be faster than the standard * operator.

Given these varied strategies, optimizing CUDA applications based on profiling data is a methodical process. The insights provided by profiling tools like NVIDIA Visual Profiler are invaluable for identifying bottlenecks and guiding optimization efforts. Addressing inefficiencies in kernel execution, memory transfers, and resource utilization is crucial for achieving optimal performance in CUDA applications.

9.10 Debugging and Profiling in Jupyter Notebooks

Jupyter Notebooks offer a versatile environment for scientific computing and development, making them a popular choice for CUDA programming with Python. This section delves into the nuances of effectively debugging and profiling CUDA applications within Jupyter Notebooks. Leveraging the interactive nature of Jupyter Notebooks enhances the process of pinpointing errors and optimizing performance.

Setting Up Jupyter Notebooks for CUDA Development

Prior to delving into debugging and profiling, ensure your Jupyter Notebook environment is configured correctly. This involves installing the necessary CUDA toolkit and libraries. To begin, verify the GPU and CUDA installation:

```
import torch
print(torch.cuda.is_available())
print(torch.cuda.device_count())
print(torch.cuda.get_device_name(0))
```

A successful output might be:

```
True
1
'NVIDIA GeForce GTX 1080'
```

This confirms that a compatible GPU is accessible, and CUDA is operational.

Debugging CUDA Code in Jupyter Notebooks

Debugging within Jupyter Notebooks can be efficiently managed using tools like '

Use the following approach to integrate CUDA-GDB, ensuring your GPU code is correctly debugged: 1. Compile the CUDA kernel with debug flags:

```
nvcc -G -g -o my_kernel my_kernel.cu
```

2. Execute the compiled kernel within Jupyter cells:

```
!./my_kernel
```

If an error occurs, CUDA-GDB provides detailed logs that can be assessed within the Notebook. Alternatively, integrating the NVIDIA Nsight Compute integration offers another robust debugging mechanism.

Profiling CUDA Code with Jupyter Notebook

Profiling within Jupyter Notebooks allows performance evaluation and optimization directly within your development workflow. Use built-in profiling tools like 'nvprof' or 'Nsight Systems', tailored for GPU performance analysis.

To profile a specific CUDA code section: 1. Execute the CUDA code with 'nvprof':

```
!nvprof ./my_kernel
```

2. Alternatively, leverage '

```
%timeit my_function()

%prun my_function()
```

The output generated by 'nvprof' might include kernel execution times, memory transfers, and other critical performance metrics:

```
==12345== Profiling application: ./my_kernel
==12345== Profiling result:
Time(%)    Time     Calls      Avg        Min        Max  Name
 99.61%  36.511s        1  36.511s  36.511s  36.511s  my_kernel
```

Nsight Systems provides a more detailed graphical interface, accessible by saving the profiling session and analyzing it with the Nsight Systems GUI.

Best Practices for Debugging and Profiling in Jupyter

1. **Modularize Code**: Divide your code into functions and classes to isolate issues and profile specific sections independently. 2. **Incremental Testing**: Regularly test code changes to catch errors early, simplifying the debugging process. 3. **Use Clear Logging**: Implement comprehensive logging within your CUDA kernels to gather runtime details, aiding in error detection. 4. **Regular Profiling**: Continuously profile your application, focusing on portions where the performance impact is most substantial. 5. **Leverage GPU Resources**: Utilize the full range of NVIDIA tools—Nsight Compute, Nsight Systems, and CUDA-GDB—to streamline debugging and profiling. 6. **Document Findings**: Maintain detailed records of profiling results and debugging steps, enabling reference and reproducibility.

Implementing these practices ensures a robust and efficient debugging and profiling workflow within Jupyter Notebooks, facilitating the development of high-performance CUDA applications.

9.11 Best Practices for Debugging and Profiling

Effective debugging and profiling of CUDA applications require a structured approach to ensure that the identified issues and performance bottlenecks are thoroughly addressed. The following best practices are essential to achieve this goal, ensuring the development of efficient and reliable CUDA applications.

Adopt a Methodical Debugging Process: When encountering a bug, it is critical to adopt a methodical approach rather than randomly guessing potential issues. Start by isolating the problem. Use print statements, assertions, or specialized debugging tools such as NVIDIA Nsight or CUDA-GDB to narrow down the location and cause of the issue. Ensure that each part of your debugging process is documented, allowing you to track changes and understand what has been tested and confirmed.

Utilize Assertions and Error Checkers: Incorporate assertions and error-checking mechanisms within your code. For example, use CUDA error-checking functions to ensure that each CUDA API call is successful. Example syntax for such functions is as follows:

```
def cuda_check_error():
    err = cudaGetLastError()
    if err != cudaSuccess:
        print(f"CUDA error: {cudaGetErrorString(err)}")
```

This function should be called after every significant CUDA call to ensure errors are caught early and the source of the problem is quickly identified.

Profile Early and Often: Profiling should not be reserved for the end of the development cycle. Regular profiling helps to identify performance degradation early, making it easier to address issues incrementally. Integrate profiling as a regular part of your development workflow using tools like the NVIDIA Visual Profiler.

Use Appropriate Profiling Tools: Select profiling tools based on the specific aspect of performance you are analyzing. For instance, use the NVIDIA Visual Profiler for a comprehensive examination of kernel execution and memory transfer times, whereas tools like Nsight Compute offer insights into detailed kernel metrics such as memory throughput and compute resource utilization.

Understand and Interpret Profiling Data: It is not enough to run a profiler; interpreting the data correctly is crucial. Look for metrics such as kernel execution time, memory bandwidth, and occupancy. Determine if kernels are compute-bound or memory-bound, and identify serialization and synchronization issues. Example output from a profiling tool might look like this:

```
Kernel execution time: 23.4 ms
Memory transfer time: 5.1 ms
Compute-to-memory ratio: 4.6
Occupancy: 75%
Memory bandwidth: 320 GB/s
```

From this, you might infer that the kernel execution time is a significant factor and further investigate the computation aspects or loop optimizations.

Iterative Optimization Approach: Optimize code iteratively. Focus on the most significant bottlenecks identified through profiling and measure the impact of each change. This iterative process ensures that optimizations yield measurable performance improvements without inadvertently introducing new issues.

Handle Memory Efficiently: Efficient use of memory is crucial for optimal performance in CUDA applications. Ensure appropriate memory allocation and deallocation, avoid unnecessary data transfers between host and device, and use shared memory judiciously within kernels. For example:

```
# Allocate unified memory
cudaMallocManaged(byref(A), size * sizeof(float))

# Explicitly free memory when no longer needed
cudaFree(A)
```

Avoid Race Conditions: Race conditions occur when multiple threads concurrently modify shared data, leading to unpredictable behavior. Use atomic operations, critical sections, or the appropriate synchronization mechanisms to prevent race conditions. For instance, utilize atomicAdd for summing values across threads:

```
__global__ void reduction_kernel(float* input, float* result){
    // Shared memory for reduction
    extern __shared__ float shared_data[];
    int index = threadIdx.x + blockIdx.x * blockDim.x;

    // Load data into shared memory
    shared_data[threadIdx.x] = input[index];

    // Ensure all threads have loaded their data
    __syncthreads();

    // Reduction within the block
    for(unsigned int s = 1; s < blockDim.x; s *= 2){
        if(threadIdx.x % (2 * s) == 0){
            shared_data[threadIdx.x] += shared_data[threadIdx.x + s];
        }
        __syncthreads();
    }

    // Write result for this block to global memory
    if(threadIdx.x == 0){
        atomicAdd(result, shared_data[0]);
    }
}
```

Checklist for CUDA Development: - Ensure proper error handling and use of error-checking functions. - Regularly profile and analyze performance using appropriate tools. - Optimize memory access patterns and minimize data transfers. - Utilize shared memory and understand its implications for performance. - Minimize thread divergence and ensure coalesced memory access. - Implement careful synchronization controls to avoid race conditions.

By adhering to these best practices, developers can systematically debug and optimize their CUDA applications, leading to more efficient, robust, and performant code.

Chapter 10

Optimization Strategies for CUDA Programs

This chapter focuses on strategies to optimize CUDA programs, covering performance metrics and effective code optimization techniques. Key topics include memory optimization, optimizing kernel launch configurations, and efficient data transfer strategies. It discusses the utilization of shared memory, reducing thread divergence, and optimizing with CUDA streams and events. Advanced topics such as leveraging CUDA libraries and case studies in optimization provide practical insights. Best practices are outlined to ensure the highest performance in CUDA applications.

10.1 Introduction to CUDA Optimization Strategies

Optimization of CUDA programs is essential to harness the true computational power of the GPU. This section introduces key optimization strategies that are crucial for improving the performance and efficiency of CUDA applications. Understanding these strategies lays the foundation for more advanced optimization techniques discussed in subsequent sections.

CUDA programming involves several aspects that influence performance, including but not limited to memory hierarchy, parallel execution models, and architectural considerations. Effective optimization requires a comprehensive understanding of these aspects and a targeted approach to modifying code and configurations.

Proper Memory Management: Memory hierarchy in CUDA consists of global, shared, and local memory, each with distinct characteristics and access speeds. Optimizing memory usage involves ensuring maximum utilization of shared memory, minimizing global memory accesses, and avoiding memory allocation/deallocation overhead within kernels. Shared memory, being much faster than global memory, should be actively employed to store frequently accessed data. An effectively optimized program often exhibits a high shared memory hit rate, reducing the need to access the slower global memory.

Efficient Kernel Launch Configurations: The choice of thread block size and grid configuration significantly affects the performance of CUDA kernels. The occupancy of streaming multiprocessors (SMs) is a key metric that determines how well the GPU resources are utilized. Higher occupancy usually translates to better performance, but it is not the only factor. Ensuring that the grid and block dimensions align well with the problem size and avoiding resource contention are critical steps in optimizing the kernel launch configurations.

The cudaOccupancyMaxPotentialBlockSize API can be utilized to find optimal block size for maximum potential occupancy:

```
int minGridSize, blockSize;
cudaOccupancyMaxPotentialBlockSize(&minGridSize, &blockSize,
                                   myKernel, 0, 0);
dim3 grid((N + blockSize - 1) / blockSize);
myKernel<<<grid, blockSize>>>(...);
```

Minimizing Data Transfer Overhead: Data transfer between the host (CPU) and the device (GPU) can become a bottleneck if not managed properly. Transfers should be minimized and overlapped with computation whenever possible. Pinned (page-locked) memory enables faster transfer speeds compared to pageable (default) memory. Leveraging CUDA streams to overlap data transfers and kernel execution also contributes to overall performance enhancement.

Using cudaMemcpyAsync allows data transfers to be asynchronous:

```
cudaMemcpyAsync(deviceArray, hostArray, size, cudaMemcpyHostToDevice, stream);
```

Optimal Thread Divergence Management: Thread divergence occurs when threads within the same warp follow different execution paths due to conditional statements. This leads to serialization of divergent warps, negatively impacting performance. Careful design of the kernel to ensure that threads within a warp follow the same execution path minimizes divergence and enhances efficiency. Utilize warp-synchronous programming techniques to reduce or eliminate divergence.

Effective Use of CUDA Streams and Events: CUDA streams allow concurrent execution of kernels and memory operations, enabling overlapping of computation and communication. Events provide mechanisms to monitor and synchronize tasks within streams. Using multiple streams efficiently requires a good understanding of dependencies and careful management to maximize GPU utilization.

An example of using streams and events:

```
cudaStream_t stream1, stream2;
cudaStreamCreate(&stream1);
cudaStreamCreate(&stream2);
cudaMemcpyAsync(deviceArray1, hostArray1, size, cudaMemcpyHostToDevice, stream1
    );
myKernel<<<grid, block, 0, stream1>>>(...);
cudaMemcpyAsync(deviceArray2, hostArray2, size, cudaMemcpyHostToDevice, stream2
    );
myKernel<<<grid, block, 0, stream2>>>(...);
cudaEventRecord(stopEvent, stream1);
cudaStreamSynchronize(stream2);
```

Leveraging Advanced CUDA Libraries: Leveraging highly optimized libraries such as cuBLAS, cuFFT, and Thrust can significantly reduce development time and improve performance over hand-written code. These libraries offer a wide range of functionalities, optimized for high performance on NVIDIA GPUs. Developers should integrate these libraries as much as possible, ensuring that they focus on the unique aspects of their application.

To summarize, introducing these optimization strategies establishes a robust foundation for developing efficient CUDA programs. This section serves as a vital starting point for delving deeper into specialized optimization techniques presented in the subsequent sections.

10.2 Understanding Performance Metrics

The optimization of CUDA programs necessitates a robust understanding of various performance metrics. These metrics help to identify bottlenecks and inefficiencies, allowing developers to make informed decisions to enhance their code's performance. The primary performance metrics in CUDA programming include execution time, occupancy, memory bandwidth, and computational throughput. This section explores each of these metrics in detail, along with methods to measure and analyze them effectively.

Execution Time

Execution time is a fundamental metric indicating how long a kernel runs on the GPU. Measuring execution time allows developers to assess the performance of their CUDA kernels and the overall efficiency of the application. Several tools and methods are available to measure execution time, including:

- **CUDA Events:** CUDA events are synchronized markers used to measure time intervals on the GPU. They provide high-resolution timing information that can be used to pinpoint performance issues in kernel code.

```
cudaEvent_t start, stop;
float milliseconds = 0;
cudaEventCreate(&start);
cudaEventCreate(&stop);

cudaEventRecord(start);
// Kernel invocation
cudaEventRecord(stop);

cudaEventSynchronize(stop);
cudaEventElapsedTime(&milliseconds, start, stop);
```

- **Prof CUDA Tool:** Profiler tools, such as NVIDIA Nsight Compute, offer detailed insights into GPU performance, including execution time. These tools provide a comprehensive analysis of the GPU's behavior during kernel execution.

Occupancy

Occupancy refers to the ratio of active warps per multiprocessor to the maximum number of possible active warps. Higher occupancy often correlates with better utilization of the GPU's resources, leading to improved performance. Factors influencing occupancy include the number of registers and shared memory used by a kernel. Maximizing occupancy can be achieved by fine-tuning these resources:

- **Register Usage:** Limiting the number of registers used per thread can increase the number of warps that can be scheduled on the SMs.

```
__global__ void kernel_function() {
    int x = threadIdx.x;
    // Register usage optimization
}
```

- **Shared Memory Usage:** Efficient use of shared memory also impacts occupancy. Excessive use of shared memory can reduce the number of active threads.

```
__global__ void kernel_function() {
    __shared__ float shared_data[256];
    // Optimize shared memory usage
}
```

Memory Bandwidth

Memory bandwidth measures the rate at which data can be read from or written to global memory. Achieving high memory bandwidth utilization is crucial for performance, especially for memory-bound applications. Strategies to enhance memory bandwidth include:

- **Memory Coalescing:** Ensuring memory accesses are coalesced can significantly improve memory bandwidth utilization. Coalesced memory accesses occur when all threads in a warp access contiguous memory locations.

```
__global__ void kernel_function(float *data) {
    int idx = threadIdx.x + blockIdx.x * blockDim.x;
    float value = data[idx];
    // Ensure coalesced memory access
}
```

- **Utilizing Shared Memory:** Shared memory has substantially higher bandwidth compared to global memory. Using shared memory for intermediate computations can alleviate global memory bandwidth constraints.

```
__global__ void kernel_function(float *data) {
    __shared__ float shared_data[256];
    int idx = threadIdx.x + blockIdx.x * blockDim.x;
    shared_data[threadIdx.x] = data[idx];
    __syncthreads();
    // Perform computations using shared memory
}
```

Computational Throughput

Computational throughput measures the number of floating-point operations per second (FLOPS) performed by the GPU. Optimizing for high computational throughput involves ensuring that the GPU executes as many operations as possible concurrently. Methods to enhance computational throughput include:

- **Instruction-Level Parallelism:** Leveraging instruction-level parallelism ensures multiple operations are pipelined within the GPU, maximizing usage of computational units.

```
__global__ void kernel_function(float *data) {
    int idx = threadIdx.x + blockIdx.x * blockDim.x;
    float value = data[idx];
    float result = value * value; // Example operation
    data[idx] = result;
}
```

- **Loop Unrolling:** Manually unrolling loops can reduce overhead and improve throughput within computationally intensive kernels.

```
__global__ void kernel_function(float *data) {
    int idx = threadIdx.x + blockIdx.x * blockDim.x;
    for (int i = 0; i < 4; i++) {
        data[idx + i] *= 2.0f; // Manually unrolled loop
    }
}
```

Understanding and optimizing these performance metrics is essential for achieving high-performance CUDA applications. Effective measurement and tuning based on these metrics ensure that computational resources are utilized to their fullest potential.

10.3 Code Optimization Techniques

Understanding how to effectively optimize CUDA code is paramount to achieving high-performing GPU-accelerated applications. This section delves into various techniques to optimize CUDA programs, employing an amalgamation of theoretical insights and practical implementations.

Before exploring individual techniques, it is crucial to acknowledge that optimization in CUDA involves a holistic approach. Every optimization strategy is interlinked with others, and often, multiple strategies need to be applied concurrently to realize substantial performance gains.

1. Profiling the Code

Profiling is the first step in optimization. Profiling tools, such as nvprof or NVIDIA Nsight Compute, provide insights into the execution of the

CUDA kernel, including time spent on each function, memory usage, and potential bottlenecks. Below is an example of how to use nvprof to profile a CUDA program:

```
$ nvprof ./your_cuda_program
```

The output will highlight the functions consuming the most time, providing a starting point for optimization.

2. Minimizing Data Transfers

Data transfer between the host (CPU) and device (GPU) can be a significant bottleneck. To reduce this overhead, minimize the frequency and volume of data transfers. Transfer data in larger chunks instead of multiple smaller transfers.

```
cudaMemcpy(device_data, host_data, data_size, cudaMemcpyHostToDevice)
```

In this code snippet, ensure data_size is as large as possible without exceeding limits to maximize efficiency.

3. Optimizing Memory Access Patterns

Ensuring coalesced memory access is critical for optimal performance. When threads within a warp access consecutive memory locations, memory transactions are minimized. In contrast, non-coalesced access patterns result in multiple, inefficient memory transactions. Here's an illustration demonstrating coalesced versus non-coalesced memory access:

```
Coalesced Access:
Thread 0 -> data[0]
Thread 1 -> data[1]
Thread 2 -> data[2]
...

Non-Coalesced Access:
Thread 0 -> data[0]
Thread 1 -> data[4]
Thread 2 -> data[8]
...
```

Below is a code example demonstrating coalesced memory access:

```
__global__ void coalesced_memory_kernel(float *data) {
    int idx = threadIdx.x + blockDim.x * blockIdx.x;
    data[idx] = some_function(data[idx]);
}
```

Ensuring idx is evaluated such that consecutive thread indices access sequential memory addresses enhances memory transaction efficiency.

4. Efficient Use of Shared Memory

Shared memory provides a high-speed, user-managed cache and can significantly reduce the latency associated with global memory accesses. The following code demonstrates using shared memory to optimize repeated global memory accesses:

```
__global__ void shared_memory_kernel(float *input, float *output) {
    __shared__ float shared_data[BLOCK_SIZE];

    int tid = threadIdx.x + blockDim.x * blockIdx.x;
    int local_tid = threadIdx.x;

    // Load data into shared memory
    shared_data[local_tid] = input[tid];
    __syncthreads();

    // Perform computation using shared data
    output[tid] = some_function(shared_data[local_tid]);
}
```

This pattern reduces the need for redundant accesses to global memory, enhancing performance.

5. Employing Loop Unrolling

Loop unrolling can significantly improve performance by reducing loop overhead and increasing instruction-level parallelism. The following example shows manual loop unrolling:

```
__global__ void loop_unrolled_kernel(float *data) {
    int idx = threadIdx.x + blockDim.x * blockIdx.x;

    // instead of
    // for (int i = 0; i < N; ++i) {
    // data[idx] += i;
    // }

    // unroll the loop
    data[idx] += 0;
    data[idx] += 1;
    data[idx] += 2;
    data[idx] += 3;
    // ... continue for loop range
}
```

Although this increases the number of instructions, it dramatically reduces the overhead caused by loop control, contributing to performance gains.

6. Reducing Divergence

Thread divergence occurs when threads in the same warp follow different execution paths due to conditional branches. Divergent warps degrade performance as the warp serially executes each taken branch path. The following example demonstrates minimizing divergence:

```
__global__ void reduce_divergence_kernel(int *data, int condition) {
    int idx = threadIdx.x + blockDim.x * blockIdx.x;

    // Reduce divergence by merging conditions
    if (condition) {
        do_task_1(data[idx]);
    } else {
        do_task_2(data[idx]);
    }
}
```

Where possible, re-arrange code to minimize the impact of divergence or leverage intrinsics provided by the CUDA toolkit to deal with divergent paths more efficiently.

Adhering to these techniques requires a deep understanding of both the hardware architecture and the nature of the problem being solved. Employing profiling tools to identify bottlenecks, refining data transfers, ensuring coalesced memory accesses, utilizing shared memory, unrolling loops, and minimizing thread divergence collectively contribute to the efficient execution of CUDA programs.

10.4 Memory Optimization Strategies

Effective memory management is paramount to achieving high performance in CUDA applications. Several facets of memory optimization include managing the various types of memory available on the GPU, minimizing memory latency, and maximizing memory bandwidth utilization. This section explores these strategies in detail, providing practical code examples and execution outputs to underscore key points.

Types of Memory: CUDA architectures provide several types of memory, each with specific characteristics:

- **Global Memory**: This is the largest and slowest memory, accessible by all threads. Optimizing access patterns to global memory is crucial for performance.
- **Shared Memory**: This on-chip memory is much faster than global memory and is shared among threads in the same block.
- **Local Memory**: Although called "local", it resides off-chip and is as slow as global memory, used for large arrays or variables with automatic storage.

- **Constant Memory**: Used for data that does not change, providing read-only access to all threads.
- **Texture and Surface Memory**: Specialized memory optimized for specific access patterns often found in graphics operations.

Global Memory Optimization: Efficient global memory access is pivotal for performance enhancement. Key strategies include coalesced memory access, proper usage of memory allocation, and avoiding unnecessary transfers between host and device.

```
# Example: Access global memory in a coalesced manner
@cuda.jit
def coalesced_memory_access(A):
    i = cuda.grid(1)
    # Coalesced access if threads access consecutive elements
    if i < A.size:
        A[i] += 1

# Memory allocation and kernel launch
A = cuda.device_array(1024, dtype=np.float32)
coalesced_memory_access[32, 32](A)
```

Ensuring that threads within a warp access consecutive memory addresses leads to coalesced global memory access, reducing memory transaction overhead and enhancing performance.

Shared Memory Utilization: Shared memory provides significant speed advantages but requires careful management. Properly using shared memory involves correctly sizing and avoiding bank conflicts.

```
@cuda.jit
def shared_memory_example(A, B):
    sA = cuda.shared.array(shape=0, dtype=numba.float32)
    tid = cuda.threadIdx.x
    # Load data into shared memory
    sA[tid] = A[tid]
    cuda.syncthreads()

    if tid < B.size:
        B[tid] = sA[tid] * 2

# Allocate and launch
A = cuda.to_device(np.arange(32, dtype=np.float32))
B = cuda.device_array_like(A)
shared_memory_example[1, 32](A, B)
print(B.copy_to_host())
```

```
[ 0., 2., 4., 6., 8., 10., 12., 14., 16., 18., 20., 22., 24., 26., 28., 30.,
 32., 34., 36., 38., 40., 42., 44., 46., 48., 50., 52., 54., 56., 58., 60., 62.]
```

This example demonstrates shared memory usage, highlighting the need for synchronous operations to ensure all threads have correctly loaded data before processing.

Constant and Texture Memory Optimizations: Leveraging constant and texture memory for specific patterns can yield better caching characteristics and optimized reads.

```
from numba import cuda, float32

const_val = cuda.const.array_like([1.0,2.0,3.0])

@cuda.jit
def const_memory_kernel(A):
    i = cuda.grid(1)
    if i < A.size:
        A[i] += const_val[i % 3]

A = cuda.device_array(1024, dtype=np.float32)
const_memory_kernel[32, 32](A)
```

Efficient Memory Transfers: Memory transfers between host and device are often costly. Strategies for reducing overhead include using pinned memory and overlapping transfers with computation using streams.

```
# Example: Using pinned memory to reduce transfer overhead
import numpy as np

pinned_array = cuda.pinned_array(1024, dtype=np.float32)
d_array = cuda.device_array_like(pinned_array)

# Populate host array
pinned_array[:] = np.arange(1024, dtype=np.float32)

# Asynchronous transfer
cuda.to_device(pinned_array, to=d_array, stream=stream)
```

Pinned memory allows for more efficient transfers, owing to reduced overhead from page-locked memory.

Memory Bandwidth Utilization: Maximizing memory bandwidth utilization requires minimizing idle periods and balancing memory access across all threads. Techniques such as loop unrolling and efficient memory access patterns are vital.

```
@cuda.jit
def optimize_bandwidth(A):
    i = cuda.grid(1)
    # Stride access to utilize memory bandwidth
    for j in range(0, A.size, cuda.blockDim.x):
        idx = i + j
        if idx < A.size:
            A[idx] += 1

A = cuda.device_array(1024, dtype=np.float32)
optimize_bandwidth[32, 32](A)
```

These techniques not only optimize memory bandwidth but also align well with hardware capabilities to enhance overall application performance.

Recommendations for practitioners include profiling memory usage and access patterns, leveraging available CUDA tools for optimization insights, and iteratively optimizing based on empirical performance data.

10.5 Optimizing Kernel Launch Configurations

Optimizing kernel launch configurations is a critical aspect of achieving high performance in CUDA programs. The configuration of a kernel launch consists of defining the grid and block dimensions. These dimensions significantly impact the execution efficiency, resource allocation, and potential parallelism.

Grid and Block Dimensions: In CUDA, a kernel launch involves specifying the number of threads per block and the number of blocks per grid. The choice of these dimensions affects how the code is executed on the hardware. An optimal configuration efficiently utilizes the available resources such as registers, shared memory, and the number of cores.

To launch a kernel, the syntax is as follows:

```
kernel<<<numBlocks, numThreadsPerBlock>>>(arguments);
```

Choosing the Number of Threads per Block: The number of threads per block is a crucial parameter. Each block can contain up to 1024 threads, but hardware specifics often guide the choice to be a multiple of 32 (a warp size).

Launching too few threads may under-utilize the device, while too many could result in resource contention or excessive register spilling. A typical approach is to start with 256 or 512 threads per block and then fine-tune based on performance profiling. For instance:

```
const int threadsPerBlock = 256;
const int blocksPerGrid = (N + threadsPerBlock - 1) / threadsPerBlock;
kernel<<<blocksPerGrid, threadsPerBlock>>>(arguments);
```

Occupancy Considerations: Occupancy refers to the ratio of active warps to the maximum number of warps supported on a multiprocessor of the CUDA device. Higher occupancy implies better resource utilization, although maximized occupancy does not always equate to best performance. The CUDA Occupancy Calculator, a tool provided by NVIDIA, helps determine optimal thread block size and register usage to balance occupancy and resource usage.

Trade-offs Between Latency and Throughput: Optimizing kernel launch configurations often involves balancing latency and throughput. Throughput-oriented configurations maximize the number of concurrently active warps, whereas latency-sensitive configurations might use fewer threads per block to minimize execution stages or synchronization overhead.

Effect of Grid Size: The grid size, determined by the number of blocks, is equally important. It must cover the entire problem space. However, if the number of blocks considerably exceeds the number of streaming multiprocessors (SMs), it may lead to excessive kernel launch overhead. There exists a sweet spot, typically ensuring that each SM has a sufficient number of blocks to keep the pipeline full.

For example, for a large data set:

```
const int threadsPerBlock = 256;
const int blocksPerGrid = (N + threadsPerBlock - 1) / threadsPerBlock;
kernel<<<blocksPerGrid, threadsPerBlock>>>(N, d_a, d_b, d_result);
```

Thread Divergence: Minimizing thread divergence within warps is essential. Thread divergence occurs when threads of the same warp follow different execution paths, generally caused by conditional statements (e.g., if-else). An optimal kernel configuration strives to allocate threads in a way that reduces divergence, ensuring all threads in a warp proceed along the same execution path as much as possible.

```
__global__ void VecAdd(float* A, float* B, float* C, int N) {
    int i = blockDim.x * blockIdx.x + threadIdx.x;
    if (i < N)
        C[i] = A[i] + B[i];
}
```

In this snippet, divergence is controlled by ensuring that only valid threads operate on the memory.

Memory Coalescing: Efficient memory accesses contribute to optimizing kernel performance. Memory coalescing involves organizing global memory accesses so they can be coalesced into as few transactions as possible.

```
__global__ void coalescedAccess(float* data) {
    int tid = threadIdx.x + blockIdx.x * blockDim.x;
    float out = data[tid];
```

```
    // Processing on out
    data[tid] = out;
}
```

Profiling and Iterative Tuning: Achieving optimal kernel configuration usually requires profiling tools like NVIDIA's nvprof or Nsight Systems. Profiling provides insights into warp execution efficiencies, resource usage, and bottlenecks. Based on profiling data, iterative adjustments to grid and block dimensions can be made to enhance performance further.

Warp Schedulers and Threadblock Scheduling: The mechanism by which the threads are scheduled on CUDA cores influences how different kernel launch configurations perform. Warp schedulers dispatch warps to available execution units considering resource availability and dependencies. Understanding this helps optimize synchronization points and reduce idle times.

To validate the performance improvements, empirical testing using different configurations and analyzing key metrics is recommended. Metrics such as achieved occupancy, warp execution efficiency, and memory throughput are critical pointers.

Effective kernel launch configuration optimizes the computation workload distributed to each thread, maximizing throughput while minimizing latency and resource contention. This requires a balance guided by empirical data and hardware specifics, ensuring an optimized runtime environment for CUDA programs.

10.6 Efficient Data Transfer Techniques

Efficient data transfer between the host (CPU) and the device (GPU) is one of the critical aspects of CUDA programming. Achieving optimal performance often requires minimizing data transfer time and maximizing bandwidth utilization. This section discusses strategies for optimizing data transfer, including the use of pinned memory, leveraging asynchronous transfers, employing zero-copy memory, and overlapping data transfer with computation.

To begin with, the choice of memory type plays a significant role in the transfer efficiency. CUDA supports different types of memory allocations, among which *pinned memory* (also known as page-locked memory) is essential for high performance.

Pinned Memory: Pinned memory is a special type of memory allocation where the memory pages are locked and cannot be swapped by the operating system. This results in higher bandwidth for memory transfers:

```
cudaMallocHost((void**)&h_data, size); // Allocate pinned host memory
cudaMemcpy(d_data, h_data, size, cudaMemcpyHostToDevice); // Copy data from
    host to device
cudaMemcpy(h_data, d_data, size, cudaMemcpyDeviceToHost); // Copy data from
    device to host
cudaFreeHost(h_data); // Free pinned host memory
```

Pinned memory is faster than pageable memory because it eliminates the page faulting overhead; hence, it is particularly useful for large data transfers. However, it should be used judiciously as it consumes more physical memory, limiting the amount of memory available to other applications.

Asynchronous Data Transfers: Another strategy to enhance data transfer efficiency is the use of asynchronous data transfers. Asynchronous transfers allow the CPU to execute other tasks while the data transfer is in progress, thereby improving overall performance. This is particularly effective when combined with kernel execution to overlap computation with communication, exploiting the full potential of the GPU.

To perform asynchronous transfers, the *cudaMemcpyAsync* function is used alongside CUDA streams:

```
cudaStream_t stream;
cudaStreamCreate(&stream);

cudaMemcpyAsync(d_data, h_data, size, cudaMemcpyHostToDevice, stream); //
    Async transfer
kernel<<<grid, block, 0, stream>>>(d_data); // Kernel execution in the same stream
cudaMemcpyAsync(h_data, d_data, size, cudaMemcpyDeviceToHost, stream); //
    Async transfer

cudaStreamSynchronize(stream); // Ensure all operations are complete
cudaStreamDestroy(stream);
```

By using streams, data transfers and kernel executions can be overlapped, leading to efficient utilization of both the CPU and GPU resources.

Zero-Copy Memory: For scenarios where data access patterns involve infrequent or small-sized data transfers, zero-copy memory can be a valuable technique. Zero-copy memory allows the GPU to directly access host memory without explicit data transfers. This can be beneficial for applications that need to share data structures between the

CPU and GPU frequently.

Enabling zero-copy memory involves creating a pointer with *cudaHostAlloc* using the *cudaHostAllocMapped* flag:

```
cudaHostAlloc((void**)&h_data, size, cudaHostAllocMapped); // Allocate zero-copy
    memory
cudaHostGetDevicePointer(&d_data, h_data, 0); // Get device pointer for host
    memory

// Kernel launches can now access h_data directly
kernel<<<grid, block>>>(d_data);
```

Zero-copy memory is most effective when data sizes are small, and frequent transfers are required. Performance may degrade for larger data sizes due to reduced bandwidth compared to dedicated device memory.

Overlapping Data Transfers with Computation: One of the most effective techniques to hide data transfer latency is overlapping communication with computation. This can be achieved using CUDA streams and asynchronous functions. The goal is to keep the GPU busy with computation while simultaneously transferring data to/from the device.

Consider a scenario of matrix multiplication where data can be divided into chunks. By transferring and computing different chunks simultaneously, overall performance can be greatly improved:

```
cudaStream_t stream1, stream2;
cudaStreamCreate(&stream1);
cudaStreamCreate(&stream2);

// Transfer chunk 1 and execute kernel on chunk 1
cudaMemcpyAsync(d_data1, h_data1, chunk_size, cudaMemcpyHostToDevice,
    stream1);
kernel<<<grid, block, 0, stream1>>>(d_data1);

// Transfer chunk 2 and execute kernel on chunk 2
cudaMemcpyAsync(d_data2, h_data2, chunk_size, cudaMemcpyHostToDevice,
    stream2);
kernel<<<grid, block, 0, stream2>>>(d_data2);

// Synchronize streams
cudaStreamSynchronize(stream1);
cudaStreamSynchronize(stream2);

cudaStreamDestroy(stream1);
cudaStreamDestroy(stream2);
```

In this example, chunks of data are transferred and processed in separate streams, allowing transfer and computation to overlap. This technique takes full advantage of the GPU's capability for concurrent execution and data transfers.

Choosing the Appropriate Transfer Techniques: Selecting the most appropriate data transfer technique depends on various factors, including data size, transfer frequency, and specific application requirements. Typically, a combination of pinned memory for fast transfers, asynchronous operations for overlapping communication with computation, and zero-copy memory for small or infrequent access patterns yields the best performance.

Effective data transfer strategies are crucial for optimizing CUDA programs. By leveraging pinned memory, asynchronous transfers, zero-copy memory, and overlapping techniques, significant improvements in performance can be achieved, enabling efficient utilization of both CPU and GPU resources.

10.7 Utilizing Shared Memory Efficiently

Shared memory in CUDA plays a critical role in achieving high performance in GPU programs. Unlike global memory, shared memory is significantly faster because it resides on-chip, allowing threads within the same block to access data in a much shorter time. The efficient use of shared memory can substantially reduce memory access latency and improve overall system performance. This section explores strategies and best practices for utilizing shared memory efficiently.

When leveraging shared memory, the primary goal is to minimize access to slower global memory and instead use shared memory for intermediate data that is accessed frequently by multiple threads. The following code snippet outlines a simple example to illustrate the application of shared memory.

```
__global__ void matrixMulShared(float* A, float* B, float* C, int N) {
    // Define shared memory with the size of a block
    __shared__ float As[BLOCK_SIZE][BLOCK_SIZE];
    __shared__ float Bs[BLOCK_SIZE][BLOCK_SIZE];

    int row = blockIdx.y * blockDim.y + threadIdx.y;
    int col = blockIdx.x * blockDim.x + threadIdx.x;
    float value = 0;

    for (int k = 0; k < (N + BLOCK_SIZE - 1) / BLOCK_SIZE; ++k) {
        // Load data into shared memory
        if (row < N && (k * BLOCK_SIZE + threadIdx.x) < N)
            As[threadIdx.y][threadIdx.x] = A[row * N + k * BLOCK_SIZE + threadIdx.
                x];
        else
            As[threadIdx.y][threadIdx.x] = 0.0;

        if (col < N && (k * BLOCK_SIZE + threadIdx.y) < N)
```

```
            Bs[threadIdx.y][threadIdx.x] = B[(k * BLOCK_SIZE + threadIdx.y) * N +
                col];
        else
            Bs[threadIdx.y][threadIdx.x] = 0.0;

        __syncthreads();

        // Perform calculations within shared memory
        for (int n = 0; n < BLOCK_SIZE; ++n)
            value += As[threadIdx.y][n] * Bs[n][threadIdx.x];

        __syncthreads();
    }

    if (row < N && col < N)
        C[row * N + col] = value;
}
```

In this example, shared memory is used to store sub-matrices from the global memory, 'A' and 'B'. By doing so, each sub-matrix is loaded only once into shared memory and reused, reducing the number of global memory accesses.

Key concepts and strategies for optimizing the usage of shared memory include:

Size and Layout of Shared Memory: Declare shared memory of appropriate size using the __shared__ keyword. The size must be carefully determined based on the problem being solved to ensure efficient memory utilization without unnecessary wastage.

Coalesced Access Pattern: Ensure that global memory loads and stores are coalesced whenever possible. Coalesced accesses occur when sequential threads access sequential memory locations, minimizing memory transaction overhead.

Bank Conflicts: Shared memory is divided into equally-sized memory banks which can be accessed simultaneously. Bank conflicts occur when multiple threads in a warp attempt to access different addresses within the same memory bank, resulting in serialized accesses. To avoid or minimize bank conflicts, ensure that accesses map to different memory banks or utilize padding strategies.

Reuse of Data: Maximize the reuse of data stored in shared memory. Instead of loading data from global memory multiple times, load it once into shared memory and have multiple threads access it as needed.

The following example demonstrates the potential pitfalls of bank conflicts and a solution:

```
__global__ void transposeNoBankConflict(float *odata, float *idata, int width, int
    height) {
```

```
    __shared__ float tile[BLOCK_SIZE][BLOCK_SIZE + 1]; // padding to avoid
        bank conflicts

    int x = blockIdx.x * BLOCK_SIZE + threadIdx.x;
    int y = blockIdx.y * BLOCK_SIZE + threadIdx.y;

    if (x < width && y < height) {
        for (int j = 0; j < BLOCK_SIZE; j += 8)
            tile[threadIdx.y + j][threadIdx.x] = idata[(y + j) * width + x];
    }

    __syncthreads();

    x = blockIdx.y * BLOCK_SIZE + threadIdx.x; // transpose block offset
    y = blockIdx.x * BLOCK_SIZE + threadIdx.y;

    if (x < height && y < width) {
        for (int j = 0; j < BLOCK_SIZE; j += 8)
            odata[(y + j) * height + x] = tile[threadIdx.x][threadIdx.y + j];
    }
}
```

The tile array in shared memory is declared with a size of BLOCK_SIZE + 1 to introduce padding and prevent bank conflicts. Without padding, access patterns may result in multiple threads accessing the same bank, causing performance degradation due to serialized accesses.

Another important practice involves utilizing atomic operations correctly when multiple threads need to read from and write to shared memory locations. Atomic functions can ensure consistent and correct results when concurrent modifications occur, although they may introduce some overhead.

Careful synchronization among threads is also essential when using shared memory. The __syncthreads() function ensures that all threads in the block have reached the same execution point and completed their shared memory operations before proceeding. Misuse or absence of synchronization can lead to race conditions, causing erroneous results or crashes.

When used judiciously, shared memory significantly enhances the performance of CUDA applications by reducing access latency and optimizing data reuse. Understanding and implementing these strategies effectively can lead to substantial performance gains in parallel computing tasks.

Finally, the efficient use of shared memory extends beyond mere implementation; it involves comprehensive profiling and iterative optimization to identify and resolve bottlenecks, ensuring maximal utilization of available hardware resources.

10.8 Reducing Divergence in GPU Threads

Thread divergence occurs when threads of the same warp follow different execution paths, leading to suboptimal utilization of the GPU's parallel processing capabilities. Reducing thread divergence is critical to maximizing performance in CUDA programs.

GPUs execute threads in groups called warps, typically consisting of 32 threads. When a divergent branch is encountered, each path of the branch is executed serially, with some threads idle while others are active. This behavior reduces the effective parallelism and overall performance. The following points elaborate on strategies to minimize thread divergence.

1. Avoiding Divergent Branches

A key strategy is to minimize conditional constructs (if, else, switch) that lead to divergent branches. When possible, refactor code to reduce or eliminate these branches. For example, replacing complex conditionals with arithmetic operations often helps. Here is an illustration:

```
__global__ void processElements(int *data, int n) {
    int idx = threadIdx.x + blockIdx.x * blockDim.x;
    if (idx < n) {
        if (data[idx] % 2 == 0) {
            data[idx] *= 2;
        } else {
            data[idx] += 1;
        }
    }
}
```

This code contains a divergent branch within the warp. A refactored version could leverage arithmetic operations to handle both conditions in a unified manner:

```
__global__ void processElementsOptimized(int *data, int n) {
    int idx = threadIdx.x + blockIdx.x * blockDim.x;
    if (idx < n) {
        int isEven = (data[idx] % 2 == 0);
        data[idx] = (data[idx] * (1 + isEven)) + (!isEven);
    }
}
```

This optimization reduces divergence by converting the branch into arithmetic expressions, maintained by each thread independently.

2. Data Layout and Access Patterns

Improving data layout can sometimes reduce thread divergence. By organizing data such that threads within a warp access contiguous memory locations sequentially, divergence can be minimized.

```
struct Data {
    int value;
    bool flag; // Determines processing path
};

__global__ void processStructs(Data *data, int n) {
    int idx = threadIdx.x + blockIdx.x * blockDim.x;
    if (idx < n) {
        if (data[idx].flag) {
            data[idx].value *= 2;
        } else {
            data[idx].value += 1;
        }
    }
}
```

An alternative is to separate the interleaved data into independent arrays, enhancing coalesced memory accesses and reducing divergence.

```
__global__ void processSeparated(int *values, bool *flags, int n) {
    int idx = threadIdx.x + blockIdx.x * blockDim.x;
    if (idx < n) {
        if (flags[idx]) {
            values[idx] *= 2;
        } else {
            values[idx] += 1;
        }
    }
}
```

This approach ensures that each warp has a unified access pattern, thereby reducing the likelihood of divergence.

3. Warp-level Primitive Functions

CUDA provides warp-level primitives, such as __all(), __any(), __ballot(), that can optimize conditional evaluations and synchronization across threads in a warp, aiding in minimizing divergence.

```
__global__ void processWithWarpPrimitives(int *data, int n) {
    int idx = threadIdx.x + blockIdx.x * blockDim.x;
    int warpId = threadIdx.x / warpSize; // Warp identifier

    if (idx < n) {
        bool pathChoice = (data[idx] % 2 == 0);
        unsigned mask = __ballot_sync(0xFFFFFFFF, pathChoice);

        if (pathChoice) {
            if (mask & (1 << warpId)) {
                data[idx] *= 2;
            }
        } else {
            data[idx] += 1;
        }
    }
```

```
}
```

In this example, the __ballot_sync function gathers predicates from all threads in a warp, allowing paths to be harmonized.

4. Loop Unrolling and Iterations Splitting

Careful loop unrolling can also mitigate thread divergence. By unrolling loops partially and running distinct loop iterations on different warps, one can control and align thread executions better.

```
__global__ void unrolledLoop(int *data, int n) {
    int idx = threadIdx.x + blockIdx.x * blockDim.x;

    for (int i = idx; i < n; i += blockDim.x * gridDim.x) {
        if (data[i] % 2 == 0) {
            data[i] *= 2;
        } else {
            data[i] += 1;
        }
    }
}
```

In practical applications, adaptive unrolling and rearrangement according to data characteristics can lead to performance benefits.

5. Cooperative Groups

Using cooperative groups, available in CUDA, allows programmers to express and manage thread groups more effectively. This can be utilized to minimize divergence within subgroups.

```
#include <cooperative_groups.h>
using namespace cooperative_groups;

__global__ void cooperativeGroupProcess(int *data, int n) {
    int idx = threadIdx.x + blockIdx.x * blockDim.x;
    auto group = coalesced_threads(); // Create a cooperative group

    if (idx < n) {
        bool pathChoice = (data[idx] % 2 == 0);
        if (group.all(pathChoice)) {
            data[idx] *= 2;
        } else {
            data[idx] += 1;
        }
    }
}
```

In this code, the coalesced_threads function forms a cooperative group, enabling unified behavior without divergence.

Incorporating these strategies helps ensure that GPU resources are optimally utilized and performance is maximized by reducing thread divergence. These approaches highlight the importance of meticulous code structuring and considerations at both the architectural and algorithmic levels.

10.9 Optimizing with CUDA Streams and Events

CUDA streams and events provide mechanisms to introduce concurrency and synchronize tasks in CUDA applications, thereby optimizing the overall execution time. Streams allow for overlapping computation with memory transfers, while events facilitate synchronization across different streams. Efficient use of these constructs can dramatically improve performance by exploiting the full potential of the GPU.

A **stream** in CUDA is a sequence of operations that are executed in order on the GPU. By default, all operations are placed in stream 0, also known as the *null stream*, which has an implicit synchronization point after each operation. Creating additional streams enables concurrent execution, allowing computations and memory transfers to overlap, thus making better use of the GPU resources.

To illustrate the use of streams, consider the following example where we create multiple streams to overlap memory transfers with kernel execution:

```
import numpy as np
from numba import cuda

# Define vector size
N = 1000000

# Allocate host memory
h_A = np.ones(N, dtype=np.float32)
h_B = np.ones(N, dtype=np.float32)
h_C = np.zeros(N, dtype=np.float32)

# Allocate device memory
d_A = cuda.device_array(N, dtype=np.float32)
d_B = cuda.device_array(N, dtype=np.float32)
d_C = cuda.device_array(N, dtype=np.float32)

# Define the kernel
@cuda.jit
def vector_add(A, B, C):
    idx = cuda.grid(1)
    if idx < A.size:
        C[idx] = A[idx] + B[idx]

# Create CUDA streams
stream1 = cuda.stream()
```

```
stream2 = cuda.stream()

# Copy data to the device
cuda.to_device(h_A, to=d_A, stream=stream1)
cuda.to_device(h_B, to=d_B, stream=stream2)

# Launch kernels in different streams
vector_add[N//256, 256, stream1](d_A, d_B, d_C)

# Copy result back to host
d_C.copy_to_host(h_C, stream=stream1)

# Synchronize streams
stream1.synchronize()
stream2.synchronize()
```

In this example, memory transfers and kernel execution are associated with different streams, allowing them to occur concurrently. Synchronization is achieved using the stream.synchronize() method, ensuring that operations in each stream complete before program execution proceeds.

CUDA events serve as markers that record the progress of a stream. They are used to monitor and synchronize tasks across different streams, measure elapsed time between events, or as conditions for stream synchronization. Events provide finer control over synchronization compared to streams alone.

Here is a refined example demonstrating the use of events to measure the time taken for a kernel execution:

```
# Create CUDA events
start = cuda.event()
end = cuda.event()

# Record events and launch kernel
start.record(stream1)
vector_add[N//256, 256, stream1](d_A, d_B, d_C)
end.record(stream1)

# Wait for the event to complete
end.synchronize()

# Calculate elapsed time
elapsed_time = cuda.event_elapsed_time(start, end)
print(f"Elapsed time: {elapsed_time} ms")
```

The cuda.event() function creates an event, which can subsequently be recorded at specific points in the code using the record() method. The synchronize() method ensures all previously issued commands on the stream have been completed. By measuring the time elapsed between two recorded events, developers can profile specific code sections for performance tuning.

Noteworthy considerations for efficient use of streams and events include:

- **Maximize Overlap:** Aim to overlap computation with data transfer as much as possible. Utilize multiple streams to schedule independent tasks concurrently.
- **Avoid Over-Subscription:** Creating too many streams can lead to overhead and degrade performance. Balance the number of streams with the workload and architecture of the GPU.
- **Use Events for Profiling:** Employ events to measure and optimize critical paths in the code, ensuring that bottlenecks are identified and addressed.
- **Stream Synchronization:** Use stream synchronization judiciously to avoid unnecessary stalls. Opt for granular synchronization with events when precise control is required.

By incorporating these strategies, CUDA streams and events can significantly contribute to optimizing performance and achieving efficient utilization of GPU resources.

10.10 Leveraging Advanced CUDA Libraries

CUDA libraries are instrumental in harnessing the full power of NVIDIA GPUs. These libraries are optimized, battle-tested, and provide high-level APIs that abstract many complexities of GPU programming. Using these libraries not only accelerates development but also enhances performance by leveraging optimizations implemented by NVIDIA. In this section, we will delve into several key CUDA libraries such as cuBLAS, cuFFT, cuDNN, Thrust, and others. We will explore their functionalities, use cases, and demonstrate how to integrate them into CUDA applications effectively.

cuBLAS: CUDA Basic Linear Algebra Subroutines

The cuBLAS library is an implementation of BLAS (Basic Linear Algebra Subroutines) on top of the NVIDIA CUDA runtime. It provides GPU-accelerated matrix operations, including vector and matrix multiplication, matrix inversion, and eigenvalue decomposition.

Consider a simple example where we perform a matrix multiplication using cuBLAS:

```
import numpy as np
import cupy as cp
import cupy.cuda.cublas as cublas

# Matrix dimensions
N = 1024

# Create random matrices A and B
A = cp.random.randn(N, N).astype(np.float32)
B = cp.random.randn(N, N).astype(np.float32)
C = cp.empty((N, N), dtype=np.float32)

# Create cublas handle
handle = cublas.create()

alpha = 1.0
beta = 0.0

# Perform matrix multiplication
cublas.sgemm(
    handle,
    cublas.CUBLAS_OP_N, cublas.CUBLAS_OP_N,
    N, N, N,
    alpha,
    A.data.ptr, N,
    B.data.ptr, N,
    beta,
    C.data.ptr, N
)

# Destroy the handle
cublas.destroy(handle)
```

The cuBLAS library allows the execution of BLAS routines on the GPU, significantly increasing the speed of linear algebra operations which are pivotal in many scientific and engineering applications.

cuFFT: CUDA Fast Fourier Transform

The cuFFT library provides a fast and efficient implementation of Fourier transforms on NVIDIA GPUs. Fourier transforms are essential in many fields, including signal processing, image processing, and solving partial differential equations.

Here is a Python example using the cuFFT library:

```
import cupy as cp
import cupy.fft as cufft

# Create a sample input data array
N = 1024
x = cp.random.randn(N).astype(cp.complex64)

# Perform forward FFT
y = cufft.fft(x)

# Perform inverse FFT
z = cufft.ifft(y)
```

```
# Verify the output
cp.testing.assert_allclose(x, z, rtol=1e-5, atol=1e-5)
```

The cuFFT library's optimized routines ensure that applications requiring Fourier transforms can perform these computations with minimal computational overhead.

cuDNN: CUDA Deep Neural Network Library

cuDNN is a GPU-accelerated library for deep neural networks. It provides highly tuned implementations for standard routines such as forward and backward convolution, pooling, normalization, and other operations critical in deep learning.

Using cuDNN can have a profound impact on the training time and performance of neural networks. Below is a simple illustration of using cuDNN in Python:

```
import numpy as np
import cupy as cp
import cupy.cudnn as cudnn

# Create input and output tensors
input_tensor = cp.random.randn(1, 1, 28, 28).astype(cp.float32)
output_tensor = cp.empty_like(input_tensor)

# Create cuDNN handle
handle = cudnn.create()

# Create tensor descriptors
input_desc = cudnn.create_tensor_descriptor(input_tensor)
output_desc = cudnn.create_tensor_descriptor(output_tensor)

# Convolution settings
filter_desc = cudnn.create_filter_descriptor(cp.random.randn(1, 1, 3, 3).astype(cp.
    float32))
conv_desc = cudnn.create_convolution_descriptor((1, 1), (1, 1))

# Forward convolution
cudnn.convolution_forward(
    handle,
    1.0, input_desc, input_tensor.data.ptr,
    filter_desc, filter_desc,
    conv_desc, cudnn.CUDNN_CONVOLUTION_FWD_ALGO_IMPLICIT_GEMM,
    None, 0,
    0.0, output_desc, output_tensor.data.ptr
)

# Destroy the handle
cudnn.destroy(handle)
```

Thrust: Parallel Algorithms Library

Thrust is a parallel algorithms library which resembles the C++ Standard Template Library (STL). It provides a rich collection of data structures and algorithms for parallel computing on GPUs. By leveraging Thrust, developers can write concise and readable code without compromising performance.

A classic example is the parallel reduction (sum of elements) using Thrust:

```
import cupy as cp
import thrust

# Create input array
N = 1024
x = cp.random.randn(N).astype(cp.float32)

# Perform parallel reduction
total_sum = thrust.reduce(x)

print(f'Total sum: {total_sum}')
```

Thrust contains many other algorithms like scan, sort, transform, and many more, making it an invaluable tool for GPU programming.

Other Libraries

Apart from the mentioned libraries, CUDA provides several other advanced libraries which can be leveraged for specific domains:

- **cuSPARSE:** For sparse matrix operations.
- **cuSOLVER:** For solving linear systems and eigenvalue problems.
- **NVIDIA OptiX:** For ray tracing.
- **nvGRAPH:** For graph analytics.

By integrating these highly optimized CUDA libraries into your applications, you can achieve performance levels far exceeding those attainable through custom implementations.

10.11 Case Studies in CUDA Optimization

In this section, we delve into detailed case studies to illustrate the application of various CUDA optimization techniques. Each case study is selected to highlight specific optimization practices and their impact on performance. By examining real-world examples, readers can gain practical insights into the challenges and solutions in CUDA programming.

To maintain a structured and informative approach, we'll explore three distinct case studies:

- Optimization of a Matrix Multiplication Kernel
- Reducing Memory Bandwidth in an Image Processing Application
- Improving Throughput in Financial Simulations

Optimization of a Matrix Multiplication Kernel

Matrix multiplication is a fundamental operation in many scientific and engineering applications. The naive implementation, although conceptually simple, is often inefficient on GPUs due to poor memory access patterns and suboptimal use of computational resources.

```
__global__ void matrixMulNaive(float *A, float *B, float *C, int N) {
    int row = blockIdx.y * blockDim.y + threadIdx.y;
    int col = blockIdx.x * blockDim.x + threadIdx.x;

    if (row < N && col < N) {
        float value = 0;
        for (int k = 0; k < N; ++k)
            value += A[row * N + k] * B[k * N + col];
        C[row * N + col] = value;
    }
}
```

In the naive implementation, each thread computes the value of a single element in the output matrix. This approach leads to suboptimal memory access patterns, causing high global memory latency. Optimizing this kernel involves leveraging shared memory to reduce global memory accesses and increase data reuse.

```
__global__ void matrixMulOptimized(float *A, float *B, float *C, int N) {
    __shared__ float s_A[TILE_SIZE][TILE_SIZE];
    __shared__ float s_B[TILE_SIZE][TILE_SIZE];

    int row = blockIdx.y * TILE_SIZE + threadIdx.y;
    int col = blockIdx.x * TILE_SIZE + threadIdx.x;
    float value = 0;

    for (int k = 0; k < (N + TILE_SIZE - 1) / TILE_SIZE; ++k) {
        if (row < N && k * TILE_SIZE + threadIdx.x < N)
            s_A[threadIdx.y][threadIdx.x] = A[row * N + k * TILE_SIZE + threadIdx.
                x];
        else
            s_A[threadIdx.y][threadIdx.x] = 0;

        if (col < N && k * TILE_SIZE + threadIdx.y < N)
```

```
            s_B[threadIdx.y][threadIdx.x] = B[(k * TILE_SIZE + threadIdx.y) * N +
                col];
        else
            s_B[threadIdx.y][threadIdx.x] = 0;

        __syncthreads();

        for (int n = 0; n < TILE_SIZE; ++n)
            value += s_A[threadIdx.y][n] * s_B[n][threadIdx.x];

        __syncthreads();
    }

    if (row < N && col < N)
        C[row * N + col] = value;
}
```

By using shared memory, the optimized kernel reduces the number of global memory accesses, resulting in better performance. Benchmarks show a significant speedup due to improved memory access patterns and increased data reuse within each thread block.

Reducing Memory Bandwidth in an Image Processing Application

Image processing workflows often involve large data sets, and memory bandwidth can become a bottleneck. Consider an edge detection filter applied to an image using the Sobel operator. The naive implementation reads and writes to global memory multiple times, resulting in high memory bandwidth usage.

```
__global__ void sobelFilterNaive(float *input, float *output, int width, int height) {
    int x = blockIdx.x * blockDim.x + threadIdx.x;
    int y = blockIdx.y * blockDim.y + threadIdx.y;

    if (x > 0 && x < width - 1 && y > 0 && y < height - 1) {
        float Gx = -input[(y - 1) * width + (x - 1)] + input[(y - 1) * width + (x + 1)]
                   - 2 * input[y * width + (x - 1)] + 2 * input[y * width + (x + 1)]
                   - input[(y + 1) * width + (x - 1)] + input[(y + 1) * width + (x + 1)];

        float Gy = input[(y - 1) * width + (x - 1)] + 2 * input[(y - 1) * width + x] +
            input[(y - 1) * width + (x + 1)]
                   - input[(y + 1) * width + (x - 1)] - 2 * input[(y + 1) * width + x] -
                       input[(y + 1) * width + (x + 1)];

        output[y * width + x] = sqrtf(Gx * Gx + Gy * Gy);
    }
}
```

To optimize, we leverage shared memory to reduce redundant global memory accesses. Loading data into shared memory once and reusing it within the tile diminishes memory bandwidth requirements.

```
__global__ void sobelFilterOptimized(float *input, float *output, int width, int height
    ) {
    __shared__ float tile[TILE_SIZE + 2][TILE_SIZE + 2];
```

```
    int x = blockIdx.x * blockDim.x + threadIdx.x;
    int y = blockIdx.y * blockDim.y + threadIdx.y;
    int tx = threadIdx.x + 1;
    int ty = threadIdx.y + 1;

    if (x < width && y < height) {
        tile[ty][tx] = input[y * width + x];
        if (threadIdx.x == 0)
            tile[ty][0] = (x > 0) ? input[y * width + (x - 1)] : 0;
        if (threadIdx.x == blockDim.x - 1)
            tile[ty][TILE_SIZE + 1] = (x < width - 1) ? input[y * width + (x + 1)] : 0;
        if (threadIdx.y == 0)
            tile[0][tx] = (y > 0) ? input[(y - 1) * width + x] : 0;
        if (threadIdx.y == blockDim.y - 1)
            tile[TILE_SIZE + 1][tx] = (y < height - 1) ? input[(y + 1) * width + x] : 0;

        __syncthreads();

        if (x > 0 && x < width - 1 && y > 0 && y < height - 1) {
            float Gx = -tile[ty - 1][tx - 1] + tile[ty - 1][tx + 1]
                       - 2 * tile[ty][tx - 1] + 2 * tile[ty][tx + 1]
                       - tile[ty + 1][tx - 1] + tile[ty + 1][tx + 1];

            float Gy = tile[ty - 1][tx - 1] + 2 * tile[ty - 1][tx] + tile[ty - 1][tx + 1]
                       - tile[ty + 1][tx - 1] - 2 * tile[ty + 1][tx] - tile[ty + 1][tx + 1];

            output[y * width + x] = sqrtf(Gx * Gx + Gy * Gy);
        }
    }
}
```

The optimized kernel shows a remarkable reduction in memory bandwidth usage, translating to improved performance metrics. This method ensures efficient usage of the memory subsystem, crucial for real-time image processing applications.

Improving Throughput in Financial Simulations

Financial simulations, such as Monte Carlo methods for option pricing, demand immense computational power. Initial implementations can suffer from inefficiencies in both computation and memory access. A naive Monte Carlo simulation might be structured as follows:

```
__global__ void monteCarloNaive(float *d_vals, int numSims, float strike, float T,
    float S0, float mu, float sigma) {
    int idx = blockIdx.x * blockDim.x + threadIdx.x;
    if (idx < numSims) {
        float dt = T / (float)numSims;
        float S = S0;
        curandState state;
        curand_init(idx, 0, 0, &state);
        for (int i = 0; i < numSims; ++i) {
            S *= expf((mu - 0.5f * sigma * sigma) * dt + sigma * sqrtf(dt) *
                    curand_normal(&state));
        }
        d_vals[idx] = fmaxf(S - strike, 0.0f);
    }
}
```

The naive kernel's performance is limited by thread-level parallelism and memory access patterns. Enhancing performance involves precomputing constants, optimizing random number generation, and improving memory coalescing.

```
__global__ void monteCarloOptimized(float *d_vals, int numSims, float strike, float
    T, float S0, float mu, float sigma) {
    int idx = blockIdx.x * blockDim.x + threadIdx.x;
    if (idx < numSims) {
        float dt = T / (float)numSims;
        float drift = (mu - 0.5f * sigma * sigma) * dt;
        float volatility = sigma * sqrtf(dt);
        float S = S0;
        curandState state;
        curand_init(idx, 0, 0, &state);
        for (int i = 0; i < numSims; ++i) {
            float gauss_bm = curand_normal(&state);
            S *= expf(drift + volatility * gauss_bm);
        }
        d_vals[idx] = fmaxf(S - strike, 0.0f);
    }
}
```

By restructuring the kernel to improve memory access patterns and reduce redundant computations, we achieve significant performance gains. These enhancements facilitate higher throughput essential for complex financial simulations where speed is critical to performance.

Examining these case studies demonstrates the profound impact of targeted CUDA optimizations on performance. They provide a practical context for understanding and applying the principles of CUDA programming in various domains.

10.12 Best Practices for CUDA Optimization

To achieve peak performance in CUDA applications, it is essential to adhere to a set of best practices that cater to various aspects of program development and execution. These practices span from code design and development to debugging and performance tuning. The objective is to maximize efficiency and ensure the program takes full advantage of the GPU capabilities.

Optimal Utilization of Memory Hierarchy: Understanding and effectively utilizing the memory hierarchy is critical. The GPU memory model comprises several types of memory, each with different access speeds, and it is crucial to minimize access to slow memory and maximize the use of fast memory.

- **Global Memory**: Avoid frequent accesses to global memory as it has high latency. Instead, read data into shared memory or registers whenever feasible.
- **Shared Memory**: Use shared memory to facilitate data sharing among threads within the same block. Ensure proper memory access patterns to avoid bank conflicts.
- **Registers**: Registers are the fastest among all memory types, but their number is limited. Efficiently use registers to store variables that are frequently accessed.
- **Constant and Texture Memory**: Utilize constant and texture memory for read-only data that does not change during kernel execution. These memories offer caching mechanisms that reduce the latency of accessing data.

Optimizing Memory Access Patterns: Ensure coalesced memory access patterns to enhance memory throughput. Coalesced access enables multiple memory operations to be combined into a single transaction, reducing the effective latency.

```
__global__ void vectorAdd(const float *A, const float *B, float *C, int N) {
    int idx = blockIdx.x * blockDim.x + threadIdx.x;
    if (idx < N) {
        C[idx] = A[idx] + B[idx];
    }
}
```

In the above kernel, if the vectors A, B, and C are aligned in memory, the memory reads and writes will be coalesced.

Minimizing Data Transfers: Data transfers between host and device can be a significant bottleneck. Reduce the frequency and volume of data transfers by:

- Transferring data in large chunks rather than many small ones.
- Keeping data on the device as much as possible.
- Overlapping computation with data transfer using CUDA streams for concurrent execution.

Efficient Kernel Configuration: Optimize the kernel launch configuration by selecting an appropriate number of blocks and threads per block. A sufficient number of blocks is necessary to keep the GPU fully occupied, while too many threads per block can lead to resource contention.

```
int numThreads = 256;
int numBlocks = (N + numThreads - 1) / numThreads;
vectorAdd<<<numBlocks, numThreads>>>(d_A, d_B, d_C, N);
```

The above configuration ensures that the number of blocks is enough to cover all elements, leveraging GPU parallelism effectively.

Avoiding Thread Divergence: Minimize thread divergence by avoiding conditional branches within warps. When threads of the same warp take different execution paths, it leads to serialization of execution, negatively impacting performance.

```
__global__ void reduce(float *data, int N) {
    int idx = blockIdx.x * blockDim.x + threadIdx.x;
    if (idx < N) {
        // Original conditional might cause divergence
        // if (...) {
        // // some code
        // } else {
        // // some code
        // }
        // Alternative approach to minimize divergence
        float val = (idx % 2 == 0) ? data[idx] * 2.0f : data[idx] / 2.0f;
        data[idx] = val;
    }
}
```

The above kernel minimizes divergence by using the ternary conditional operator for uniform thread execution paths.

Leveraging Asynchronous Operations: Use asynchronous operations to overlap computation with data transfer. Utilize CUDA streams to achieve concurrent kernel execution and data transfer.

```
cudaStream_t stream1, stream2;
cudaStreamCreate(&stream1);
cudaStreamCreate(&stream2);
cudaMemcpyAsync(d_A, h_A, size, cudaMemcpyHostToDevice, stream1);
cudaMemcpyAsync(d_B, h_B, size, cudaMemcpyHostToDevice, stream2);
vectorAdd<<<numBlocks, numThreads, 0, stream1>>>(d_A, d_B, d_C, N);
cudaMemcpyAsync(h_C, d_C, size, cudaMemcpyDeviceToHost, stream1);
cudaStreamSynchronize(stream1);
cudaStreamSynchronize(stream2);
cudaStreamDestroy(stream1);
cudaStreamDestroy(stream2);
```

This example demonstrates how to use two streams to perform data transfer and computation in parallel.

Profiling and Tuning: Use profiling tools like nvprof, nsight, and cuda-memcheck to identify performance bottlenecks. Regular profiling helps in understanding the behavior of the application and the impact of optimizations.

```
$ nvprof ./vectorAdd
==12345== Profiling application: ./vectorAdd
==12345== Profiling result:
Time(%)     Time     Calls      Avg       Min       Max  Name
100.00%  1.6782ms        1  1.6782ms  1.6782ms  1.6782ms  vectorAdd(float const *, float const *, float *, int)
```

The profiling output indicates the time spent in the vectorAdd kernel. Analyze such outputs to refine and enhance kernel performance.

Managing Compute Capability: Ensure that the code leverages features specific to the compute capability of the target GPU. This includes utilizing advanced instructions, efficient use of warp-level primitives like shfl, and exploiting hardware capabilities.

```
if (deviceProp.major >= 7) {
    // Use features available in CUDA Compute Capability 7.x or higher
}
```

By following these best practices, one can ensure that CUDA applications are optimized for performance, leverage the GPU resources efficiently, and provide improved execution speed that fully capitalizes on the parallel processing power of modern GPUs.

Made in the USA
Monee, IL
05 November 2026

67845307R00177